1 · 9 · 9 · 8

STOCK · TRADER'S

ALMANAC

BY YALE HIRSCH

THE HIRSCH ORGANIZATION INC • 184 CENTRAL AVENUE • OLD TAPPAN NJ 07675

Editor/Publisher: Yale Hirsch
Production Coordinator: Elizabeth Ross
Associate Editor: Jeffrey A. Hirsch
Page Layout and Design: Brendan M. Stewart
Data Coordinator: Scott Barrie
Director of Research: Robert Cardwell

The *Stock Trader's Almanac* is an organizer. It puts investing on a business basis by making things easier.

1. It is a monthly reminder and refresher course.

2. It updates investment knowledge; informs you of new techniques and tools.

3. It alerts you to seasonal opportunities and dangers.

4. It provides an historical viewpoint by providing pertinent statistics on past market behavior.

5. It supplies every form needed for portfolio-planning, record-keeping and tax preparation.

For several years prior to the publication of our first *Stock Trader's Almanac*, we collected items from financial columns, books and articles that pointed to seasonal tendencies in the stock market. It occurred to us that these intriguing phenomena should be thoroughly researched and arranged in calendar order. So we did it! We also examined various investment, record-keeping forms and found some hadn't been updated for 20-30 years. Others were so cumbersome they were beyond anyone's patience. So we designed new and more practical forms.

We are constantly searching for new insights and nuances about the stock market and welcome any suggestions from our readers.

Have a healthy and prosperous 1998!

This symbol signifies THIRD FRIDAY OF THE MONTH on calendar pages and tells you to be alert to extraordinary volatility due to expiration of equity and index options and index future contracts. Triple-witching days appear during March, June, September and December.

The bull symbol on calendar pages signifies very favorable trading days (see pages 64, 66, 108, 114, 120 and 134) near the ends and beginnings of months, before holidays and around Thanksgiving and Christmas.

This Thirty-First Edition is respectfully dedicated to

David L. Brown

Co-author of *Cyber Investing* and President of Telescan,
who showed the average investor with a PC and Telescan's
software and database, how to spot the stocks that the hottest
money managers are buying.

INTRODUCTION TO THE
THIRTY-FIRST EDITION

It is with a great feeling of celebration that I introduce the Thirty-First Annual Edition of the *Stock Trader's Almanac*. I am pleased and proud to have brought significant and useful information to investors over the years. This edition, as well as those that follow, continues in that tradition.

J.P. Morgan's classic retort when questioned about the future course of the stock market was, "Stocks will fluctuate." This remark is often quoted with a wink-of-the-eye implication that the only prediction one can truly make about the market is that it will go up, down, or sideways. Many investors wholeheartedly believe that no one ever really knows which way the market will go. Nothing could be further from the truth—as Almanac readers well know.

During the past thirty one years I have made many exceptionally accurate forecasts in the *Stock Trader's Almanac*. These forecasts were based on thousands of hours of research into recurring patterns. I learned that while stocks do indeed fluctuate, they do so in well-defined, often predictable patterns which recur too frequently to be the result of chance or coincidence.

The Almanac is a practical working tool. Its wealth of information is organized on a calendar basis. It alerts you to those little-known market patterns and tendencies on which shrewd professionals maximize profit potential. You will be able to forecast market trends with accuracy and confidence when you use the Almanac to help you understand:

1. How our quadrennial presidential elections unequivocally affect the economy and the stock market—just as the moon affects the tides. Many investors have made fortunes following the political cycle. You can be certain that money managers who control hundreds of millions of dollars are also political cycle watchers. Sharp people are not likely to ignore a pattern that has been working like a charm for decades.

2. How the passage of the Twentieth Amendment to the Constitution fathered the January Barometer which has a super record for predicting the course of the stock market each year and a perfect record in odd-numbered years.

3. That there is significant market bias at certain times of the day, week, month and year.

Even if you are an investor who pays scant attention to cycles, indicators and patterns, your investment survival could hinge on your interpretation of one of the recurring patterns found within these pages. One of the most intriguing and important patterns is the symbiotic relationship between Washington and Wall Street. Aside from the potential profitability in seasonal patterns, there's the pure joy of seeing the market very often do just what you expected.

As the Dow approached the Twentieth Century, it gained 21.3% in 1897. Next year it was up 22.5% and 1899's gain was 9.2%. The streak continued in 1900 for another 7.0%.

Such exuberance is likely as we approach both a new century and a new millennium. From the low of 1998, I expect a gain of at least 2000 Dow points to the high of 1999.

THE 1998 STOCK TRADER'S ALMANAC

CONTENTS

DIRECTORY OF SEASONAL TRADING PATTERNS & DATABANK

STRATEGY PLANNING AND RECORD SECTION

	MONDAY	TUESDAY	WEDNESDAY	THURSDAY	FRIDAY	SATURDAY	SUNDAY
JANUARY	29	30	31	**1** JANUARY New Year's Day	2	3	4
	5	6	7	8	9	10	11
	12	13	14	15	(16)	17	18
	19 Martin Luther King Day	20	21	22	23	24	25
	26	27	28	29	30	31	**1** FEBRUARY
FEBRUARY	2	3	4	5	6	7	8
	9	10	11 Ash Wednesday	12	13	14 ♥	15
	16 Presidents' Day	17	18	19	(20)	21	22
	23	24	25	26	27	28	**1** MARCH
MARCH	2	3	4	5	6	7	8
	9	10	11	12	13	14	15
	16	17 ♣	18	19	(20)	21	22
	23	24	25	26	27 Good Friday	28	29 Easter
	30	31	**1** APRIL	2	3	4	5
APRIL	6	7	8	9	10	11 Passover	12
	13	14	15	16	(17)	18	19
	20	21	22	23	24	25	26
	27	28	29	30	**1** MAY	2	3
MAY	4	5	6	7	8	9	10 Mother's Day
	11	12	13	14	(15)	16	17
	18	19	20	21	22	23	24
	25 Memorial Day	26	27	28	29	30	31
JUNE	**1** JUNE	2	3	4	5	6	7
	8	9	10	11	12	13	14
	15	16	17	18	(19)	20	21 Father's Day
	22	23	24	25	26	27	28

1998 STRATEGY CALENDAR
(Option expiration dates encircled)

MONDAY	TUESDAY	WEDNESDAY	THURSDAY	FRIDAY	SATURDAY	SUNDAY	
29	30	1 JULY	2	3	4 Independence Day	5	JULY
6	7	8	9	10	11	12	
13	14	15	16	(17)	18	19	
20	21	22	23	24	25	26	
27	28	29	30	31	1 AUGUST	2	
3	4	5	6	7	8	9	AUGUST
10	11	12	13	14	15	16	
17	18	19	20	(21)	22	23	
24	25	26	27	28	29	30	
31	1 SEPTEMBER	2	3	4	5	6	SEPTEMBER
7 Labor Day	8	9	10	11	12	13	
14	15	16	17	(18)	19	20	
21 Rosh Hashanah	22	23	24	25	26	27	
28	29	30 Yom Kippur	1 OCTOBER	2	3	4	OCTOBER
5	6	7	8	9	10	11	
12 Columbus Day	13	14	15	(16)	17	18	
19	20	21	22	23	24	25	
26	27	28	29	30	31 Boo!	1 NOVEMBER	
2	3 Election Day	4	5	6	7	8	NOVEMBER
9	10	11 Veteran's Day	12	13	14	15	
16	17	18	19	(20)	21	22	
23	24	25	26 Thanksgiving	27	28	29	
30	1 DECEMBER	2	3	4	5	6	DECEMBER
7	8	9	10	11	12	13	
14 Chanukah	15	16	17	(18)	19	20	
21	22	23	24	25 Christmas	26	27	
28	29	30	31				

PROGNOSTICATING TOOLS AND PATTERNS FOR 1998

For 31 years, Almanac readers profited from being able to predict the timing of the Political Market Cycle. To help you gain perspective in 1998, a Midterm Election year, a valuable array of tables, charts and pertinent information are presented on the pages noted:

THE EIGHTH YEAR OF DECADES
Graphic presentation reveals "eight" years are great years, though not as dazzling as "fives." *Page 16.*

THE INCREDIBLE JANUARY BAROMETER
ONLY THREE MAJOR ERRORS IN 47 YEARS
Since 1935 the January Barometer has compiled a perfect record in all odd-numbered years and a very good one in the others. *Page 20 and 28.*

MARKET CHARTS OF MIDTERM ELECTION YEARS
Individual charts for each of the century's last 21 midterm election years. *Page 32.*

MIDTERM ELECTION YEARS: WHERE BOTTOM
PICKERS FIND PARADISE
Graphic presentation of midterm election years along with the midterm election year record since 1914. *Page 36.*

MARKET REACTIONS TO CAPITAL GAINS TAX CUTS
Would a capital gains tax cut be good news for the stock market. The answer may surprise you. *Page 74.*

DOW COULD GAIN WELL OVER 2000 POINTS
FROM ITS 1998 LOW TO ITS HIGH IN 1999
An average gain of 50.0% has been recorded since 1914 between the Dow's midterm low and its pre-election year high. *Page 76.*

LOOKING TO THE YEAR 2000
WHY YOU SHOULD REMAIN BULLISH
The excitement over the new millennium should infect investors. One hundred years ago, the oncoming 20th Century produced five up years in a row. This bodes well for the approaching millenium. *Page 112.*

PRESIDENTIAL ELECTION/STOCK MARKET CYCLE
Stock prices have been impacted by elections for 165 years, gaining more in the midterm years than in the post-election years. *Page 139.*

DECEMBER

MONDAY
 1

*Keep away from people who try to belittle
your ambitions. Small people always do that, but the really great
make you feel that you, too, can become great.*
— Mark Twain

TUESDAY
 2

*Two advertisements:
"Free trip to Disneyland.
Driver needed to deliver new car from New York."
(Got 3 responses.)
"Drive free from New York to Disneyland
delivering new air-conditioned Cadillac."
(Got 103 responses.)*

WEDNESDAY
 3

*The Edison Company offered me
the general superintendency of the
company but only on the condition that I would
give up my gas engine and devote myself to
something really useful.*
— Henry Ford (1922)

THURSDAY
 4

*Establish a no-excuses environment
and watch your productivity and earnings soar.*
— Jordan Kimmel, Private Money Manager

Chanukah

FRIDAY
5

*To see a World in a grain of sand
and a Heaven in a wild flower
Hold infinity in the palm of your hand
and eternity in an hour.*
— William Blake

SATURDAY
6

SUNDAY
7

BEAT THE DOW WITH ONE ARM TIED BEHIND YOUR BACK

A simple system any investor can use to outperform the market was presented in the book *Beating the Dow*, by Michael O'Higgins and John Downes (available from us at $25.00 postpaid).

TEN HIGHEST YIELDERS

Investing in the ten highest-yielding Dow Jones industrial stocks at the start of each year between 1973 and 1996 produced a cumulative total gain of 5,362%, an 18.2% annual compounded return. The Dow average of 30 industrials during this 24-year period gained 1,610%, or 12.6% annually.

FIVE LOWEST PRICED

Choosing just the five lowest-priced issues among the ten highest yielders each year resulted in a 9,787% total return, equal to 21.1% per year.

SECOND LOWEST-PRICED

Remarkably, picking one Dow stock each year, the second lowest-priced stock of the ten highest yielders, did best of all, a 23,287% return, or 25.5% a year.

Isn't it amazing that you can beat the Dow from within, using a few of its own components? However, to rely on just one stock can be dangerous in some years.

A SIMPLE BEATING-THE-DOW SYSTEM (1973-1996)

	Total Return	Annual Return
30 Dow Jones Industrials	1,610%	12.6%
10 highest-yielding Dow stocks	5,362%	18.2%
5 lowest-priced of 10 high yielders	9,787%	21.1%
2nd lowest-priced of 10 high yielders	23,287%	25.5%

THREE WEEKS EACH YEAR AVERAGE 4.9%
THAT'S A COMPOUNDED ANNUAL RETURN OF 125%

Want an interesting way to average 4.9% for a particular three-week period every year? Investing in the five worst Dow losers in the two weeks prior to the last trading day in December and getting out on the fourth trading day in January has produced the 4.9% return over the past 21 years.

BEATING THE DOW NEWSLETTER

For a FREE copy of the latest monthly *Beating the Dow* newsletter, published by the Hirsch Organization, send a stamped, self-addressed envelope to: Beating the Dow, P O Box 2069, River Vale NJ 07675.

DECEMBER

MONDAY
8

*In an uptrend, if a higher high
is made but fails to carry through,
and prices dip below the previous high,
the trend is apt to reverse.
The converse is true for downtrends.*
— Victor Sperandeo

TUESDAY
9

*It's a buy when the 10-week moving
average crosses the 30-week moving
average and the slope of both averages is up.*
— Victor Sperandeo

WEDNESDAY
10

*Pullbacks near the 30-week moving
average are often good times to take action*
— Michael Burke, Chartcraft

THURSDAY
11

MURPHY & MURPHY 1:00PM

Review 1997 P&L 2½HRS ✓

MURPHY & SLW7 1 HR ✓
REVIEW

*News on stocks is not important.
How the stock reacts to it is important.*
— Michael Burke, Chartcraft

FRIDAY
12

*The first stocks to double in a bull market
will usually double again.*
— Michael Burke, Chartcraft

SATURDAY
13

SUNDAY
14

BEING AN EARLY BIRD IN DECEMBER IMPROVES YOUR BEATING-THE-DOW PERFORMANCE

Outperforming the stock market by investing in the ten highest-yielding Dow industrial stocks at the start of each year has produced numerous Dow beating strategies.

An investment stampede occurred in recent years to use these various Dow strategies to outperform the stock market. All the major wire houses now have unit trusts that each year enable investors to take advantage of the superior returns garnered by the selection of Dow stocks over the Dow's performance as a whole. In addition, there are several mutual funds that utilize these Dow strategies.

Each year on the last trading day, a number of money managers and brokers and thousands of individual investors religiously purchase a portfolio of a select group of Dow stocks. Consequently, billions of dollars in Dow strategy portfolios handled by money managers are reshuffled in tandem on the last trading day of the year.

The table reveals a superior strategy to beat these money managers at their own game. December's Dow point and percentage changes for 24 years are shown in the first section of the table. However, the next section shows that December lows usually come far earlier than the year-end close.

It seems wiser to make investment decisions utilizing the Dow strategy earlier in the month—most likely, the first week. Over the last 12 years (1985-1996) the Dow on December's first trading day was 2.7% lower than the last. The strategy of buying earlier obviously has an enormous performance advantage over the long term. Of course, on the occasions a bear market strikes, one's short-term performance could suffer.

DECEMBER DOW INDUSTRIAL CHANGES

	Nov Close	Dec Close	Point Change	% Change	December Low Day	December Low Close	Next Year's % Change Five Stock Strategy	Next Year's % Change What The Dow Did
1972	1018.21	1020.02	1.81	0.2%	21	1000.00	19.6%	—13.1%
1973	822.25	850.86	28.61	3.5	5	788.31	— 3.8	—23.1
1974	618.66	616.24	— 2.42	—0.4	6	577.60	70.1	44.4
1975	860.67	852.41	— 8.26	—1.0	5	818.80	40.8	22.7
1976	947.22	1004.65	57.43	6.1	2	946.64	4.5	—12.7
1977	829.70	831.17	1.47	0.2	20	806.22	1.7	2.7
1978	799.03	805.01	5.98	0.7	18	787.51	9.9	10.5
1979	822.35	838.74	16.39	2.0	3	819.62	40.5	21.4
1980	993.34	963.99	—29.35	—3.0	11	908.45	0.0	— 3.4
1981	888.98	875.00	—13.98	—1.6	29	868.25	37.4	25.8
1982	1039.28	1046.54	7.26	0.7	16	990.25	36.1	25.7
1983	1276.02	1258.64	—17.38	—1.4	15	1236.79	12.6	1.1
1984	1188.94	1211.57	22.63	1.9	7	1163.21	37.8	32.8
1985	1472.13	1546.67	74.54	5.1	2	1457.91	27.9	26.9
1986	1914.23	1895.95	—18.28	—1.0	31	1895.95	11.1	6.1
1987	1833.55	1938.83	105.28	5.7	4	1766.74	18.4	16.0
1988	2114.51	2168.57	54.06	2.6	2	2092.28	10.5	31.7
1989	2706.27	2753.20	46.93	1.7	20	2687.93	—15.2	— 0.4
1990	2559.65	2633.66	74.01	2.9	3	2565.59	61.9	23.9
1991	2894.68	3168.83	274.15	9.5	10	2863.82	23.1	7.4
1992	3305.16	3301.11	— 4.05	—0.1	16	3255.18	34.3	16.8
1993	3683.95	3754.09	70.14	1.9	1	3697.08	8.6	4.9
1994	3739.23	3834.44	95.21	2.5	8	3685.73	30.5	36.4
1995	5074.49	5117.12	42.63	0.8	20	5059.32	26.0	28.9
1996	6521.70	6448.27	—73.43	—1.1	16	6268.35	?	?

What $1,000 grew to: $98,945 $17,152

DECEMBER

MONDAY
15

*Mr. Bell, after careful consideration of
your invention, while it is a very interesting
novelty, we have come to the conclusion
that it has no commercial possibilities.*
— J.P. Morgan, after a demonstration of the telephone (1876)

TUESDAY
16

Every crowd has a silver lining.
— P.T. Barnum

WEDNESDAY
17

*Ah, but a man's reach should exceed his grasp
Or what's a heaven for?*
— Robert Browning

THURSDAY
18

*When people are free to do as they please,
they usually imitate each other.*
— Eric Hoffer

FRIDAY
 # 19

*The fireworks begin today
Each diploma is a lighted match.
Each one of you is a fuse.*
— NYC Mayor Edward Koch, Commencement Address, 1983

SATURDAY
20

SUNDAY
21

THE EIGHTH YEAR OF DECADES

"Eight" years are great years, though not as dazzling as the "fives." Most of them had up, up markets. The 10% November drop after Truman beat Dewey left 1948 a loser; following 1978's "October Massacre," the Dow ended the year slightly down while the S&P was up a bit. A new century approaching will uplift people and businesses worldwide. Add a new millennium and 1998 should be a bull year.

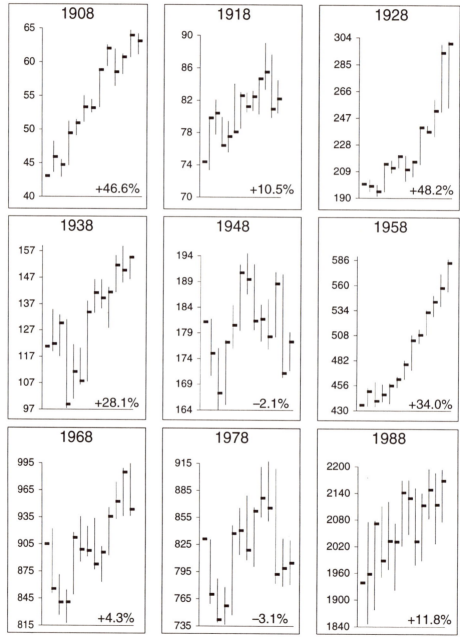

Based on Dow Jones industrial average monthly ranges and closing prices

DECEMBER

MONDAY
22

The heights by great men reached and kept
Were not attained by sudden flight,
But they, while their companions slept,
Were toiling upward in the night.
— Henry Wadsworth Longfellow
"The Ladder of Saint Augustine," 1858

TUESDAY
23

In democracies, nothing is more great
or brilliant than commerce; it attracts
the attention of the public and fills the
imagination of the multitude; all passions
of energy are directed towards it.
— Alexis de Tocqueville, *Democracy in America*, 1840

Chanukah

WEDNESDAY
24

There are three ingredients in the good life:
learning, earning and yearning.
— Christopher Morley

Christmas
(Market Closed)

THURSDAY
25

This is the biggest fool thing we have ever done.
The (atom) bomb will never go off, and I
speak as an expert in explosives.
— Admiral William Leahy to President Truman (1945)

FRIDAY
26

Eighty percent of success is showing up.
— Woody Allen

SATURDAY
27

SUNDAY
28

20th Amendment made "Lame Ducks" disappear
Now, "As January goes, so goes the odd-numbered year."

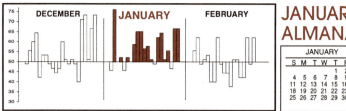

JANUARY ALMANAC

	JANUARY								FEBRUARY					
S	M	T	W	T	F	S		S	M	T	W	T	F	S
					1	2	3							1
4	5	6	7	8	9	10		2	3	4	5	6	7	
11	12	13	14	15	16	17		8	9	10	11	12	13	14
18	19	20	21	22	23	24		15	16	17	18	19	20	21
25	26	27	28	29	30	31		22	23	24	25	26	27	28

See Market Probability Chart on page 125.

❑ As January goes, so goes the year (pgs 20-30) ❑ Greatest concentration of turndowns since 1949 occurred in month's first six trading days ❑ January Barometer outperforms all other monthly barometers in predicting the next 11 months ❑ More Dow points gained than any other month ❑ Low-priced stocks beat quality in early weeks of year ❑ Worst five Dow stocks average 4.9% gain in the last two weeks plus the first week of the new year.

JANUARY DAILY POINT CHANGES DOW JONES INDUSTRIALS

Previous Months	1988	1989	1990	1991	1992	1993	1994	1995	1996	1997
Close	1938.83	2168.57	2753.20	2633.66	3168.83	3301.11	3754.09	3834.44	5117.12	6448.27
1	H	H	H	H	H	H	H	H	H	H
2	—	—	56.95	−23.02	3.58	–	—	—	60.33	– 5.78
3	—	−23.93	– 0.42	−37.13	29.07	—	2.51	4.04	16.62	101.60
4	76.42	33.04	−13.65	– 7.42	—	8.11	27.30	19.17	−20.23	—
5	16.25	12.86	−22.83	—	—	– 1.35	14.92	– 6.73	7.59	—
6	6.30	3.75	—	—	– 1.35	– 2.71	5.06	16.49	—	23.09
7	14.09	—	—	−43.32	4.70	−36.20	16.89	—	—	33.48
8	−140.58	—	21.12	−13.36	0.89	−17.29	—	—	16.25	−51.18
9	—	5.17	−28.37	−39.11	5.59	—	—	– 6.06	−67.55	76.19
10	—	– 6.25	−15.36	28.46	−10.07	—	44.74	5.39	−97.19	78.12
11	33.82	13.22	10.03	2.73	—	11.08	−15.20	– 4.71	32.16	—
12	16.58	15.89	−71.46	—	—	1.89	– 1.68	– 3.03	– 3.98	—
13	– 3.82	3.75	—	—	−13.86	– 1.08	– 6.20	49.46	—	5.39
14	– 8.62	—	—	−17.58	60.60	4.32	24.77	—	—	53.11
15	39.96	—	−19.84	6.68	12.30	3.24	—	—	−17.34	−35.41
16	—	– 1.43	23.25	18.32	– 8.95	—	—	23.88	44.44	38.49
17	—	−10.00	−33.49	114.60	15.43	—	3.09	– 1.68	−21.32	67.73
18	7.79	24.11	7.25	23.27	—	3.79	N/C	– 1.68	57.45	—
19	– 27.52	0.36	11.52	—	—	−18.92	14.08	−46.77	60.33	—
20	– 57.20	– 3.75	—	—	−10.95	−14.04	7.59	−12.78	—	10.77
21	0.17	—	—	−17.57	−30.64	11.07	22.52	—	—	40.03
22	24.20	—	−77.45	−25.99	32.42	3.79	—	—	34.68	−33.87
23	—	−16.97	14.87	15.84	−29.07	—	—	– 2.02	−27.09	−94.28
24	—	38.04	−10.82	24.01	6.04	—	– 1.69	– 4.71	50.57	−59.27
25	42.94	9.46	−43.46	16.34	—	35.39	−17.45	8.75	−26.01	—
26	– 25.86	25.18	– 1.81	—	—	6.75	12.66	– 1.01	54.92	—
27	– 9.45	31.79	—	—	7.83	– 7.56	18.30	−12.45	—	−35.79
28	18.90	—	—	– 4.95	31.53	14.86	19.13	—	—	– 4.61
29	28.18	—	– 5.85	8.16	−47.18	4.05	—	—	33.23	84.66
30	—	1.25	−10.14	50.50	19.90	—	—	−25.91	76.23	83.12
31	—	18.21	47.30	23.27	−21.47	—	32.93	11.78	14.09	−10.77
Close	1958.22	2342.32	2590.54	2736.39	3223.39	3310.30	3978.36	3843.86	5395.30	6813.09
Change	19.39	173.75	−162.66	102.73	54.56	9.19	224.27	9.42	278.18	364.82

DECEMBER/JANUARY

MONDAY
 29

*Days between the 26th through the 10th
of months outperform middle
11th through 25th days.*
— Yale Hirsch (see page 48)

TUESDAY

*Better to sell "too late" than "too soon"
in a momentum driven market as stocks
often go much, much higher.
Let your stock hit at least two lower
tops and bottoms before you sell.*
— Jordan Kimmel, Private Money Manager

WEDNESDAY
 31

*I was in search of a one-armed economist so
that the guy could never make a statement
and then say: "on the other hand."*
— Harry S. Truman

**New Year's Day
(Market Closed)**

THURSDAY
1

*As far as paying off debt is concerned, there
are very few instances in history when any
government has ever paid off debt.*
— Walter Wriston

FRIDAY

*In Boston they ask, "How much does he know?"
In New York, "How much is he worth?" In
Philadephia, "Who were his parents?"*
— Mark Twain

SATURDAY
3

SUNDAY
4

THE INCREDIBLE JANUARY BAROMETER
ONLY THREE MAJOR ERRORS IN 47 YEARS

Since 1950, the January Barometer has predicted the annual course of the stock market with amazing accuracy. Based on whether Standard & Poor's composite index is up or down in January, most years have, in essence, followed suit—42 out of 47 times—for an 89% batting average. However, there were **no errors in odd years** when new congresses convened.

January performance chronologically and by rank is shown below. The top 27 Januarys (except 1994) had gains of 1% and launched the best market years. Twenty-one Januarys were losers or had miniscule gains. Only one very good year—1982—followed a January loss. 1966, 1968, and 1982 were significant errors—Vietnam affected the first two.

AS JANUARY GOES, SO GOES THE YEAR

	Market Performance in January				January Performance by Rank			
	Previous Year's Close	January Close	January Change	Rank			January Change	Year's Change
1950	16.76	17.05	1.7%	1	1987		13.2%	2.0%
1951	20.41	21.66	6.1	2	1975		12.3	31.5
1952	23.77	24.14	1.6	3	1976		11.8	19.1
1953	26.57	26.38	− 0.7	4	1967		7.8	20.1
1954	24.81	26.08	5.1	5	1985		7.4	26.3
1955	35.98	36.63	1.8	6	1989		7.1	27.3
1956	45.48	43.82	− 3.6	7	1980		6.7	25.8
1957	46.67	44.72	− 4.2	8	1961		6.3	23.1
1958	39.99	41.70	4.3	9	1997		6.1	??
1959	55.21	55.42	0.4	10	1951		6.1	16.5
1960	59.89	55.61	− 7.1	11	1954		5.1	45.0
1961	58.11	61.78	6.3	12	1963		4.9	18.9
1962	71.55	68.84	− 3.8	13	1958		4.3	38.1
1963	63.10	66.20	4.9	14	1991		4.1	26.3
1964	75.02	77.04	2.7	15	1971		4.0	10.8
1965	84.75	87.56	3.3	16	1988		4.0	12.4
1966	92.43	92.88	0.5	17	1979		4.0	12.3
1967	80.33	86.61	7.8	18	1965		3.3	9.1
1968	96.47	92.24	− 4.4	19	1983		3.3	17.3
1969	103.86	103.01	− 0.8	20	1996		3.3	20.3
1970	92.06	85.02	− 7.6	21	1994		3.3	− 1.5
1971	92.15	95.88	4.0	22	1964		2.7	13.0
1972	102.09	103.94	1.8	23	1995		2.4	34.1
1973	118.05	116.03	− 1.7	24	1972		1.8	15.6
1974	97.55	96.57	− 1.0	25	1955		1.8	26.4
1975	68.56	76.98	12.3	26	1950		1.7	21.8
1976	90.19	100.86	11.8	27	1952		1.6	11.8
1977	107.46	102.03	− 5.1	28	1993		0.7	7.1
1978	95.10	89.25	− 6.2	29	1966		0.5	−13.1
1979	96.11	99.93	4.0	30	1959		0.4	8.5
1980	107.94	115.12	6.7	31	1986		0.2	14.6
1981	135.76	129.55	− 4.6	32	1953		− 0.7	− 6.6
1982	122.55	120.40	− 1.8	33	1969		− 0.8	−11.4
1983	140.64	145.30	3.3	34	1984		− 0.9	1.4
1984	164.93	163.42	− 0.9	35	1974		− 1.0	−29.7
1985	167.24	179.63	7.4	36	1973		− 1.7	−17.4
1986	211.28	211.78	0.2	37	1982		− 1.8	14.8
1987	242.16	274.08	13.2	38	1992		− 2.0	4.5
1988	247.09	257.07	4.0	39	1956		− 3.6	2.6
1989	277.72	297.48	7.1	40	1962		− 3.8	−11.8
1990	353.40	329.07	− 6.9	41	1957		− 4.2	−14.3
1991	330.23	343.93	4.1	42	1968		− 4.4	7.7
1992	417.09	408.79	− 2.0	43	1981		− 4.6	− 9.7
1993	435.71	438.78	0.7	44	1977		− 5.1	−11.5
1994	466.45	481.61	3.3	45	1978		− 6.2	1.1
1995	459.27	470.42	2.4	46	1990		− 6.9	− 6.6
1996	615.93	636.02	3.3	47	1960		− 7.1	− 3.0
1997	740.74	786.16	6.1	48	1970		− 7.6	0.1

Based on S&P composite index

JANUARY

MONDAY

5

Big Business breeds bureaucracy and bureacrats exactly as big government does.
— T.K. Quinn

TUESDAY

6

All organizations are at least 50 percent waste— waste people, waste effort, waste space, and waste time.
— Robert Townsend

WEDNESDAY

7

A committee is a cul de sac down which ideas are lured and then quietly strangled.
— Barnett Cocks

Murphy, & Slots — W-2's & UD 1 ½ HR ✗

Murphy & Murphy — W-2's & Update
Expense Analysis 4 HRS ✗

THURSDAY

8

A good new chairman of the Federal Reserve Bank is worth a $10 billion tax cut.
— Paul H. Douglas

Buy Jan SPX Puts
Feb SXB

SPX 1110.67 +9.02
OEX 533.20 +4.84

FRIDAY

9

An entrepreneur tends to lie some of the time. An entrepreneur in trouble tends to lie most of the time.
— Anonymous

SATURDAY

10

SUNDAY

11

JANUARY BAROMETER IN GRAPHIC FORM

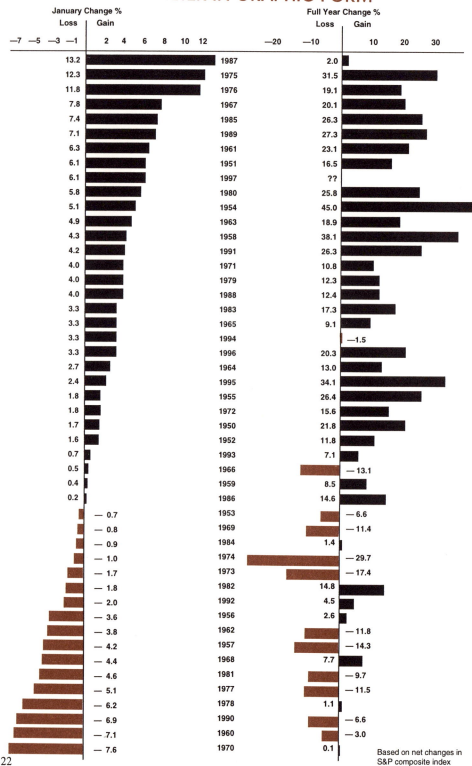

January Change %		
Loss	Gain	

—7 —5 —3 —1   2   4   6   8   10   12

		Full Year Change %
	Loss	Gain

—20   —10   10   20   30

January Change %	Year	Full Year Change %
13.2	1987	2.0
12.3	1975	31.5
11.8	1976	19.1
7.8	1967	20.1
7.4	1985	26.3
7.1	1989	27.3
6.3	1961	23.1
6.1	1951	16.5
6.1	1997	??
5.8	1980	25.8
5.1	1954	45.0
4.9	1963	18.9
4.3	1958	38.1
4.2	1991	26.3
4.0	1971	10.8
4.0	1979	12.3
4.0	1988	12.4
3.3	1983	17.3
3.3	1965	9.1
3.3	1994	—1.5
3.3	1996	20.3
2.7	1964	13.0
2.4	1995	34.1
1.8	1955	26.4
1.8	1972	15.6
1.7	1950	21.8
1.6	1952	11.8
0.7	1993	7.1
0.5	1966	—13.1
0.4	1959	8.5
0.2	1986	14.6
—0.7	1953	—6.6
—0.8	1969	—11.4
—0.9	1984	1.4
—1.0	1974	—29.7
—1.7	1973	—17.4
—1.8	1982	14.8
—2.0	1992	4.5
—3.6	1956	2.6
—3.8	1962	—11.8
—4.2	1957	—14.3
—4.4	1968	7.7
—4.6	1981	—9.7
—5.1	1977	—11.5
—6.2	1978	1.1
—6.9	1990	—6.6
—7.1	1960	—3.0
—7.6	1970	0.1

Based on net changes in
S&P composite index

22

JANUARY

MONDAY
12

There is always plenty of capital for those who can create practical plans for using it.
— Napoleon Hill

TUESDAY
13

In business, the competition will bite you if you keep running; if you stand still, they will swallow you.
— William Knudsen

WEDNESDAY
14

All the features and achievements of modern civilization are, directly or indirectly, the products of the capitalist process.
— Joseph A. Schumpeter

THURSDAY
15

Andy Musser Ltd
Photocopy returns   1 INK
Review termination   1 INK

The political problem of mankind is to combine three things: economic efficiency, social justice, and individual liberty.
— John Maynard Keynes

FRIDAY
 # 16

The only thing that saves us from the bureaucracy is its inefficiency.
— Eugene McCarthy

SATURDAY
17

SUNDAY
18

JANUARY'S FIRST FIVE DAYS
AN "EARLY WARNING" SYSTEM

January followers can often get a glimpse of what lies ahead by watching the market's action during the first five trading days of the month. These five days serve as an excellent "early warning" system with a batting average almost equal to the January Barometer's 89%.

Early January gains since 1950 (excluding 1994) were matched by whole-year gains with just three war related exceptions: The start of the Vietnam war triggered big military spending which delayed the start of the 1966 bear market; and the imminence of a final ceasefire raised stock prices temporarily in early January 1973; Saddam Hussein's actions in Kuwait brought the market down in 1990. Seventeen Januarys got off to a bad start and eight of those ended on the downside. The nine that didn't follow suit were 1955, 1956, 1978, 1982, 1985, 1986, 1988, 1991, and 1993.

Remember that five days is a brief span and some extraordinary event could sidetrack this indicator as on 1986's fifth day and again on 1990's fifth day.

THE FIRST-FIVE-DAYS-IN-JANUARY INDICATOR

	Chronological Data				Ranked By Performance		
	Previous Year's Close	5th Day In January	Change 1st 5 Days	Rank		Change 1st 5 Days	Change For Year
1950	16.76	17.09	2.0%	1	1987	6.2%	2.0%
1951	20.41	20.88	2.3	2	1976	4.9	19.1
1952	23.77	23.91	0.6	3	1983	3.3	17.3
1953	26.57	26.22	− 1.3	4	1967	3.1	20.1
1954	24.81	24.93	0.5	5	1979	2.8	12.3
1955	35.98	35.33	− 1.8	6	1963	2.6	18.9
1956	45.48	44.51	− 2.1	7	1958	2.5	38.1
1957	46.67	46.25	− 0.9	8	1984	2.4	1.4
1958	39.99	40.99	2.5	9	1951	2.3	16.5
1959	55.21	55.40	0.3	10	1975	2.2	31.5
1960	59.89	59.50	− 0.7	11	1950	2.0	21.8
1961	58.11	58.81	1.2	12	1973	1.5	−17.4
1962	71.55	69.12	− 3.4	13	1972	1.4	15.6
1963	63.10	64.74	2.6	14	1964	1.3	13.0
1964	75.02	76.00	1.3	15	1961	1.2	23.1
1965	84.75	85.37	0.7	16	1989	1.2	27.3
1966	92.43	93.14	0.8	17	1997	1.0	??
1967	80.33	82.81	3.1	18	1980	0.9	25.8
1968	96.47	96.62	0.2	19	1966	0.8	−13.1
1969	103.86	100.80	− 2.9	20	1994	0.7	− 1.5
1970	92.06	92.68	0.7	21	1965	0.7	9.1
1971	92.15	92.19	0.0	22	1970	0.7	0.1
1972	102.09	103.47	1.4	23	1952	0.6	11.8
1973	118.05	119.85	1.5	24	1954	0.5	45.0
1974	97.55	96.12	− 1.5	25	1996	0.4	20.3
1975	68.56	70.04	2.2	26	1959	0.3	8.5
1976	90.19	94.58	4.9	27	1995	0.3	34.1
1977	107.46	105.01	− 2.3	28	1992	0.2	4.5
1978	95.10	90.64	− 4.7	29	1968	0.2	7.7
1979	96.11	98.80	2.8	30	1990	0.1	− 6.6
1980	107.94	108.95	0.9	31	1971	0.0	10.8
1981	135.76	133.06	− 2.0	32	1960	− 0.7	− 3.0
1982	122.55	119.55	− 2.4	33	1957	− 0.9	−14.3
1983	140.64	145.23	3.3	34	1953	− 1.3	− 6.6
1984	164.93	168.90	2.4	35	1974	− 1.5	−29.7
1985	167.24	163.99	− 1.9	36	1988	− 1.5	12.4
1986	211.28	207.97	− 1.6	37	1993	− 1.5	7.1
1987	242.16	257.28	6.2	38	1986	− 1.6	14.6
1988	247.09	243.40	− 1.5	39	1955	− 1.8	26.4
1989	277.72	280.98	1.2	40	1985	− 1.9	26.3
1990	353.40	353.79	0.1	41	1981	− 2.0	− 9.7
1991	330.23	314.90	− 4.6	42	1956	− 2.1	2.6
1992	417.09	418.10	0.2	43	1977	− 2.3	−11.5
1993	435.71	429.05	− 1.5	44	1982	− 2.4	14.8
1994	466.45	469.90	0.7	45	1969	− 2.9	−11.4
1995	459.27	460.83	0.3	46	1962	− 3.4	−11.8
1996	615.93	618.46	0.4	47	1991	− 4.6	26.3
1997	740.74	748.41	1.0	48	1978	− 4.7	1.1

Based on S&P composite index

JANUARY

MONDAY
19

Without development there is no profit,
without profit, no development.
— Joseph A. Schumpeter

TUESDAY
20

The most valuable executive is one who is
training somebody to be a better man than he is.
— Robert G. Ingersoll

WEDNESDAY
21

Love of money is either the chief or a
secondary motive at the bottom of everything
the Americans do.
— Alexis de Tocqueville

THURSDAY
22

Economy is the art of making the most of life.
The love of economy is the root of all virtue.
— George Bernard Shaw

FRIDAY
23

Jones Termite & Pest Control
Payroll 45 Net
Worksheet 3 Hrs

How can I adopt a creed (socialism) which
exalts the boorish proletariat above the
bourgeois and the intelligentsia who, with
whatever faults, are the quality of life and surely
carry the seeds of all human advancement?
— John Maynard Keynes

SATURDAY
24

SUNDAY
25

Big January moves ebb
When they spill into Feb

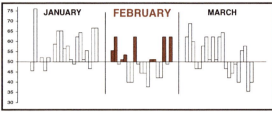

	FEBRUARY					
S	M	T	W	T	F	S
1	2	3	4	5	6	7
8	9	10	11	12	13	14
15	16	17	18	19	20	21
22	23	24	25	26	27	28

	MARCH					
S	M	T	W	T	F	S
1	2	3	4	5	6	7
8	9	10	11	12	13	14
15	16	17	18	19	20	21
22	23	24	25	26	27	28
29	30	31				

See Market Probability Chart on page 125.

❑ Sharp January moves tend to consolidate in February ❑ If January is up, stay in; if down, move to sidelines ❑ RECORD: S&P 27 up, 21 down ❑ February's average change is 0.1% since 1950 (page 50) ❑ Many analysts may revise annual forecasts at the beginning of February, as the rest of the year tends to follow the lead of January's performance, especially in odd years ❑ Tends to follow whatever major market trend we're in, bull or bear. ❑ FLASH: February has been the fourth best month in the last 12 years as the Dow was gaining about 6500 points (pages 50 and 146).

FEBRUARY DAILY POINT CHANGES DOW JONES INDUSTRIALS

	1988	1989	1990	1991	1992	1993	1994	1995	1996	1997
Previous Month	19 89	173.75	−162.66	+102.73	+ 54.56 +	9.19	+224.27 +	9.42 +	278.18	+364.82
Close	1958.22	2342.32	2590.54	2736.39	3223.39	3310.03	3978.36	3843.86	5395.30	6813.09
1	−13.59	− 4.11	− 4.28	− 5.70	—	22.15	−14.35	3.70	9.76	—
2	8.29	− 4.46	16.44	—	—	− 3.51	11.53	23.21	−31.07	—
3	−28.35	− 2.50	—	—	10.73	45.12	− 7.88	57.87	—	− 6.93
4	− 1.00	—	—	41.59	38.69	42.95	−96.24	—	—	27.32
5	−13.09	—	19.82	16.09	−15.21	25.40	—	—	33.60	−86.58
6	—	−10.18	−16.21	42.57	− 2.01	—	—	9.09	52.02	26.16
7	—	26.07	33.78	−20.30	−30.19	—	34.90	− 0.34	32.51	82.74
8	−14.76	− 3.93	4.28	20.05	—	− 4.60	− 0.29	− 2.02	47.33	—
9	18.74	−20.17	3.83	—	—	−22.96	25.89	− 2.69	2.17	—
10	47.58	−36.97	—	—	19.68	− 2.16	−36.58	6.39	—	−49.26
11	−0.50	—	—	71.54	6.49	10.27	− 0.56	—	—	51.57
12	21.72	—	−29.06	−27.48	25.26	−30.26	—	—	58.53	103.52
13	—	− 3.57	4.96	34.41	−30.18	—	—	15.14	1.08	60.81
14	—	− 1.25	0.22	−31.93	− 0.68	—	9.28	4.04	−21.68	−33.48
15	H	22.68	25.23	57.42	—	H	24.21	27.92	−28.18	—
16	22.71	7.50	−13.96	—	—	−82.94	9.00	1.35	−48.05	—
17	− 4.98	13.39	—	—	H	2.70	−14.63	−33.98	—	H
18	−14.58	—	—	H	−21.24	−10.00	−35.18	—	—	78.50
19	28.18	—	H	− 2.47	5.59	19.99	—	—	H	−47.33
20	—	H	−38.74	−33.17	50.32	—	—	H	−44.79	−92.75
21	—	1.61	−13.29	− 7.18	− 0.45	—	H	10.43	57.44	4.24
22	25.70	−42.50	− 8.79	− 2.47	—	20.81	24.20	9.08	92.49	—
23	− 1.17	5.53	−10.58	—	—	−19.72	−19.98	30.28	22.03	—
24	0.83	−43.92	—	—	2.23	33.23	−51.78	8.41	—	76.58
25	−22.38	—	—	− 1.49	−24.59	8.64	− 1.12	—	—	29.63
26	5.64	—	38.29	−23.27	25.49	5.67	—	—	−65.39	−54.65
27	—	4.82	14.64	24.51	−13.87	—	—	−23.17	−15.89	−58.11
28	—	8.03	10.13	− 6.93	− 1.78	—	− 6.76	22.48	−43.00	N/C
29	48.41								−20.59	
Close	2071.62	2258.39	2627.25	2882.18	3267.67	3370.81	3832.02	4011.05	5485.62	6925.07
Change	113.40	−83.93	36.71	145.79	44.28	60.78	−146.34	167.19	90.32	111.98

MONDAY

26

Free trade, one of the great blessings
a government can confer on a people, is in
almost every country unpopular.
— Thomas Macauley

TUESDAY

27

If you can take twenty thousand dollars in
one-hundred dollar bills and walk up on a windy hill
and tear them up and watch them blow away,
and it doesn't bother you, then
you should go into the commodities market.
— attributed to Don Tyson, The New Yorker

WEDNESDAY

 # 28

You know you're right
when the other side
starts to shout.
— I. A. O'Shaughnessy

THURSDAY

 # 29

If you bet on a horse, that's gambling.
If you bet you can make three spades,
that's entertainment. If you bet cotton
will go up three points, that's business.
See the difference?
— Blackie Sherrod

FRIDAY

 # 30

I always know we are
very close to a rally
when I start to question
my own work.
— Elaine Garzarelli

J. & J. BOZZELLI - 11:00 AM

SATURDAY

31

SUNDAY

1

1933 "LAME DUCK" AMENDMENT REASON JANUARY BAROMETER WORKS

Between 1901 and 1933 the market's direction in January was similar to that of the whole year 19 times and different 14 times. Comparing January to the 11 subsequent months, 16 were similar and 17 dissimilar.

A dramatic change occurred in 1934—the Twentieth Amendment to the Constitution! Since then it has essentially been "As January goes, so goes the year." January's direction has been correct in most of the subsequent years.

January Barometer (Odd Years)
LAME DUCK AMENDMENT RATIFIED 1933
JANUARY BAROMETER IS BORN

January % Change	12 Month % Change	Same	Opposite
−4.2%	41.2%		1935
3.8	−38.6		1937
−6.9	−5.4	1939	
−4.8	−17.9	1941	
7.2	19.4	1943	
1.4	30.7	1945	
2.4	0.0	1947	
0.1	10.3	1949	
6.1	16.5	1951	
−0.7	−6.6	1953	
1.8	26.4	1955	
−4.2	−14.3	1957	
0.4	8.5	1959	
6.3	23.1	1961	
4.9	18.9	1963	
3.3	9.1	1965	
7.8	20.1	1967	
−0.8	−11.4	1969	
4.0	10.8	1971	
−1.7	−17.4	1973	
12.3	31.5	1975	
−5.1	−11.5	1977	
4.0	12.3	1979	
−4.6	−9.7	1981	
3.3	17.3	1983	
7.4	26.3	1985	
13.2	2.0	1987	
7.1	27.3	1989	
4.2	26.3	1991	
0.7	7.1	1993	
2.4	34.1	1995	
6.1	??	1997?	

12 month's % change includes January's % change
Based on S&P composite index

Prior to 1934, new Congresses generally convened the first Monday in December (except when new Presidents were inaugurated). Newly elected Senators and Representatives did not take office until December of the following year, **13 months later**. Defeated Congressmen stayed in Congress for all of the following session. They were known as "lame ducks."

Since the Twentieth (Lame Duck) Amendment was ratified in 1933, Congress convenes January 3 and includes those members newly elected the previous November. Inauguration Day was also moved up from March 4 to January 20. As a result several events have been squeezed into January which affect our economy and our stock market and quite possibly those of many nations of the world. During January, Congress convenes, the President gives the State of the Union message, presents the annual budget and sets national goals and priorities. Switch these events to any other month and chances are the January Barometer would become a memory.

The table shows the January Barometer and its predecessors in odd years. In 1935 and 1937, the Democrats already had the most lopsided congressional margins in history, so when these two Congresses convened it was anticlimactic. The January Barometer in all subsequent odd years compiled a **perfect record**.

(continued on page 30)

FEBRUARY

MONDAY

Beware of inside information...
all inside information.
— Jesse Livermore, *How to Trade In Stocks*

TUESDAY

Life is an illusion.
You are what you
think you are.
— Yale Hirsch

WEDNESDAY

What the superior man seeks is
in himself. What the inferior
man seeks is in others.
— Confucious

THURSDAY

During the first period of a
man's life, the greatest danger is:
not to take the risk.
— Soren Kierkegaard

FRIDAY

We are all in the gutter,
but some of us are looking
at the stars.
— Oscar Wilde

SATURDAY
7

SUNDAY
8

(continued from page 28)

Prior to the Twentieth Amendment in this century, we had a "March Barometer" when newly-elected Presidents (Taft, Wilson, Harding, Hoover, and Roosevelt) were inaugurated on March 4. Newly elected Congresses convened in March for the occasion. Score 5 out of 5 for the "March Barometer" prior to the Twentieth Amendment.

Between 1900 and 1933, eight new Congresses convened on the first Monday in December (13 months after the election). But because of annual year-end reinvestment, it would be misleading to use December as a barometer. I used a "November Barometer" instead and the score was almost perfect. In 1903, the only time Congress actually convened in November, the barometer was in error. The Panic of 1903 took the Dow down 37.7% and the new Congress was called in one month earlier, ostensibly to "stem the tide." The Panic ended on November 9, the day Congress convened, but the month remained negative while the market moved up over the next 11 months.

Three other new Congresses were convened in other months for different reasons—April in 1911 and 1917 and May in 1919. The record is a double bulls-eye for the "April Barometer." As for the one-shot "May Barometer" a post-Armistice 30.9% surge in four months (February to May) took May up 13.6% but the 12-month period (including May) almost lost it all. President Wilson spent six months in Europe trying to win the peace.

New Congress Barometers (Odd Years)
NEWLY ELECTED PRESIDENT INAUGURATED MARCH 4TH

March % Change	12 Month's % Change	Same	Opposite
5.2%	11.6%	1909	
0.7	2.4	1913	
1.0	14.0	1921	
− 2.7	− 14.6	1929	
7.8	101.3	1933	

12 month's % change includes March

NEW CONGRESS CONVENES FIRST WEEK IN DECEMBER 13 MONTHS AFTER ELECTION

November % Change	12 Month's % Change	Same	Opposite
0.9%	2.5%	1901	
− 1.8	39.7		1903*
7.3	10.9	1905	
1.2	4.3	1907	
0.7	8.9	1915	
4.3	17.5	1923	
3.5	3.9	1925	
9.1	38.8	1927	
− 11.0	− 41.3	1931	

*Panic of 1903 ends 11/9 as Congress convenes (off 37.7%)
12 month's % change includes November

NEW CONGRESS CONVENES IN APRIL OR MAY EARLIER THAN USUAL, NO CHANGE IN PRESIDENCY

Month's % Change	12 Month's % Change	Same	Opposite
0.5%	6.0%	1911	
− 2.3	− 19.6	1917	
13.6	0.7	1919**	

**Wilson in Europe 6 months; Post-Armistice surge (up 30.9% Feb to May)
12 month's % change includes applicable month

Based on Dow Jones industrial average (1901-1933)

This "New Congress Barometer" performed rather impressively until the passage of the Twentieth Amendment. Since then, it's successor, the January Barometer has compiled the best record in odd-numbered years of all other known indicators. A perfect record since 1937 is hard to beat.

FEBRUARY

MONDAY
9

*In the realm of ideas, everything
depends on enthusiasm; in the real
world, all rests on perseverance.*
— Goethe

TUESDAY
10

*For a country, everything will be lost
when the jobs of an economist
and a banker become highly
respected professions.*
— Montesquieu

Ash Wednesday

WEDNESDAY
11

Wallace   10:00 AM

Hunter   1:00 PM

*Those heroes of finance are like
beads on a string, when one slips off,
the rest follow.*
— Henrik Ibsen

THURSDAY
12

*Every man is the architect of
his own fortune.*
— Appius Claudius

FRIDAY
13

*All a parent can give a child
is roots and wings.*
— Chinese proverb

St. Valentine's Day

SATURDAY
14

SUNDAY
15

MARKET CHARTS OF POST-PRESIDENTIAL ELECTION YEARS

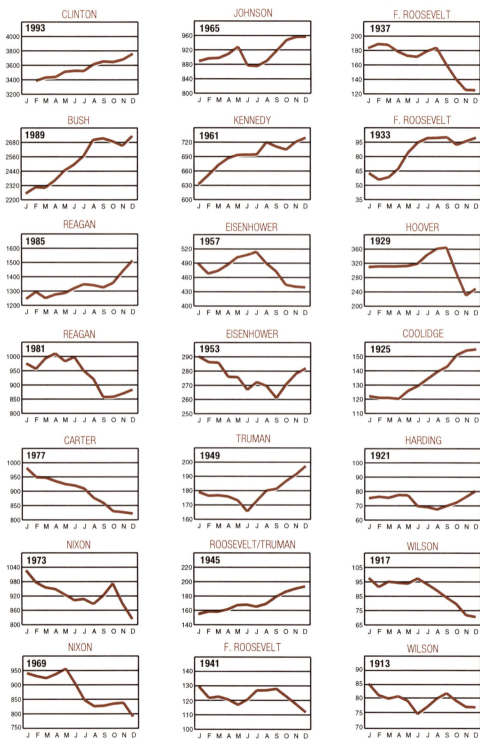

Based on Dow Jones industrial average mean of the month

FEBRUARY

MONDAY 16

P. Devit 10:00 AM

*The worse a situation becomes the less
it takes to turn it around, the bigger
the upside.*
— George Soros

TUESDAY 17

RAYNER VENDING - 237-3430

Mcbride - 2½ mi. 3 mi. Gorstin
420 Right) Pearla V. Sion
Maple Nery Alu
Parker r vice

3020
Martin Branville Ltt on Parker
Mailbox

*Poor Mexico, so far from God, but so
close to the United States.*
— Quoted on CNBC May 1993

WEDNESDAY 18

DR. DEAL - CLEANING 1:45PM

*There is only one side of the market
and it is not the bull side or the bear side,
but the right side.*
— Jesse Livermore

THURSDAY 19

*Drawing on my fine command of
language, I said nothing.*
— Robert Benchley

FRIDAY 20

*Markets are constantly in a state of
uncertainty and flux and money is made
by discounting the obvious and betting on
the unexpected.*
— George Soros

SATURDAY 21

W. Ricker

SUNDAY 22

Up, up in March is the Dow's direction
In the year before a Presidential election

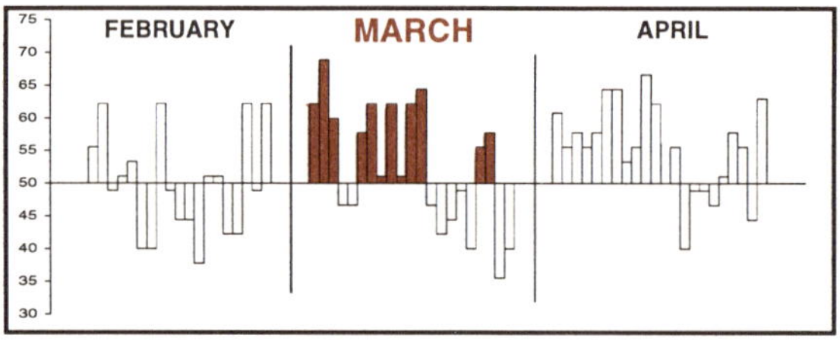

See Market Probability Chart on page 125.

MARCH ALMANAC

MARCH

S	M	T	W	T	F	S
1	2	3	4	5	6	7
8	9	10	11	12	13	14
15	16	17	18	19	20	21
22	23	24	25	26	27	28
29	30	31				

APRIL

S	M	T	W	T	F	S
			1	2	3	4
5	6	7	8	9	10	11
12	13	14	15	16	17	18
19	20	21	22	23	24	25
26	27	28	29	30		

❑ "In like a lion, out like a lamb" describes stronger first half than second ❑ Many substantial rallies of at least 5% started here since 1949 ❑ RECORD: S&P 31 up, 17 down ❑ Average S&P gain 0.9%, sixth best ❑ Gain of 241.46 Dow points, eighth best over 47 years (gained 146 points in 1995 but lost 294 points in 1997) ❑ March fares much better when the market takes a hit in February (1994 was an exception). ❑ March 20th will be a triple expiration day and potentially volatile.

MARCH DAILY POINT CHANGES DOW JONES INDUSTRIALS

Previous Month Close	1988	1989	1990	1991	1992	1993	1994	1995	1996	1997
	2071.62	**2258.39**	**2627.25**	**2882.18**	**3267.67**	**3370.81**	**3832.02**	**4011.05**	**5485.62**	**6877.74**
1	– 1.16	–15.35	8.34	27.72	—	–15.40	–22.79	–16.25	50.94	—
2	0.83	22.67	24.77	—	7.60	45.12	22.51	–14.87	—	—
3	– 7.80	8.58	—	–	14.98	3.51	– 7.32	9.68	—	41.18
4	– 5.63	—	–	4.21	–21.69	– 5.13	7.88	—	63.59	– 66.20
5	—	—	–10.81	58.41	–27.06	5.67	—	—	42.27	93.13
6	—	20.53	27.25	0.75	–19.90	—	—	7.95	– 12.65	– 1.15
7	– 1.49	– 4.11	– 7.21	– 9.90	—	—	23.92	–34.93	11.92	56.19
8	24.70	4.83	26.58	– 8.17	—	64.84	– 4.50	16.60	–171.24	—
9	– 6.80	– 4.11	–12.84	—	– 6.48	2.70	1.69	4.16	—	—
10	–48.24	– 9.29	—	—	15.87	6.22	–22.79	52.22	—	78.50
11	8.95	—	—	–15.84	–22.36	–21.34	32.08	—	110.55	5.77
12	—	—	3.38	–16.84	N/C	–29.18	—	—	2.89	– 45.79
13	—	24.11	–12.16	32.68	27.28	—	—	–10.38	– 15.17	–160.48
14	15.09	N/C	13.29	– 2.97	—	—	0.28	23.52	17.34	56.57
15	– 2.66	14.29	7.88	– 3.96	—	14.59	–13.39	–10.38	– 1.09	—
16	16.91	20.17	45.50	—	0.45	0.54	– 1.44	30.78	—	—
17	21.72	–48.57	—	—	19.68	–16.21	16.99	4.50	—	20.02
18	1.33	—	—	–18.32	– 1.79	38.90	30.51	—	98.63	– 58.92
19	—	—	14.41	–62.13	7.15	5.94	—	—	– 14.09	– 18.88
20	—	–29.64	–16.89	4.21	14.99	—	—	10.03	– 14.09	– 57.40
21	–20.23	3.75	–10.81	–16.58	—	—	–30.80	–11.07	– 28.54	– 15.49
22	– 0.99	– 3.04	–32.21	3.46	—	– 8.10	– 2.30	10.38	9.76	—
23	1.49	–20.17	8.56	—	– 4.25	– 1.62	6.91	4.84	—	—
24	–43.77	—	—	—	–11.18	–16.48	–48.37	50.84	—	100.46
25	–44.92	—	—	6.93	– 1.57	15.94	–46.36	—	7.22	– 29.08
26	—	—	3.38	49.01	8.28	–21.34	—	—	26.74	4.53
27	—	14.82	29.28	2.72	–36.23	—	—	18.67	– 43.72	–140.11
28	0.82	17.68	6.75	–3.71	—	—	–12.38	– 5.53	3.97	H
29	18.57	5.98	–15.99	—	—	15.12	–63.33	8.99	– 43.71	—
30	–20.22	– 0.18	–20.49	—	3.80	2.17	–72.27	11.76	—	—
31	9.94	12.28	—	—	0.23	–22.16	9.21	–14.87	—	–157.11
Close	**1988.06**	**2293.62**	**2707.21**	**2913.86**	**3235.47**	**3435.11**	**3635.96**	**4157.69**	**5587.14**	**6583.48**
Change	**–83.56**	**35.23**	**79.96**	**31.68**	**–32.20**	**64.30**	**–196.06**	**146.64**	**101.52**	**–294.26**

FEBRUARY/MARCH

MONDAY
23

It isn't as important to buy as cheap as possible as it is to buy at the right time.
— Jesse Livermore

TUESDAY
24

Writing a book is an adventure. To begin with it is a toy, an amusement; then it is a mistress, and then a master, and then a tyrant.
— Winston Churchill

WEDNESDAY
25

I don't know where speculation got such a bad name, since I know of no forward leap which was not fathered by speculation.
— John Steinbeck

THURSDAY

To affect the quality of the day, that is the highest of the arts.
— Henry David Thoreau

FRIDAY

Imagination is more important than knowledge.
— Albert Einstein

SATURDAY
28

SUNDAY
1

MIDTERM ELECTION YEARS:
WHERE BOTTOM PICKERS FIND PARADISE

American presidents have danced the Quadrennial Quadrille over the past two centuries. After the midterm congressional election and the invariable seat loss by his party, the president during the next two years jiggles fiscal policies to get federal spending, disposable income and social security benefits up and interest rates and inflation down. By Election Day, he will have danced his way into the wallets and hearts of the electorate and, hopefully, will have choreographed four more years in the White House for his party.

After the Inaugural Ball is over, however, we pay the piper. Practically all bear markets began and ended in the two years after presidential elections. Bottoms often occurred in an air of crisis: the Cuban Missile Crisis in 1962, tight money in 1966, Cambodia in 1970, Watergate and Nixon's resignation in 1974, and threat of international monetary collapse in 1982. But remember, the word for "crisis" in Chinese is composed of two characters: the first, the symbol for danger; the second, opportunity. Of the 16 quadrennial cycles in the past 64 years, only three bottoms were reached in the post-presidential year. All others came in midterm years, including the six in a row prior to 1986.

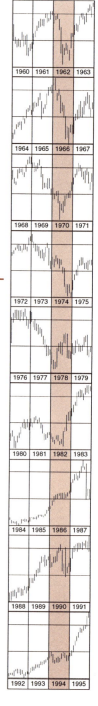

MIDTERM ELECTION YEAR RECORD SINCE 1914

1914	Wilson (D)	Bottom in July. War closed markets.
1918	Wilson (D)	Bottom 12 days prior to start of year.
1922	Harding (R)	Bottom 4½ months prior to start of year.
1926	Coolidge (R)	Only drop (7 wks, –17%) ends Mar. 30.
1930	Hoover (R)	Crash of '29 continues through 1930. **No bottom.**
1934	Roosevelt (D)	First Roosevelt bear, February to July 26 bottom (–23%).
1938	Roosevelt (D)	Big 1937 break ends in March, DJI off 49%.
1942	Roosevelt (D)	World War II bottom in April.
1946	Truman (D)	Market tops in May, bottoms in October.
1950	Truman (D)	June 1949 bottom, but June 1950 Korean War outbreak causes 14% drop.
1954	Eisenhower (R)	September 1953 bottom, then straight up.
1958	Eisenhower (R)	October 1957 bottom, then straight up.
1962	Kennedy (D)	Bottoms in June and October.
1966	Johnson (D)	Bottom in October.
1970	Nixon (R)	Bottom in May.
1974	Nixon, Ford (R)	December Dow bottom, S&P bottom in October.
1978	Carter (D)	March bottom, despite October massacre later.
1982	Reagan (R)	Bottom in August.
1986	Reagan (R)	**No bottom in 1985 or 1986.**
1990	Bush (R)	Bottom in October (Kuwaiti Invasion).
1994	Clinton (D)	Bottom on April 4th after 10% drop.

MONDAY
  2

From listening comes wisdom, and from speaking repentance.
— Italian proverb

TUESDAY
  3

He who knows nothing is confident of everything.
— Anonymous

WEDNESDAY
  4

I must create a system or be enslaved by another man's.
— William Blake

THURSDAY
  5

SKITARSLIE

I just wait until the fourth year, when the business cycle bottoms, and buy whatever I think will have the biggest bounce.
— Larry Tisch's investment style

FRIDAY
  6

SKITARSLER   1:00 PM

MCCUNLOGUE   11:00 AM

*How a minority
Reaching majority
Seizing authority
Hates a minority.*
— Leonard H. Robbins

SATURDAY
7

SUNDAY
8

PROFITING ON ST. PATRICK'S DAY—MORE THAN LUCK!

Most savvy traders know that the day before major holidays strongly tends to be bullish. Dan Turov, editor of *Turov On Timing* (published by the Hirsch Organization), calls the market daily using the S&P cash index, is operating at over a 400% average annual rate of return for the past 45 months. Turov has investigated the seasonality of market trading around St. Patrick's Day. Results appear in the table below.

Note the stellar performance of the market on the day before St. Patrick's Day. The average gain of 0.26% on the S&P is equivalent to more than 21 Dow points (at current levels for the Dow). That's equal to an annualized rate of return of almost 100%! So the day before St. Patrick's Day compares quite favorably with the day before more conventional holidays.

In 1998 St. Patrick's Day falls on Tuesday, March 17th. Therefore, it's more than likely that Monday, March 16th will provide you with an added edge to make a little extra profit in the market.

During the past 45 years St. Patrick's Day has posted an average gain of 0.02%. The record for this day would be improved quite a bit if we could discount the 3% loss in 1980 during the Hunt Silver Crisis. The average gain then would be 0.09%.

St. Patrick's Day Trading Record (Days Before And After)

Year	% Change 2 Days Prior	% Change 1 Day Prior	% Change St. Patrick's Day	S&P Day After St. Patrick's Day	% Change Day After
1953	0.19%	0.15%	0.42%	26.24%	−0.34%
1954	−0.45	−0.04	0.23	26.73	0.41
1955	2.15	0.76	0.39	36.18	0.17
1956	0.97	0.31	0.93	48.87	0.58
1957	0.07	−0.05	−0.45	44.04	0.43
1958	0.12	−0.31	−0.69	41.89	−0.36
1959	0.12	−1.08	0.82	56.39	−0.23
1960	0.77	0.55	−0.15	55.01	0.09
1961	0.30	1.01	0.61	64.86	0.40
1962	0.21	−0.17	−0.13	70.66	−0.27
1963	−0.47	0.50	−0.49	65.47	−0.21
1964	0.08	0.00	0.23	79.38	0.08
1965	0.03	−0.13	−0.13	86.81	−0.24
1966	−0.57	0.58	0.35	88.53	0.41
1967	0.95	1.01	0.18	90.20	−0.06
1968	−1.90	0.88	0.55	88.99	−0.67
1969	−0.67	−0.40	0.26	98.49	0.24
1970	−0.53	−1.08	0.44	87.54	0.29
1971	1.14	0.50	−0.09	101.19	0.07
1972	0.13	−0.23	0.39	107.59	−0.31
1973	−0.75	−0.51	−1.21	111.95	−0.20
1974	−0.09	−0.37	−1.24	97.23	−0.84
1975	0.18	1.22	1.47	85.13	−1.02
1976	−1.05	1.12	−0.06	100.45	−0.41
1977	0.55	0.19	−0.09	101.86	−0.22
1978	−0.26	0.44	0.77	90.82	0.69
1979	0.15	0.83	0.37	100.50	−0.55
1980	−1.17	−0.18	−3.01	104.10	1.80
1981	−0.06	1.18	−0.56	134.22	0.22
1982	0.77	−0.16	−0.18	110.30	1.12
1983	0.35	−1.03	−0.14	149.90	0.21
1984	0.41	1.18	−0.94	158.86	0.68
1985	−0.20	−0.74	0.20	179.54	1.50
1986	0.28	1.44	−0.79	235.78	0.47
1987	−0.46	−0.57	1.47	292.78	0.11
1988	−0.09	0.95	0.96	271.12	−0.04
1989	0.52	0.93	−2.25	289.92	−0.95
1990	0.36	1.14	0.47	341.57	−0.57
1991	−0.29	0.02	−0.40	366.59	−1.48
1992	0.48	0.14	0.78	409.15	−0.10
1993	0.36	−0.01	−0.68	451.88	0.80
1994	−0.08	0.52	0.31	471.06	0.04
1995	−0.20	0.72	0.02	496.14	0.13
1996	0.37	0.09	1.75	651.69	−0.15
1997	−1.83%	0.46%	0.32%	789.66	−0.76%
Average	**0.02%**	**0.26%**	**0.02%**		**0.02%**

MARCH

MONDAY
9

Spend at least as much time
researching a stock as you would
choosing a refrigerator.
— Peter Lynch

TUESDAY
10

The world will not see another such talent
for a hundred years.
— Franz Joseph Haydn, after Mozart's death at 35

WEDNESDAY
11

6:00 Dr, Urban

1:00 · LaPlante

The mass of men lead lives
of quiet desperation.
— Henry David Thoreau (a favorite Ross Perot quote)

THURSDAY
12

The first rule is not to lose. The second
rule is not to forget the first rule.
— Warren Buffett

FRIDAY
13

Press on. Nothing in the world can take the place of persistence.
Talent will not: nothing is more common than unrewarded talent.
Education alone will not: the world is full of educated failures.
Persistence alone is omnipotent.
— Calvin Coolidge

SATURDAY
14

SUNDAY
15

SPRING PORTFOLIO REVIEW

NO. OF SHARES	SECURITY	A ORIGINAL COST	B CURRENT VALUE	C GAIN (B – A) OR LOSS (A – B)	D % CHANGE (C ÷ A)	E MONTHS HELD	F CHANGE PER MO. (D ÷ E)	G ANNUAL RETURN (F × 12)
200	Sample Corp.	$10,000	$10,400	$400	4.0%	8	0.5%	6.0%
	TOTALS							

Stocks which have achieved their potential
1
2
3

Candidates for addition to portfolio
1
2
3

Stocks which have been disappointments
1
2
3

Investment decisions
1
2
3

MARCH

MONDAY
 16

*Companies already dominant in a field
rarely produce the breakthroughs that
transform it.*
—George Gilder

TUESDAY
17

4:00 Chadwick

5:00 Krams

*Nothing will ever be attempted if all possible
objections must first be overcome.*
—Plaque on J.R. Simplot's desk

WEDNESDAY
18

*With enough inside information and a million dollars,
you can go broke in a year*
—Warren Buffett

THURSDAY
19

5:00 MRS. KRAMER

*You can get everything in life you want, if
you help enough other people get what
they want.*
— Zig Ziglar

FRIDAY
20

1:00 PM → LOIS KIRCLEY

*The greatest trouble with most of us is that
our demands upon ourselves are so feeble,
the call upon the great within us so weak
and intermittent that it makes no
impression upon the creative energies.*
— Orlson Swett Marden

SATURDAY
21

SUNDAY
22

FIRST HALF OF APRIL OUTPERFORMS SECOND HALF

Most people believe Uncle Sam has a chilling effect on stock prices in early April. They assume many investors sell some of their holdings to pay income taxes. Once the April 15 tax deadline passes, they guess the market will turn up as tax selling ceases. However, the obvious is seldom true in investing. From 1955 through 1997, the first half of April outperformed the second half 28 out of 43 times. Note: last four second halves have been superior.

MARKET PERFORMANCE IN APRIL

	End of March	Mid-April Tax Deadline	End of April	April 1-15	April 16-30
1955	36.58	37.96	37.96	3.8%	0.0%
1956	48.48	47.96	48.38	—1.1	0.9
1957	44.11	44.95	45.74	1.9	1.8
1958	42.10	42.43	43.44	0.8	2.4
1959	55.44	56.96	57.59	2.7	1.1
1960	55.34	56.59	54.37	2.3	—3.9
1961	65.06	66.68	65.31	2.5	—2.1
1962	69.55	67.60	65.24	—2.8	—3.5
1963	66.57	69.09	69.80	3.8	1.0
1964	78.98	80.09	79.46	1.4	—0.8
1965	86.16	88.15	89.11	2.3	1.1
1966	89.23	91.99	91.06	3.1	—1.0
1967	90.20	91.07	94.01	1.0	3.2
1968	90.20	96.59	97.46	7.1	0.9
1969	101.51	101.53	103.69	0.0	2.1
1970	89.63	86.73	81.52	—3.2	—6.0
1971	100.31	103.52	103.95	3.2	0.4
1972	107.20	109.51	107.67	2.2	—1.7
1973	111.52	111.44	106.97	—0.1	—4.0
1974	93.98	92.05	90.31	—2.1	—1.9
1975	83.36	86.30	87.30	3.5	1.2
1976	102.77	100.67	101.64	—2.0	1.0
1977	98.42	101.04	98.44	2.7	—2.6
1978	89.21	94.45	96.83	5.9	2.5
1979	101.59	101.12	101.76	—0.5	0.6
1980	102.09	102.83	106.29	0.7	3.4
1981	136.00	134.17	132.87	—1.3	—1.0
1982	111.96	116.35	116.44	3.9	0.1
1983	152.96	158.75	164.43	3.8	3.6
1984	159.18	158.32	160.04	—0.5	1.1
1985	180.66	180.92	179.83	0.1	—0.6
1986	238.90	237.73	235.52	—0.5	—0.9
1987	291.70	284.43	288.35	—2.5	1.4
1988	258.89	259.77	261.33	0.3	0.6
1989	294.87	301.72	309.64	2.3	2.6
1990	339.94	344.74	330.80	1.4	—4.0
1991	375.22	381.19	375.35	1.6	—1.5
1992	403.69	416.27	414.95	3.1	—0.3
1993	451.67	448.40	440.19	—0.7	—1.8
1994	445.76	446.18	450.99	0.1	1.1
1995	500.71	506.13	514.71	1.1	1.7
1996	645.50	642.49	654.18	—0.5	1.8
1997	795.08	754.72	801.34	—5.1	6.2
Based on S&P composite index			**Average**	**1.2**	**0.0%**

Five of the eleven Aprils with losses in the first half of the month were in bear market years. These declining years had more of an adverse effect on the last two weeks of the month. The table begins with 1955, as March 15 was the income tax deadline in prior years. When April 15 falls on the weekend and the IRS extends its deadline, the following Monday's market close is used. (See page 46 for market performance of first half of all months vs. second half.)

MARCH

MONDAY
23

*The greatest discovery of my generation
is that human beings can alter their
lives by altering their attitudes.*
— William James

TUESDAY
24

*Follow the course opposite to custom and
you will almost always do well.*
— Jean-Jacques Rousseau

WEDNESDAY
25

11:00 Bement
1:00 wilson. >
3:00 Keller

*If all the financial experts in this
country were laid end to end, they'd still
point in all directions.*
— Sam Ewing

THURSDAY
 ## 26

*The quality of a person's life is in direct
proportion to their commitment to
excellence, regardless of their chosen
field of endeavor.*
— Vince Lombardi

**Good Friday
(Market Closed)**

FRIDAY
27

*Quality is never an accident; it is always
the result of high intention, genuine
effort, intelligent direction,
and skillful execution.*
— Willa A. Foster

SATURDAY
28

Easter

SUNDAY
29

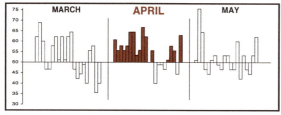

Market does better, two weeks before taxes
Remainder of April, Dow often relaxes

APRIL ALMANAC

APRIL						
S	M	T	W	T	F	S
				1	2	3	4
5	6	7	8	9	10	11
12	13	14	15	16	17	18
19	20	21	22	23	24	25
26	27	28	29	30		

MAY						
S	M	T	W	T	F	S
					1	2
3	4	5	6	7	8	9
10	11	12	13	14	15	16
17	18	19	20	21	22	23
24	25	26	27	28	29	30
31						

See Market Probability Chart on page 125.

❏ More ground gained in the two weeks prior to federal tax deadline than in the last two ❏ New trend may be starting in last four years (See page 42) ❏ When a company's first quarter earnings double, its stock tends to score a 25.2% gain the previous 30 days and only 5.0% more in the next 30 ❏ RECORD: S&P 33 up, 15 down ❏ Fourth best S&P gain of 1.4% (page 50) ❏ Not usually dangerous except in certain sharp bear markets (1962, 1970, 1973, 1974) ❏ Best Aprils often follow great Januarys ❏ Expect a down month during a bear market.

APRIL DAILY POINT CHANGES DOW JONES INDUSTRIALS

Previous Month Close	1988 1988.06	1989 2293.62	1990 2707.21	1991 2913.86	1992 3235.47	1993 3435.11	1994 3635.96	1995 4157.69	1996 5587.14	1997 6583.48
1	H	—	–	–32.67	13.86	4.33	H	—	50.58	27.57
2	—	—	– 6.76	63.86	–15.21	–68.63	—	–	33.96	94.04
3	—	11.18	36.26	–18.32	14.99	—	—	10.72	18.06	– 39.66
4	– 7.46	– 6.60	–17.34	– 2.23	—	—	–42.61	33.20	– 6.86	48.72
5	16.91	6.60	1.80	–27.72	—	8.38	82.06	– 1.04	H	—
6	64.16	–12.83	– 4.05	—	26.38	– 1.62	4.32	4.84	—	—
7	0.50	12.83	—	—	–61.94	19.45	13.53	–12.79	—	29.84
8	28.02	—	–	21.78	–32.20	– 0.54	–19.00	—	–88.51	53.25
9	—	—	4.95	–45.54	43.61	H	—	–	–33.96	– 45.32
10	—	– 2.93	9.01	1.48	30.41	—	—	5.53	–74.43	– 23.79
11	5.80	9.71	– 1.35	30.95	—	—	14.57	–11.07	1.09	–148.36
12	14.09	8.07	22.07	15.34	—	31.61	– 7.14	10.73	45.52	—
13	– 2.98	–23.65	H	—	14.53	15.94	–20.22	10.37	—	—
14	–101.46	41.06	—	—	36.23	11.61	1.78	H	—	60.21
15	8.29	—	—	12.38	47.63	0.28	– 1.78	—	60.33	135.26
16	—	—	11.26	53.71	12.74	22.69	—	–	27.10	92.71
17	—	0.73	2.71	17.58	H	—	–	–12.80	–70.09	– 21.27
18	– 5.81	41.61	–32.89	– 5.20	—	—	–41.05	–16.25	1.81	44.95
19	– 8.62	7.51	–20.94	–33.67	—	–11.62	– 0.60	28.36	–16.26	—
20	– 14.09	– 9.53	–15.99	—	–30.19	–23.50	–21.11	23.17	—	—
21	1.99	32.08	—	–	6.94	– 4.05	53.83	39.43	—	– 43.34
22	27.69	—	–	–37.87	– 4.48	–10.27	– 3.86	—	29.26	173.38
23	—	—	–29.28	2.73	9.84	–15.40	—	—	23.85	– 20.87
24	—	– 6.78	–12.17	19.05	–24.15	—	—	33.89	–34.69	– 20.47
25	20.88	–15.77	11.94	–28.46	—	—	57.10	– 3.81	13.01	– 53.38
26	8.79	2.20	10.14	– 8.66	—	–15.40	– 6.24	– 0.34	1.08	—
27	3.15	29.88	–31.53	—	–19.90	17.56	H*	14.87	—	—
28	– 6.63	– 0.19	—	—	3.36	– 2.43	–31.23	6.57	—	44.15
29	– 8.95	—	–	–35.40	25.26	11.62	13.38	—	5.42	179.01
30	—	—	11.71	10.89	25.94	2.43	—	–	– 4.33	46.96
Close	2032.33	2418.80	2656.76	2887.87	3359.12	3427.55	3681.69	4321.27	5569.08	7008.99
Change	44.27	125.18	–50.45	–25.99	123.65	–7.56	45.73	163.58	–18.06	425.51

* Nixon Memorial

MONDAY

 30

It is a funny thing about life; if you refuse to accept anything but the best, you very often get it.
— W. Somerset Maugham

TUESDAY

 31

1

Urbain - Tues 6:00. 6:30

Muvphy & Slotz - 1 HR ☓
Review records for 5500 problem
Call Brooklyn IRS Re: 5500 filing
Spoke with agent Cruz

Capitalism without bankruptcy is like Christianity without hell.
— Frank Borman, CEO, Eastern Airlines, April 1986

WEDNESDAY

 1

Management is always going to be biased, either they're too close to the company to see what's really going on, or they're not totally upfront.
— D.H. Blair, Morton Davis Chairman

THURSDAY

  2

I'm always turned off by an overly optimistic letter from the president in the annual report. If his letter is mildly pessimistic to me that's a good sign.
— Philip Carret

FRIDAY

  3

When I talk to a company that tells me the last analyst showed up three years ago, I can hardly contain my enthusiasm.
— Peter Lynch

SATURDAY

4

SUNDAY

5

FIRST HALVES OF ALL MONTHS
OUTPERFORM SECOND HALVES

Investors have observed that institutions tend to invest funds early in the month (pages 64 and 66). I thought it would be interesting to divide the months into two parts and compare one to another. I went back 34 years and the results are presented in the tables below.

FIRST HALVES OF ALL MONTHS VS. SECOND HALVES (BASED ON S&P 500)

	1963–1973		1974–1984		1985–1997		Avg All Months 1963–Apr 1997	
	1st Half	2nd Half	1st Half	2nd Half	1st Half	2nd Half	1st Half	2nd Half
Jan	1.2%	—0.2%	0.9%	0.9%	0.9%	2.2%	0.9%	1.0%
Feb	0.3	—0.9	—0.7	0.1	1.9	—0.1	0.5	—0.2
Mar	0.7	0.5	0.4	—0.3	1.2	—0.8	0.8	—0.1
Apr	1.5	—0.3	1.6	0.5	1.1	0.1	1.4	0.04
May	—1.2	—0.4	—0.1	—1.2	0.8	2.2	—0.1	0.2
Jun	—0.9	—1.1	1.2	0.1	—0.04	0.1	0.1	—0.3
Jul	1.1	—0.7	0.4	—1.1	0.3	0.6	0.6	—0.4
Aug	0.4	0.5	0.6	0.3	0.0	0.5	0.3	0.4
Sep	1.0	0.2	—0.1	—0.9	—0.4	—0.2	0.2	—0.3
Oct	0.8	0.2	2.6	—1.1	—0.8	—0.4	0.8	—0.4
Nov	0.01	—0.2	0.0	1.3	0.1	0.4	0.02	0.5
Dec	0.4	1.3	—1.4	2.0	1.0	1.3	0.03	1.5
Total	5.4%	—1.1%	5.4%	0.5%	5.8%	6.0%	5.5%	2.0%
Avg	0.5%	—0.1%	0.5%	0.0%	0.5%	0.5%	0.5%	0.2%

The gain for the first half of all the months averaged 0.5%. This is two and a half times the 0.2% average gain for the second half of all months.

I separated the entire period into three sections because the 6500-point gain in the Dow in the 1985-1997 years altered previous patterns.

In the 1963-1973 and the 1974-1984 periods, the first half of the month outperformed the second half by an extremely wide margin. However, during the latest period, which contained the greatest bull market ever, second halves have actually outperformed first halves, though only slightly.

The first half of January, March, April and July were gainers in all periods. The best second half during all periods was December. January was second best on average and August, third, was a gainer in all periods.

The biggest surprise was May's spectacular showing in the latest period, especially its average 2.2% gain during the second half of the month. May was tied with January for top honors while December ran third with 1.3%.

When we separated the months into different segments the results were quite dramatic. We divided them into the 26th through the 10th days vs. the 11th through the 25th days. Please turn to page 48 and see how the better half of the month has outperformed the other half four to one.

BROADCASTERS CONVENTION THIS WEEK
IN LAS VEGAS

MONDAY

6

Dr. Urbin

Analysts are supposed to be critics of corporations. They often end up being public relations spokesmen for them.
— Ralph Wanger

TUESDAY

7

6:00 - 6:20 p.

It's a lot of fun finding a country nobody knows about. The only thing better is finding a country everybody's bullish on and shorting it.
— Jim Rogers

WEDNESDAY

8

Short-term volatility is greatest at turning points and diminishes as a trend becomes established.
— George Soros

THURSDAY

9

Patriotism is when love of your own people comes first; nationalism, when hate for people other than your own comes first.
— Charles DeGaulle, *Life* May 9, 1969

FRIDAY

10

The bigger a man's head gets, the easier it is to fill his shoes.
— Anonymous

Passover   **SATURDAY**

11

SUNDAY

12

DAYS BETWEEN 26TH THROUGH 10TH OF MONTHS OUTPERFORM MIDDLE 11TH THROUGH 25TH DAYS

It is evident that the first half of all months outperforms the second half (see page 46). What would happen if months were divided into two different segments? Since the greatest gains come at the ends and beginnings of months I contrasted the days between the twenty-sixth of one month and the tenth of the following month with those days between the eleventh and the twenty-fifth. An interesting pattern develops.

The timespan is separated into three periods because the 6500-point gain in the Dow during 1985-1997 altered previous patterns.

HALF OF MONTHS INCLUDING ENDS AND BEGINNINGS VS. REST OF DAYS BETWEEN 11TH AND 25TH

	1963–1973		1974–1984		1985–April 1997		Avg All Months 1963–Apr 1997	
	26 to 10	11 to 25	26 to 10	11 to 25	26 to 10	11 to 25	26 to 10	11 to 25
Jan	1.2%	0.4%	1.8%	0.1%	0.02%	1.9%	0.9%	0.9%
Feb	—0.1	—0.4	0.1	—0.1	2.7	0.5	1.0	0.1
Mar	0.3	0.1	0.4	0.3	0.6	0.1	0.4	0.2
Apr	1.9	0.1	0.2	1.5	0.2	0.7	0.7	0.8
May	—0.2	—1.6	0.7	—0.9	0.6	1.2	0.4	—0.4
Jun	—0.1	—1.0	1.1	0.9	1.1	0.4	0.7	0.1
Jul	1.1	—0.6	—1.3	0.5	0.3	—0.2	0.05	—0.1
Aug	—0.2	0.6	0.4	—0.3	0.8	0.4	0.3	0.2
Sep	1.0	0.9	0.01	—0.1	0.1	—1.0	0.4	—0.1
Oct	0.2	0.8	1.5	—1.7	0.1	—0.8	0.6	—0.6
Nov	—0.2	—1.1	1.5	0.7	0.8	0.5	0.7	0.1
Dec	1.7	—0.5	—0.8	0.6	0.9	1.5	0.6	0.6
Avg Yr	**6.5%**	**—2.3%**	**5.4%**	**1.4%**	**7.8%**	**5.2%**	**6.8%**	**1.6%**
Avg Mo	**0.5%**	**—0.2%**	**0.5%**	**0.1%**	**0.7%**	**0.4%**	**0.56%**	**0.14%**

Based on S&P composite index

During the 1963-1997 period, the first 11 whole years averaged puny annual gains of 4.2% (6.5% *minus* 2.3%). The next 11 years gained 6.8% per year while the third and current period had an average annual gain of 13.0%.

The table shows the prime halves of the month during 1963-1973 averaged annual gains of 6.5% while the other halves lost 2.3% per year. During 1974-1984 the results were 5.4% versus 1.4%. A vast improvement occurs during 1985-1997 with the prime days gaining 7.8% on average annually and the remaining days also improving considerably to 5.2% per year.

All months from 1963 through April 1997 show an annual gain of 6.8% for the prime days, compared to only 1.6% for the remaining days. The average month gained 0.56% during the twenty-sixth through the tenth day of the following month. A gain of 0.14% was registered for days eleven through twenty five. The four to one advantage is far higher than the 2.5 to one ratio when the months are split in half right down the middle as on page 46.

MONDAY
13

The test of success is not what you do when you are on top. Success is how high you bounce when you hit bottom.
— General George S. Patton

TUESDAY
14

When an old man dies, a library burns down.
— African proverb

Murphy & Murphy — Phila. Returns
— Norristown Returns
4 HRS

MURPHY & SLOTA
1 HR PHL/BPS

WEDNESDAY
15

Do your work with your whole heart and you will succeed — there is so little competition.
— Elbert Hubbard

THURSDAY
16

The usual bull market successfully weathers a number of tests until it is considered invulnerable, whereupon it is ripe for a bust.
— George Soros

FRIDAY
 # 17

The people who sustain the worst losses are usually those who overreach. And it's not necessary: Steady, moderate gains will get you where you want to go.
— John Train

SATURDAY
18

SUNDAY
19

BEST MONTHS IN PAST 47⅓ YEARS

Seasonality for different months of the year is usually based on the number of times the month has closed higher in either the Dow industrials or the S&P 500.

December ranks Number One with an average monthly gain of 1.7% since 1950 based on the S&P 500. Next comes January 1.7%, November 1.6%, and April 1.2%. Using Dow points as a measuring stick is misleading as the Dow was mostly under 1000 prior to 1982. The worst two months since 1950 are September, down 217.39 on the Dow and 22.1% on the S&P. Next-to-last comes October on the Dow and June on the S&P. See the graphic presentation on page 135.

MONTHLY % AND POINT CHANGES (JANUARY 1950-APRIL 1997)

	Standard & Poor's 500						Dow Jones Industrials			
Month	**Total % Change**	**Avg. % Change**	**# Up**	**# Down**		**Month**	**Total Points Change**	**Avg. Points Change**	**# Up**	**# Down**
Jan	79.5%	1.7%	31	17		Jan	1622.11	33.79	34	14
Feb	6.6	0.1	27	21		Feb	538.84	11.23	28	20
Mar	42.1	0.9	31	17		Mar	241.46	5.03	30	18
Apr	64.9	1.4	33	15		Apr	1236.90	25.77	30	18
May	9.2	0.2	27	20		May	622.17	13.24	25	22
June	3.1	0.1	23	24		Jun	— 78.43	—1.67	23	24
July	55.6	1.2	27	20		Jul	759.95	16.17	29	18
Aug	19.9	0.4	26	21		Aug	174.94	3.72	27	20
Sep	—22.1	—0.5	19	28		Sep	—217.39	—4.63	17	30
Oct	22.3	0.5	27	20		Oct	—102.08	—2.17	26	21
Nov	72.9	1.6	30	17		Nov	958.22	20.39	31	16
Dec	80.4	1.7	35	12		Dec	1055.07	22.45	33	14
% Rank						**Points Rank**				
Dec	80.4%	1.7%	35	12		Jan	1622.11	33.79	34	14
Jan	79.5	1.7	31	17		Apr	1236.90	25.77	30	18
Nov	72.9	1.6	30	17		Dec	1055.07	22.45	33	14
Apr	64.9	1.4	33	15		Nov	958.22	20.39	31	16
July	55.6	1.2	27	20		Jul	759.95	16.17	29	18
Mar	42.1	0.9	31	17		May	622.17	13.24	25	22
Oct	22.3	0.5	27	20		Feb	538.84	11.23	28	20
Aug	19.9	0.4	26	21		Mar	241.46	5.03	30	18
May	9.2	0.2	27	20		Aug	174.94	3.72	27	20
Feb	6.6	0.1	27	21		Jun	— 78.43	—1.67	23	24
June	3.1	0.1	23	24		Oct	—102.08	—2.17	26	21
Sep	—22.1	—0.5	19	28		Sep	—217.39	—4.63	17	30

One must always be diligent when analyzing long periods of seasonal data as market seasonality can change just like the weather. While the Dow was gaining over 6000 points in the last 12 years and more than quadrupling, the total S&P percent changes for each month in ranking order were: May 37.4%, January 35.6%, December 29.1%, February 23.6%, July 15.9%, April 12.1%, November 10.7%, August 6.3%, March 5.7%, June 3.3%, October *minus* 5.1%, and September *minus* 11.5%.

APRIL

MONDAY
20

The best time to buy long-term bonds is when short-term rates are higher than long-term rates.
— George Soros

TUESDAY
21

Most periodicals and trade journals are deadly dull, and indeed full of fluff provided by public relations agents.
— Jim Rogers

WEDNESDAY
22

A poor stock market will discourage both consumer and business outlays. Also a decline in the value of stocks reduces their value as collateral, a further depressant.
— George Soros

THURSDAY
23

You try to be greedy when others are fearful, and fearful when others are greedy.
—Warren Buffett

FRIDAY
24

I never hired anybody who wasn't smarter than me.
— Don Hewett, Producer, *60 Minutes*

SATURDAY
25

SUNDAY
26

In the very merry month of May
Bulls have lately romped away

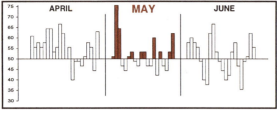

MAY
ALMANAC

		MAY							JUNE			
S	M	T	W	T	F	S		S	M	T	W	T	F	S
					1	2						1	2	3	4	5	6
3	4	5	6	7	8	9		7	8	9	10	11	12	13
10	11	12	13	14	15	16		14	15	16	17	18	19	20
17	18	19	20	21	22	23		21	22	23	24	25	26	27
24	25	26	27	28	29	30		28	29	30				
31													

See Market Probability Chart on page 125.

❑ Between 1964 and 1984 May was the "disaster month" with the S&P 500 down 15 out of 20 times ❑ S&P has now been up thirteen straight years since then (page 140) ❑ May ranks fourth from last on the S&P since 1950 ❑ However, in the latest twelve years, May beat all other months, gaining a spectacular 37.4% (page 50) ❑ Why the turnabout? Short (3-month) bear markets in 1987 and 1990 ending in October and almost 10% drops ending March 1994 and April 1997 left May unscathed.

MAY DAILY POINT CHANGES DOW JONES INDUSTRIALS

Previous Month	1987	1988	1989	1990	1991	1992	1993	1994	1995	1996
Close	2286.36	2032.33	2418.80	2656.76	2887.87	3359.12	3427.55	3681.69	4321.27	5569.08
1	−5.96	—	− 3.84	12.16	42.33	−23.03	—	—	− 5.19	6.14
2	—	10.94	−12.10	20.72	8.41	—	—	19.33	12.80	−76.95
3	—	15.09	− 9.16	6.53	0.25	—	18.91	13.39	44.27	−20.24
4	5.82	−22.05	− 8.80	14.19	—	42.04	− 0.27	−16.66	−13.49	—
5	51.85	−16.08	− 2.94	—	—	−18.78	2.91	− 1.78	−16.26	—
6	4.12	−12.77	—	—	2.78	10.06	− 7.20	−26.47	—	−13.72
7	− 7.53	—	—	11.26	−24.15	− 6.04	− 4.71	—	—	−43.36
8	−12.36	—	− 5.49	11.94	13.41	6.04	—	—	40.47	53.11
9	—	−10.11	− 5.14	− 0.68	40.25	—	—	−40.46	6.91	1.08
10	—	6.30	3.12	5.63	−50.98	—	6.09	27.37	13.84	43.00
11	−15.00	−37.80	8.43	63.07	—	28.17	25.47	−27.37	6.57	—
12	15.30	2.15	56.82	—	—	−12.46	13.56	23.80	19.37	—
13	7.08	22.55	—	—	4.25	6.86	−34.32	6.84	—	64.46
14	− 4.19	—	—	19.95	−37.57	−23.10	− 4.98	—	—	42.11
15	−52.97	—	24.19	0.92	−21.47	−15.79	—	—	6.91	0.73
16	—	17.08	−10.44	− 2.77	28.63	—	—	11.82	− 2.42	9.61
17	—	−21.22	8.98	12.03	− 7.38	—	6.92	49.11	−12.45	52.45
18	−13.86	−35.32	7.69	−11.80	—	22.94	− 5.54	12.28	−81.96	—
19	−37.38	7.63	30.98	—	—	21.96	55.64	26.09	0.69	—
20	− 5.41	− 6.13	—	—	5.59	− 4.15	23.25	7.37	—	61.32
21	9.90	—	0.92	24.77	13.86	−15.13	−30.45	—	—	−12.56
22	17.43	—	—	7.55	4.25	8.06	—	—	54.30	41.74
23	—	−11.11	−24.01	4.03	−10.29	—	—	−23.94	40.81	−15.88
24	—	21.05	5.86	− 0.71	13.87	—	14.95	2.76	1.72	0.74
25	H	− 1.16	− 1.28	−34.63	—	H	8.85	10.13	−25.93	—
26	54.74	5.38	11.18	—	—	−22.56	23.53	− 1.84	−43.23	—
27	− 2.13	−10.31	—	—	H	6.23	14.67	3.68	—	H
28	14.87	—	—	H	44.95	27.99	−27.40	—	—	−53.19
29	−19.11	—	H	49.57	10.73	− 1.55	—	—	H	−35.84
30	—	—	−18.22	8.07	30.86	—	—	H	9.68	19.58
31	—	74.68	4.60	− 1.90	27.05	—	H	1.23	86.46	−50.23
Close	2291.57	2031.12	2480.15	2876.66	3027.50	3396.88	3527.43	3758.37	4465.14	5643.18
Change	5.21	−1.21	61.35	219.90	139.63	37.76	99.88	76.68	143.87	74.10

MONDAY
27

*With its circular flows of purchasing power, its invisible-handed
markets, its intricate interplays of goods and money,
all modern economics resembles a vast mathematical drama,
on an elaborate stage of theory, without a protagonist to
animate the play.*
—George Gilder

TUESDAY
28

*I've never been poor, only broke. Being poor is a
frame of mind. Being broke is only a temporary situation.*
—Mike Todd, 1958

WEDNESDAY
 ## 29

*There are now more than a million U.S. dollar-based
millionaires in China.*
—John Naisbitt, *Megatrends Asia*

THURSDAY
 ## 30

Murphy e Slota
Post e Close   2 1/2 Hrs
  1997
Murphy e Murphy
Post e Close   2 1/2 Hrs ✕
  1997

*There is nothing good or bad, only
thinking makes it so.*
— William Shakespeare

FRIDAY
 ## 1

Chance favors the informed mind.
—Louis Pasteur

SATURDAY
2

SUNDAY
3

DOW GAINS 5635.90 NOVEMBER THROUGH APRIL, BUT ONLY 1159.16 MAY THROUGH OCTOBER IN 47 YEARS

To have invested in the market between November First and April Thirtieth each year, and to have switched into fixed income securities for the other six months of the year, back and forth, would have been an excellent strategy during the second half of the century. A glance at the "Best Months" table on page 50, or the chart on page 135, shows that November, December, January, March, and April have been outstanding months of the year since 1950. Add February, and a new strategy is born. These six consecutive months gained 5635.90 points for the Dow industrials in 47 years, while the remaining six May through October months gained only 1159.16 points.

Percentage changes in the Standard & Poor's composite index for each six-month segment since 1950 are shown alongside a compounding $10,000 investment. May/October's puny $8,747 gain is overshadowed by November/April's $227,066. Just two November/April losses were double-digited and were due to exogenous factors: our April 1970 Cambodian invasion and the fall 1973 OPEC oil embargo.

Don't tell the big boys about this! Let's keep this one to ourselves.

SIX-MONTH SWITCHING STRATEGY

	S&P % Change May 1 Through Oct 31	Investing $10,000		S&P % Change Nov 1 Through Apr 30	Investing $10,000
1950	8.1%	$10,810		14.8%	$ 11,480
1951	2.3	11,059		1.7	11,675
1952	5.1	11,623		0.4	11,722
1953	— 0.3	11,588		15.2	13,504
1954	12.1	12,990		19.8	16,177
1955	11.5	14,484		14.3	18,491
1956	— 5.8	13,644		0.4	18,565
1957	—10.2	12,252		5.8	19,641
1958	18.2	14,482		12.2	22,038
1959	— 0.1	14,467		— 5.5	20,826
1960	— 1.8	14,207		22.3	25,470
1961	5.1	14,932		— 4.9	24,222
1962	—13.4	12,931		23.5	29,914
1963	6.0	13,707		7.4	32,127
1964	6.8	14,639		5.0	33,734
1965	3.7	15,180		— 1.5	33,228
1966	—11.9	13,374		17.2	38,943
1967	— 0.8	13,267		4.5	40,695
1968	6.1	14,076		0.3	40,817
1969	— 6.3	13,189		—16.1	34,246
1970	2.1	13,466		24.9	42,773
1971	— 9.4	12,200		14.3	48,889
1972	3.6	12,640		— 4.1	46,885
1973	1.2	12,791		—16.6	39,102
1974	—18.2	10,463		18.1	46,180
1975	2.0	10,673		14.2	52,737
1976	1.2	10,801		— 4.3	50,469
1977	— 6.2	10,131		4.9	52,942
1978	— 3.8	9,746		9.2	57,813
1979	0.1	9,756		4.4	60,357
1980	19.9	11,697		4.2	62,892
1981	— 8.3	10,726		— 4.5	60,062
1982	14.8	12,314		23.0	73,876
1983	— 0.5	12,252		— 2.1	72,325
1984	3.8	12,718		8.3	78,327
1985	5.6	13,430		24.1	97,204
1986	3.6	13,913		18.2	114,896
1987	—12.7	12,146		3.8	119,262
1988	6.8	12,972		11.0	132,380
1989	9.9	14,257		— 2.8	128,674
1990	— 8.1	13,102		23.5	158,912
1991	4.6	13,705		5.7	167,970
1992	0.9	13,828		5.1	176,536
1993	6.3	14,699		— 3.6	170,181
1994	4.7	15,390		9.0	185,497
1995	13.0	17,391		12.5	208,685
1996	7.8	18,747		13.6	237,066

47-Year Gain $8,747   47-Year Gain $227,066

MAY

MONDAY   4

CABLE TV CONVENTION
ATLANTA   MAY 4-6

The man who masters himself,
masters the universe.
— Robert Krausz

TUESDAY   5

Murphy & Slota — 1 Hr
Review corporate returns
for corporate liquidation

The measure of success is not whether
you have a tough problem to deal with,
but whether its the same problem
you had last year.
— John Foster Dulles

WEDNESDAY   6

Don't be scared to take big steps—you
can't cross a chasm in two small jumps.
— David Lloyd George

THURSDAY   7

Choose a job you love, and you will never
have to work a day in your life.
— Confucius

FRIDAY 8

I cannot give you a formula for success
but I can give you a formula for failure:
Try to please everybody.
— Herbert Swope

SATURDAY 9

Mother's Day   SUNDAY 10

SURPRISE! MONDAY NOW BEST DAY OF WEEK

What's going on here? For many years Fridays were the recipient of the best market performances of the year and Mondays the worst. Separating the last seven years in the table below shows that Mondays and Fridays have reversed roles. Meanwhile, Wednesdays keep climbing! See pages 132 and 133.

ANNUAL DOW POINT CHANGES FOR DAYS OF THE WEEK SINCE 1953

	Monday	Tuesday	Wednesday	Thursday	Friday	Year's Closing D.J.I.	Year's Point Change
1953	— 37.39	— 6.70	19.63	7.25	6.21	280.90	— 11.00
1954	9.80	9.15	24.31	36.05	44.18	404.39	123.49
1955	— 56.09	34.31	45.83	0.78	59.18	488.40	84.01
1956	— 30.15	— 16.36	— 15.30	9.86	63.02	499.47	11.07
1957	—111.28	— 5.93	64.12	4.26	— 14.95	435.69	— 63.78
1958	14.36	26.73	29.10	24.25	53.52	583.65	147.96
1959	— 35.69	20.25	4.11	20.49	86.55	679.36	95.71
1960	—104.89	— 9.90	— 5.62	10.35	46.59	615.89	— 63.47
1961	— 17.66	4.29	87.51	— 5.74	46.85	731.14	115.25
1962	— 88.44	13.03	9.97	— 4.46	— 9.14	652.10	— 79.04
1963	— 43.61	81.85	16.23	26.07	30.31	762.95	110.85
1964	— 3.89	— 14.34	39.84	21.96	67.61	874.13	111.18
1965	— 70.23	36.65	57.03	2.75	68.93	969.26	95.13
1966	—126.73	— 54.24	56.13	— 45.69	— 13.04	785.69	—183.57
1967	— 73.17	35.94	25.50	98.37	32.78	905.11	119.42
1968*	3.28	37.97	25.16	— 59.00	31.23	943.75	38.64
1969	—152.05	— 48.82	18.33	17.79	21.36	800.36	—143.39
1970	— 99.00	— 47.14	116.07	1.81	66.82	838.92	38.56
1971	— 15.89	22.44	13.70	6.23	24.80	890.20	51.28
1972	— 85.08	— 3.55	65.24	6.14	147.07	1020.02	129.82
1973	—192.68	29.09	— 5.94	41.56	— 41.19	850.86	—169.16
1974	—130.99	29.13	— 20.31	— 12.60	— 99.85	616.24	—234.62
1975	59.80	—129.96	56.93	129.48	119.92	852.41	236.17
1976	81.16	61.32	50.88	— 26.79	— 14.33	1004.65	152.24
1977	— 66.38	— 43.66	— 79.61	8.53	7.64	831.17	—173.48
1978	— 31.79	— 70.34	71.33	— 65.71	70.35	805.01	— 26.16
1979	— 27.72	4.72	— 18.84	73.97	1.60	838.74	33.73
1980	— 89.40	137.92	137.77	—112.78	51.74	963.99	125.25
1981	— 55.47	— 39.72	— 13.95	— 13.66	33.81	875.00	— 88.99
1982	21.69	70.22	28.37	14.65	36.61	1046.54	171.54
1983	39.34	— 39.75	149.28	48.30	14.93	1258.64	212.10
1984	— 40.48	44.70	—129.24	84.36	— 6.41	1211.57	— 47.07
1985	86.96	43.97	56.19	49.45	98.53	1546.67	335.10
1986	— 56.03	113.72	178.65	32.17	80.77	1895.95	349.28
1987	—651.77	338.45	382.03	142.47	—168.30	1938.83	42.88
1988	139.28	295.28	— 60.48	—220.90	76.56	2168.57	229.74
1989	— 3.23	93.25	233.25	70.08	191.28	2753.20	584.63
Sub Total	**—2041.51**	**1053.97**	**1713.20**	**422.10**	**1313.54**		**2461.30**
1990	153.11	41.57	47.96	—330.48	— 31.7	2633.66	—119.54
1991	174.58	64.52	174.53	251.08	—129.54	3168.83	535.17
1992	302.94	—114.81	3.12	90.38	—149.35	3301.11	132.28
1993	441.72	—155.93	243.87	— 0.04	— 76.64	3754.09	452.98
1994	133.77	— 22.69	29.98	—159.66	98.95	3834.44	80.35
1995	203.99	269.04	357.02	150.44	302.19	5117.12	1282.68
1996	631.88	150.08	— 34.24	261.66	321.77	6448.27	1331.15
Sub Total	**2041.99**	**231.78**	**822.24**	**263.38**	**335.68**		**3695.07**
Totals	**0.48**	**1285.75**	**2535.44**	**685.48**	**1649.22**		**6156.37**

56 * Most Wednesdays closed last 7 months of 1968

MONDAY
11

*Under capitalism, the seller chases after
the buyer, and that makes both of them
work better; under socialism, the buyer
chases the seller, and neither has
time to work.*
— Andrei Sakharov's Uncle Ivan

TUESDAY
12

*Get inside information from the president and you
will probably lose half your money. If you get it from the
chairman of the board, you will lose all your money.*
—Jim Rogers

WEDNESDAY
13

*Things may come to those who wait, but
only the things left by those who hustle.*
— Abraham Lincoln

THURSDAY
14

*There is one thing stonger than all the armies in the world,
and this is an idea whose time has come.*
—Victor Hugo

FRIDAY
 # 15

*He who wants to persuade should put his
trust not in the right argument, but in the
right word. The power of sound
has always been greater than
the power of sense.*
— Joseph Conrad

SATURDAY
16

SUNDAY
17

1996 DAILY DOW POINT CHANGES
(Dow Jones Industrial Average)

WEEK #	MONDAY	TUESDAY	WEDNESDAY	THURSDAY	FRIDAY	WEEKLY DOW CLOSE	NET POINT CHANGE
					1995 Close	5117.12	
1	H	60.33	16.62	—20.23	7.59	5181.43	64.31
2	16.25	— 67.55	—97.19	32.16	— 3.98	5061.12	—120.31
3	— 17.34	44.44	—21.32	57.45	60.33	5184.68	123.56
4	34.68	— 27.09	50.57	—26.01	54.92	5271.75	87.07
5	33.23	76.23	14.09	9.76	— 31.07	5373.99	102.24
6	33.60	52.02	32.51	47.33	2.17	5541.62	167.63
7	58.53	1.08	—21.68	—28.18	— 48.05	5503.32	— 38.30
8	H	— 44.79	57.44	92.49	22.03	5630.49	127.17
9	— 65.39	— 15.89	—43.00	—20.59	50.94	5536.56	— 93.93
10	63.59	42.27	—12.65	11.92	—171.24	5470.45	— 66.11
11	110.55	2.89	—15.17	17.34	— 1.09	5584.97	114.52
12	98.63	— 14.09	—14.09	—28.54	9.76	5636.64	51.67
13	7.22	26.74	—43.72	3.97	— 43.71	5587.14	— 49.50
14	50.58	33.96	18.06	— 6.86	H	5682.88	95.74
15	— 88.51	— 33.96	—74.43	1.09	45.52	5532.59	—150.29
16	60.33	27.10	—70.09	1.81	— 16.26	5535.48	2.89
17	29.26	23.85	—34.69	13.01	1.08	5567.99	32.51
18	5.42	— 4.33	6.14	—76.95	— 20.24	5478.03	— 89.96
19	— 13.72	— 43.36	53.11	1.08	43.00	5518.14	40.11
20	64.46	42.11	0.73	9.61	52.45	5687.50	169.36
21	61.32	— 12.56	41.74	—15.88	0.74	5762.86	75.36
22	H	— 53.19	—35.84	19.58	— 50.23	5643.18	—119.68
23	— 18.47	41.00	31.77	—30.29	29.92	5697.11	53.93
24	— 9.24	— 19.21	— 0.37	—10.34	— 8.50	5649.45	— 47.66
25	3.33	— 24.75	20.32	11.08	45.80	5705.23	55.78
26	12.56	1.48	—36.57	— 5.17	— 22.90	5654.63	— 50.60
27	75.35	— 9.60	—17.36	H	—114.88*	5588.14	— 66.49
28	— 37.31	31.03	21.79	—83.11	— 9.98	5510.56	— 77.58
29	—161.05	9.25	18.12	87.30	— 37.36	5426.82	— 83.74
30	— 35.88	— 44.39	8.14	67.32	51.05	5473.06	46.24
31	— 38.47	47.34	46.98	65.84	85.08	5679.83	206.77
32	— 5.55	21.83	22.56	— 5.18	— 32.18	5681.31	1.48
33	23.67	— 57.70	19.60	— 1.10	23.67	5689.45	8.14
34	9.99	21.82	—31.44	43.65	— 10.73	5722.74	33.29
35	— 28.85	17.38	1.11	—64.73	— 31.44	5616.21	—106.53
36	H	32.18	8.51	—49.94	52.90	5659.86	43.65
37	73.98	— 6.66	27.74	17.02	66.58	5838.52	178.66
38	50.68	— 0.37	—11.47	— 9.62	20.72	5888.46	49.94
39	6.28	— 20.71	3.33	— 8.51	4.07	5872.92	— 15.54
40	9.25	22.73	29.07	— 1.12	60.01	5992.86	119.94
41	— 13.05	— 13.04	—36.15	— 8.95	47.71	5969.38	— 23.48
42	40.62	— 5.22	16.03	38.39	35.03	6094.23	124.85
43	— 3.36	— 29.07	—25.34	—43.98	14.54	6007.02	— 87.21
44	— 34.29	34.29	—13.79	36.15	— 7.45	6021.93	14.91
45	19.75	39.50	96.53	28.33	13.78	6219.82	197.89
46	35.78	10.44	8.20	38.76	35.03	6348.03	128.21
47	— 1.12	50.69	32.42	—11.55	53.29	6471.76	123.73
48	76.03	— 19.38	—29.07	H	22.36*	6521.70	49.94
49	N/C	— 79.01	—19.75	14.16	— 55.16	6381.94	—139.76
50	82.00	9.31	—70.73	—98.81	1.16	6304.87	— 77.07
51	— 36.52	39.98	38.44	126.87	10.76	6484.40	179.53
52	4.62	33.83*	H	23.83	14.23	6560.91	76.51
53	— 11.54	—101.10				6448.27	—112.64†
TOTALS	**631.88**	**150.08**	**—34.24**	**261.66**	**321.77**		**1331.15**

*Shortened trading day †Partial week

MAY

MONDAY
18

*I have brought myself, by long meditation,
to the conviction that a human being with a
settled purpose must accomplish it, and that
nothing can resist a will which will stake
even existence upon its fulfillment.*
— Benjamin Disraeli

TUESDAY
19

*Great works are performed not by
strength, but perseverance.*
— Samuel Johnson

WEDNESDAY
20

*You've got to think about "big things"
while you're doing small things, so that
all the small things go in the right direction.*
— Alvin Toffler

THURSDAY
21

*Obstacles are those frightful things you
see when you take your eyes off the goal.*
— Hannah More

FRIDAY
22

*There have been three great inventions
since the beginning of time. The fire, the
wheel, and central banking.*
— Will Rogers

SATURDAY
23

SUNDAY
24

MEMORIAL DAY WEEK
UP 12 YEARS IN A ROW UNTIL 1996

This time of the year used to be known as "The May-June Disaster Area." Durings the '60s, '70s, and early '80s we cautioned, "If one month doesn't get you, the other one would."

However, investors returning from the three-day Memorial Day weekend, the first big weekend of the summer season, must have returned in very good spirits for twelve years starting in 1984. Records show that the market gained ground in all these abbreviated four-day weeks.

Some of the credit for this phenomenon is due to the big bull market since 1982 during which May surprisingly has been the best month of all. Also contributing to this latest phenomenon is the favorable month-end period which usually tends to coincide with this holiday week. Page 66 shows what the last plus the first four days of each month have done since 1967. Page 52 (May Almanac) and page 62 (June Almanac) show where the Memorial Day week Dow point changes occurred on the calendar.

It's always dangerous to publicize a favorable seasonal pattern. A pattern

---

DOW POINT CHANGES DURING MEMORIAL DAY WEEK

	Memorial Day	Tuesday	Wednesday	Thursday	Friday	Points Change	Percent Change	Week's Closing DJIA
1984		— 5.86	1.35	2.26	19.50	**17.25**	**1.6%**	1124.35
1985	C	— 0.45	1.46	2.80	9.63	**13.44**	**1.0**	1315.41
1986		29.74	25.25	4.07	— 5.64	**53.42**	**2.9**	1876.71
1987	L	54.74	— 2.13	14.87	—19.11	**48.37**	**2.2**	2291.57
1988		74.68	32.89	—11.56	18.85	**114.86**	**5.8**	2081.30
1989	O	—18.22	4.60	10.48	27.20	**24.06**	**1.0**	2517.83
1990		49.57	8.07	— 1.90	24.31	**80.05**	**2.8**	2900.97
1991	S	44.95	10.73	30.86	27.05	**113.59**	**3.9**	3027.50
1992		—22.56	6.23	27.99	— 1.55	**10.11**	**0.3**	3396.88
1993	E	24.91	1.11	— 8.58	0.27	**17.71**	**0.5**	3545.14
1994		1.23	2.46	1.84	13.23	**18.76**	**0.5**	3772.22
1995	D	9.68	88.46	7.61	—28.36	**75.39**	**1.7**	4444.39
1996		— 53.19	— 35.84	19.58	— 50.23	**—119.68**	**— 2.1**	5643.18
1997		37.50	— 26.18	— 27.05	0.86	**— 14.87**	**— 0.2**	7331.04

that has been in effect for a long time is bound to attract a multitude of traders, who will obviously want to take advantage of this bullish phenomenon.

The absence of the Memorial Day week rally in 1996 can be attributed to the threat of rising interest rates and the market's short term top after a 1000-point move over the previous seven months. In 1997, a 1000-point surge in six weeks paused during the Holiday week before resuming its climb in June. Let's keep watching the next year or two before we kiss this 12-year phenomenon goodbye.

MAY

MONDAY
25

*I measure what's going on, and I adapt to
it. I try to get my ego out of the way. The
market is smarter than I am so I bend.*
— Martin Zweig

TUESDAY
26

Financial genius is a rising stock market.
—John Kenneth Galbraith

WEDNESDAY
27

*We go to the movies to be entertained, not
see rape, ransacking, pillage and looting.
We can get all that in the stock market.*
— Kennedy Gammage

THURSDAY
 # 28

*Liberals have practiced tax and tax, spend
and spend, elect and elect but conservatives
have perfected borrow and borrow, spend
and spend, elect and elect.*
— George Will, *Newsweek*, 1989

FRIDAY
 # 29

*The worst mistake investors make
is taking their profits too soon,
and their losses too long.*
— Michael Price, Mutual Shares Fund

SATURDAY
30

SUNDAY
31

O "Summer Rally" start in June
Lift my portfolio to the moon!

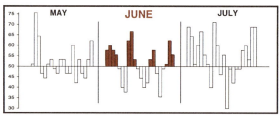

JUNE ALMANAC

JUNE						
S	M	T	W	T	F	S
		1	2	3	4	5	6
7	8	9	10	11	12	13
14	15	16	17	18	19	20
21	22	23	24	25	26	27
28	29	30				

JULY						
S	M	T	W	T	F	S
				1	2	3	4
5	6	7	8	9	10	11
12	13	14	15	16	17	18
19	20	21	22	23	24	25
26	27	28	29	30	31	

See Market Probability Chart on page 125.

❑ After rising just three times between 1965 and 1974, the S&P rose in eleven of the following fourteen Junes ❑ Autos used to begin major moves here ❑ RECORD: very little ground gained in 47 Junes ❑ 1997 was biggest June % gain since 1955, Dow was up 341 points ❑ Many sharp spring declines accelerate into June ❑ June is the leading rallying point after October during both bull and bear markets ❑ 1997 was first time June busted out in past eight years on the S&P and Dow.

JUNE DAILY POINT CHANGES DOW JONES INDUSTRIALS

Previous Month Close	1987 2291.57	1988 2031.12	1989 2480.15	1990 2876.66	1991 3027.50	1992 3396.88	1993 3527.43	1994 3758.37	1995 4465.14	1996 5643.18
1	− 3.34	32.89	10.48	24.31	—	16.33	24.91	2.46	7.61	—
2	−10.01	−11.56	27.20	—	—	−17.11	1.11	− 1.84	−28.36	—
3	42.47	18.85	—	—	7.83	10.89	− 8.58	13.23	—	−18.47
4	16.39	—	—	34.22	− 7.38	− 7.26	0.27	—	—	41.00
5	−10.93	—	−37.13	−10.19	−22.58	− 1.04	—	—	32.16	31.77
6	—	3.91	15.62	−13.35	−10.51	—	− 3.70	8.65	−30.29
7	—	−20.62	16.00	−14.32	−18.12	—	−13.01	−12.61	−23.17	29.92
8	25.49	48.36	4.59	−34.95	—	5.44	−21.59	− 6.46	− 3.46	—
9	1.06	− 9.60	− 3.49	—	—	−34.21	1.39	3.69	−34.58	—
10	0.91	8.36	—	—	− 1.34	−26.70	−20.21	20.31	—	− 9.24
11	6.52	—	—	30.19	10.51	8.29	13.29	—	—	−19.21
12	17.60	—	5.42	40.85	−23.92	2.85	—	—	22.47	− 0.37
13	—	− 2.31	−15.30	− 3.72	3.13	—	—	9.67	38.05	−10.34
14	—	25.07	− 0.18	− 1.48	35.33	—	9.68	31.71	6.57	− 8.50
15	13.81	6.93	−28.36	7.67	—	0.54	−22.69	−24.42	5.19	—
16	15.81	−37.16	11.38	—	—	−25.41	19.65	20.93	14.52	—
17	N/C	9.78	—	—	− 6.49	−41.73	10.24	−34.56	—	3.33
18	0.78	—	—	−53.71	− 7.15	−13.64	−27.12	—	—	−24.75
19	12.72	—	− 6.49	11.38	−31.31	11.23	—	—	42.89	20.32
20	—	−20.09	− 7.01	1.74	− 1.56	—	—	−34.88	− 3.12	11.08
21	—	25.24	− 7.97	6.43	11.62	—	16.05	−33.93	− 3.46	45.80
22	24.66	43.03	17.26	−44.55	—	− 4.55	−13.29	16.80	42.54	—
23	− 5.78	− 3.91	49.70	—	—	4.82	−30.72	−25.68	− 3.80	—
24	−11.32	− 5.33	—	—	−52.55	5.08	23.80	−62.15	—	12.56
25	22.64	—	—	−12.13	− 2.90	− 6.69	0.28	—	—	1.48
26	−14.19	—	−20.49	−2.72	2.90	− 1.60	—	—	−34.59	−36.57
27	—	−34.50	14.99	19.80	21.92	—	—	48.56	− 8.64	− 5.17
28	—	22.41	−21.63	16.58	−28.18	—	39.31	−15.86	14.18	−22.90
29	10.05	− 8.89	−46.47	1.98	—	37.45	−11.35	− 2.59	− 6.23	—
30	−28.38	19.73	−18.21	—	—	− 1.34	− 2.77	−42.09	5.54	—
Close	2418.53	2141.71	2440.06	2880.69	2906.75	3318.52	3516.08	3624.96	4556.10	5654.63
Change	126.96	110.59	−40.09	4.03	−120.75	−78.36	−11.35	−133.41	90.96	11.45

MONDAY

  1

KNAPP EXTENSION

*People's spending habits depend more on how
wealthy they feel than with the actual amount of their
current income.*
—A.S. Pigou

TUESDAY

  2

*Stock prices tend to discount what
has been unanimously reported
by the mass media.*
— Louis Ehrenkrantz

WEDNESDAY

  3

*When prices are high
They want to buy;
When prices are low
They let them go.*
— Ian Notley

THURSDAY

  4

*It is the growth of total government
spending as a percentage of gross national
product— not the way it is financed—
that crowds out the private sector.*
— Paul Craig Roberts, *Business Week*, 1984

FRIDAY

  5

*Governments last as long as the
under-taxed can defend themselves
against the over-taxed.*
— Bernard Berenson

SATURDAY

6

SUNDAY

7

LAST + FIRST FOUR DAYS VS. REST OF MONTH 1989-97

Quite obviously, the "best five days" may no longer be the last plus the first four. The many investors trying to take advantage of this lucrative seasonality pattern may have caused it to change. Now, the last three days of the month and the first two of the following month appear to be the best days. (Also, see page 66.)

NET DOW POINT CHANGES SHOWING MONTHLY BIAS

	Best 5 Days	Rest of Month	Best 5 Days	Rest of Month	Best 5 Days	Rest of Month
	1989		**1990**		**1991**	
Jan	11.61	129.82	40.95	—230.01	—106.44	190.35
Feb	— 3.04	— 70.71	63.07	10.81	117.82	58.17
Mar	44.46	— 13.48	59.68	50.90	84.16	— 55.70
Apr	10.63	127.02	— 6.53	— 76.12	6.93	— 47.52
May	—34.09	90.65	65.31	168.20	64.66	58.81
Jun	20.77	— 38.05	33.09	— 32.94	— 5.59	— 59.93
Jul	29.59	147.38	26.24	12.38	— 2.46	83.85
Aug	18.21	74.70	—200.99	—123.02	10.96	22.36
Sep	—21.27	— 11.97	26.23	—192.07	— 38.01	— 5.59
Oct	78.65	—170.08	89.35	— 68.81	— 44.28	110.02
Nov	—21.31	106.61	37.13	33.66	— 33.32	—138.42
Dec	47.99	— 4.47	83.67	26.73	— 10.95	274.82
Totals	**182.20**	**367.42**	**317.20**	**—420.29**	**43.48**	**491.22**
Average	**15.18**	**30.62**	**26.43**	**— 35.02**	**3.62**	**40.94**
	1992		**1993**		**1994**	
Jan	40.92	40.03	— 52.14	37.29	28.00	141.55
Feb	10.73	13.86	110.49	— 51.60	— 74.01	— 32.64
Mar	—27.95	— 6.26	33.77	58.36	— 6.48	—205.55
Apr	40.25	57.69	— 79.70	47.55	66.51	— 24.95
May	36.23	29.02	16.78	112.93	27.66	61.17
Jun	1.30	— 79.87	— 9.69	— 26.29	11.38	—101.47
Jul	—24.69	96.72	— 43.18	91.75	21.37	42.41
Aug	—51.33	— 72.95	— 18.45	95.02	34.96	151.51
Sep	14.32	— 15.13	— 36.89	— 40.80	— 31.05	— 31.62
Oct	—88.61	68.08	32.69	88.87	— 79.07	155.10
Nov	— 2.43	38.36	— 62.88	52.82	—123.14	— 68.97
Dec	6.48	32.42	32.41	65.67	7.40	87.48
Totals	**—44.78**	**201.97**	**— 76.79**	**531.57**	**—116.47**	**174.02**
Average	**— 3.73**	**16.83**	**— 6.40**	**44.30**	**— 9.71**	**14.50**
	1995		**1996**		**1997**	
Jan	33.98	— 35.33	85.63	199.78	51.29	223.20
Feb	105.65	50.84	78.40	46.60	— 50.80	152.01
Mar	8.99	175.00	123.56	1.08	19.63	—204.11
Apr	32.85	109.29	52.03	—109.47	—214.52	435.96
May	44.96	19.02	—109.10	229.10		
Jun	106.52	65.36	— 26.22	10.34		
Jul	152.17	12.78	— 89.39	—106.21		
Aug	—32.05	— 78.89	214.18	— 48.46		
Sep	65.15	117.92	12.21	213.06		
Oct	—24.93	— 6.14	119.94	0.37		
Nov	57.44	291.55	184.48	321.63		
Dec	93.57	—103.33	— 62.24	112.27		
Totals	**644.30**	**618.07**	**583.48**	**870.09**	**—194.40**	**607.06**
Average	**53.69**	**51.51**	**48.62**	**72.51**	**— 48.60**	**151.77**

		Best Five Days		**Rest of Month (16 Days)**	
100	Net D.J. Points	1338.22	Net D.J. Points	3441.13
MONTH	Average Period	13.38	Average Period	34.41
TOTALS	Average Day	2.68	Average Day	2.15

JUNE

MONDAY
8

*Marketing is our No. 1 priority...
A marketing campaign isn't worth doing
unless it serves three purposes. It must
grow the business, create news, and
enhance our image.*
— James Robinson III, American Express

TUESDAY
9

*Average earnings of an English worker in 1900 came to
half an ounce of gold a week and in 1979 after world wars,
a world slump, and a world inflation, the British worker
has average earnings of half an ounce of gold a week.*
—William Rees Mogg

WEDNESDAY
10

*Never lend money to someone who must
borrow money to pay interest [on other
money owed].*
— A Swiss Banker's First Rule quoted by Lester Thurow

THURSDAY
11

*If you don't keep your employees happy,
they won't keep the customers happy.*
— Red Lobster V.P., *New York Times* 4/23/89

FRIDAY
12

*A man isn't a man until he has
to meet a payroll.*
— Ivan Shaffer

SATURDAY
13

SUNDAY
14

MARKET GAINS MORE ON FIVE DAYS OF MONTH THAN ON ALL REMAINING DAYS COMBINED

Being invested only during the last trading day of the month and the first four of the following month (the "best five days") then switching into money market funds for the remaining days, alternating back and forth each month, was a smart strategy over the years.

From the beginning of 1967 (Dow 785.69) to April 30, 1997 (Dow 7008.99) the Dow Jones industrial average gained 6223.30. However, it is incredible that the "best five days" of the 364 months of the 30⅓ year period produced a gain of 2747.97 in contrast to a gain of 3475.33 points on the rest of the 16 (on average) trading days of the month, a period three times as long.

NET DOW POINT CHANGE FOR PRIME FIVE DAYS (1967-1997)

	JAN	FEB	MAR	APR	MAY	JUNE	JUL	AUG	SEP	OCT	NOV	DEC
1967	22.39	7.01	5.56	— 8.74	7.13	— 2.27	7.11	22.24	14.45	— 2.25	— 31.33	9.13
1968	3.41	1.68	— 7.51	37.40	6.19	14.92	13.84	— 6.44	26.92	22.88	— 0.43	1.92
1969	— 19.39	4.54	10.51	— 12.10	27.96	— 6.21	13.45	22.30	— 8.91	— 8.64	4.69	— 13.99
1970	7.13	1.91	23.10	6.53	— 19.00	22.38	—13.55	— 11.91	5.34	21.57	18.00	34.71
1971	— 3.49	9.65	9.38	9.34	— 10.76	16.37	13.58	— 11.97	15.04	16.72	5.55	25.99
1972	19.42	0.30	25.89	26.42	— 8.66	—19.72	11.81	25.06	16.10	— 13.85	38.38	8.73
1973	39.81	—13.02	31.08	— 35.68	31.68	—10.69	—24.53	— 20.99	16.10	2.63	— 55.46	— 20.99
1974	28.83	—37.70	16.43	4.54	9.46	41.77	—11.89	8.21	21.04	—37.39	— 3.91	— 32.23
1975	37.94	17.75	30.66	— 23.00	31.68	27.15	—12.04	— 17.99	6.50	14.43	1.50	— 29.44
1976	46.28	— 3.94	— 8.19	9.52	— 12.60	— 1.67	— 9.49	7.39	27.67	—31.50	9.56	11.72
1977	— 19.20	— 9.64	20.03	— 6.48	16.12	4.21	— 3.82	— 1.82	17.50	1.99	— 12.74	— 20.36
1978	— 36.90	— 3.82	— 5.63	4.33	— 2.51	32.31	— 9.18	32.14	12.99	15.16	3.03	31.79
1979	24.77	—28.93	19.58	10.83	— 9.10	13.34	3.12	9.81	— 9.55	2.64	— 17.33	3.33
1980	— 6.91	— 0.08	—26.37	9.31	4.95	12.45	16.38	2.05	10.58	43.77	14.67	— 19.20
1981	18.86	— 2.13	— 2.19	2.08	— 30.98	— 7.51	—30.44	7.80	—30.54	8.37	26.16	6.75
1982	— 11.32	—17.22	—18.27	14.84	18.26	—19.98	—12.55	— 16.36	20.98	37.99	59.23	52.80
1983	23.55	13.16	20.02	—25.64	0.20	— 1.90	— 3.40	— 33.26	48.07	28.66	— 5.19	17.89
1984	26.48	—47.21	— 4.61	— 40.20	3.76	31.25	— 3.98	92.98	—15.90	—29.37	26.84	— 22.97
1985	— 13.58	— 7.29	— 0.66	— 1.66	— 11.93	17.70	2.24	— 20.94	0.56	7.95	27.87	7.22
1986	15.25	48.51	—17.39	— 82.50	— 37.94	— 2.91	—46.26	0.14	— 0.42	29.25	13.22	22.92
1987	85.34	41.48	59.75	127.13	87.93	26.40	2.87	26.79	—77.97	—41.94	47.08	—143.74
1988	101.79	— 6.47	34.65	84.05	— 21.05	118.77	0.71	44.27	27.56	—11.56	— 4.09	47.83
1989	11.61	— 3.04	44.46	10.63	— 34.09	20.77	29.59	18.21	—21.27	78.65	— 21.31	47.99
1990	40.95	63.07	59.68	— 6.53	65.31	33.09	26.24	—200.99	26.23	89.35	37.13	83.67
1991	—106.44	117.82	84.16	6.93	64.66	— 5.59	— 2.46	10.96	—38.01	—44.28	— 33.32	— 10.95
1992	40.92	10.73	—27.95	40.25	36.23	1.30	—24.69	— 51.33	14.32	—88.61	— 2.43	6.48
1993	— 52.14	110.49	33.77	— 79.70	16.78	— 9.69	—43.18	— 18.45	—36.89	32.69	— 62.88	32.41
1994	28.00	—74.01	— 6.48	66.51	27.66	11.38	21.37	34.96	—31.05	—79.07	—123.14	7.40
1995	33.98	105.65	8.99	32.85	44.96	106.52	152.17	— 32.05	65.15	—24.93	57.44	93.57
1996	85.63	78.40	123.56	52.03	—109.10	—26.22	—89.39	214.18	12.21	119.94	184.48	— 62.24
1997	51.29	—50.80	19.63	—214.52								
Totals	524.26	326.85	555.64	0.15	185.68	437.72	—26.37	134.99	123.29	161.25	182.15	142.36
Up	22	16	20	18	17	18	14	17	20	18	16	19
Down	9	15	11·	13	13	12	16	13	10	12	14	11

The most Dow points during the "best five days" were gained in March (555) followed by January (524), June (437), and February (326). July was the worst month, losing 26.37 Dow points.

New SEC mandated three-day settlement of trades effective June 1995 could have an effect on month-end seasonality. Five-day settlements were the rule in prior years. As noted on page 64, too many investors chasing this seasonal quirk seem to be altering it.

MONDAY

15

*Wall Street has a uniquely hysterical way of thinking the world
will end tomorrow but be fully recovered in the long run, then a
few years later believing the immediate future is rosy but that the
long term stinks.*
— Kenneth L. Fisher, *Wall Street Waltz*

TUESDAY

16

*Early in March (1960), Dr. Arthur F. Burns called on me…Burns'
conclusion was that unless some decisive action was taken, and
taken soon, we were heading for another economic dip which
would hit its low point in October, just before the elections.*
— Richard M. Nixon, *Six Crises*

WEDNESDAY

17

*If you can buy all you want of a new issue,
you do not want any;
if you cannot obtain any,
you want all you can buy.*
— Rod Fadem, Oppenheimer & Co.

THURSDAY

18

*Make money and the whole nation
will conspire to call you a gentleman.*
— George Bernard Shaw

FRIDAY

19

*Central Bankers are brought up
pulling the legs off ants.*
— Paul Volker, quoted by William Grieder, *Secrets of the Temple*

SATURDAY

20

Father's Day

SUNDAY

21

SUMMER PORTFOLIO REVIEW

NO. OF SHARES	SECURITY	A ORIGINAL COST	B CURRENT VALUE	C GAIN (B – A) OR LOSS (A – B)	D % CHANGE (C ÷ A)	E MONTHS HELD	F CHANGE PER MO. (D ÷ E)	G ANNUAL RETURN (F × 12)
200	Sample Corp.	$10,000	$10,400	$400	4.0%	8	0.5%	6.0%
	TOTALS							

Stocks which have achieved their potential	Candidates for addition to portfolio
1	1
2	2
3	3

Stocks which have been disappointments	Investment decisions
1	1
2	2
3	3

JUNE

MONDAY
22

*The power to tax involves the
power to destroy.*
— John Marshall, U. S. Supreme Court, 1819

TUESDAY
23

*The fear of capitalism has compelled
socialism to widen freedom, and the fear
of socialism has compelled capitalism to
increase equality.*
— Will and Ariel Durant

WEDNESDAY
24

*Nothing contributes so much to
the prosperity and happiness of a
country as high profits.*
— David Ricardo, *On Protection to Agriculture*, 1820

THURSDAY
25

*One machine can do the work of fifty
ordinary men. No machine can do
the work of one extraordinary man.*
— Elbert Hubbard

FRIDAY
26

Speed is God and time is the devil.
—David Hancock, Hitachi
(on launching new technical products)

SATURDAY
27

SUNDAY
28

Stocks like to rocket in July, and how!
Up seven straight, Dow take a bow

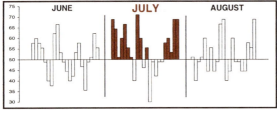

JULY ALMANAC

JULY								AUGUST					
S	M	T	W	T	F	S		S	M	T	W	T	F	S
				1	2	3	4							1
5	6	7	8	9	10	11		2	3	4	5	6	7	8
12	13	14	15	16	17	18		9	10	11	12	13	14	15
19	20	21	22	23	24	25		16	17	18	19	20	21	22
26	27	28	29	30	31			23	24	25	26	27	28	29
								30	31					

See Market Probability Chart on page 125.

❑ Last 47 years July was up 14 times on the Dow in first 17 years, down 14 in next 22, and up 7 straight until 1996's loss ❑ July fifth best in S&P 500, up 1.2% on average since 1950 ❑ Best July of all time was 1989, Dow was up 220.60, 9.0% ❑ Great Julys (up 3% or more) during bull markets invariably precede better buying opportunities sometime in the fall ❑ Four big losers 1969, 1974, 1975, and 1986: down 6.0%, 7.8%, 6.8%, and 5.9%.

JULY DAILY POINT CHANGES DOW JONES INDUSTRIALS

Previous Month Close	1987 2418.53	1988 2141.71	1989 2440.06	1990 2880.69	1991 2906.75	1992 3318.52	1993 3516.08	1994 3624.96	1995 4556.10	1996 5654.63
1	− 8.77	−10.13	—	—	51.66	35.58	− 5.54	21.69	—	75.35
2	26.94	—	—	18.57	14.31	−23.81	−26.57	—	—	− 9.60
3	—	—	12.71	12.37	−38.02	—	—	—	29.05	− 17.36
4	H	H	H	H	H	H	H	H	H	H
5	—	27.03	3.79	−32.42	− 2.23	—	—	5.83	30.08	−114.88*
6	− 7.17	−28.45	5.88	25.74	—	8.91	−34.04	22.02	48.77	—
7	20.25	− 7.47	25.42	—	—	−44.03	25.74	13.92	38.73	—
8	14.19	−16.54	—	—	29.52	− 1.89	38.75	20.72	—	− 37.31
9	−12.76	—	—	9.16	−14.76	30.80	6.64	—	—	31.03
10	4.78	—	14.80	−23.27	− 2.46	6.48	—	—	− 0.34	21.79
11	—	5.16	11.95	41.83	14.98	—	—	− 6.15	−21.79	− 83.11
12	—	−18.67	18.02	37.13	21.02	—	3.32	− 0.33	46.69	− 9.98
13	− 3.02	11.73	5.69	10.40	—	6.75	− 8.94	1.62	0.19	—
14	28.38	9.25	16.50	—	—	21.08	27.11	34.97	−18.66	—
15	2.39	15.83	—	—	9.84	−12.97	8.38	14.56	—	−161.05
16	13.23	—	—	19.55	− 6.71	16.21	−22.64	—	—	9.25
17	13.07	—	− 1.33	N/C	− 5.14	−29.99	—	—	27.47	18.12
18	—	−11.56	− 8.73	−18.07	37.56	—	—	1.62	−50.01	87.30
19	—	−20.63	39.65	12.13	N/C	—	6.99	− 7.12	−57.41	− 37.36
20	−22.32	13.34	− 8.92	−32.67	—	−28.64	9.50	−21.04	12.68	—
21	−19.77	−24.01	31.87	—	—	5.41	10.62	5.18	N/C	—
22	2.23	−25.60	—	—	− 3.35	−30.80	−30.18	2.59	—	− 35.88
23	1.76	—	—	−56.44	−29.74	12.43	21.52	—	—	− 44.39
24	13.39	—	−22.38	17.82	−17.00	− 4.33	—	'	27.12	8.14
25	—	10.84	− 1.90	8.42	13.87	—	—	6.80	45.78	67.32
26	—	2.14	29.97	−10.15	− 7.60	—	20.96	− 6.16	− 7.39	51.05
27	8.61	−20.27	22.38	−22.28	—	− 3.51	− 2.24	−15.21	25.71	—
28	35.83	28.63	− 0.19	—	—	51.87	−12.01	10.36	−17.26	—
29	9.77	46.40	—	—	12.74	45.12	13.97	33.67	—	− 38.47
30	27.90	—	—	18.82	31.08	12.70	−27.95	—	—	47.34
31	4.63	—	25.42	−12.13	8.50	1.89	—	—	− 7.04	46.98
Close	2572.07	2128.73	2660.66	2905.20	3024.82	3393.78	3539.47	3764.50	4708.47	5528.91
Change	153.54	−12.98	220.60	24.51	118.07	75.26	23.39	139.54	152.37	−125.72

* Post-July 4th shortened trading day

JUNE/JULY

File Forms 5500
Chadwick Funeral Home
Andy Musser Ltd
Jones Termite & Pest Control

MONDAY

29

*I am first and foremost a catalyst. I bring
people and situations together.*
— Armand Hammer

TUESDAY

30

*The average man... is always waiting for
something to happen to him instead of
setting to work to make things happen.*
— A.A. Milne

WEDNESDAY

1

*It is impossible to please all the world
and one's father.*
— Jean de La Fontaine

THURSDAY
2

*Good judgment is usually the result of
experience and experience frequently
is the result of bad judgment.*
— Robert Lovell, quoted by Robert Sobel, *Panic on Wall Street*

FRIDAY

(Market Closed)

3

*Every human being, no matter how
beaten down, dreams of a better life
and will work like a champion for
it given the opportunity.*
— Mildred & Glen Leet, Founders of "Trickle Up"

Independence Day

SATURDAY
4

SUNDAY
5

A RALLY FOR ALL SEASONS

In any year when the market is a disappointment, you hear talk of a summer rally. Parameters for this "rally" were defined by the late Ralph Rotnem as the lowest close in the Dow industrial average in May or June to the highest close in July, August, or September. Such a big deal is made of the "summer rally" that one might get the impression the market puts on its best razzle-dazzle performance in the summertime. Nothing could be further from the truth! Not only does the market "rally" in every season of the year, but it does so with more gusto in the winter, spring, and fall than in the summer.

Winters in 34 years averaged a 13.7% gain as measured from the low in November or December to the first quarter closing high. Spring was up 10.1% followed by fall with 10.1%. Last and least was the average 9.4% "summer rally."

Nevertheless, no matter how thick the gloom or grim the outlook, don't despair! There's always a rally for all seasons, statistically.

SEASONAL GAINS IN DOW JONES INDUSTRIALS

	WINTER RALLY Nov/Dec Low to 1 Q. High	SPRING RALLY Feb/Mar Low to 2 Q. High	SUMMER RALLY May/Jun Low to 3 Q. High	FALL RALLY Aug/Sep Low to 4 Q. High
1964	15.3%	6.2%	9.4%	8.3%
1965	5.7	6.6	11.6	10.3
1966	5.9	4.8	3.5	7.0
1967	11.6	8.7	11.2	4.4
1968	7.0	11.5	5.2	13.3
1969	0.9	7.7	1.9	6.7
1970	5.4	6.2	22.5	19.0
1971	21.6	9.4	5.5	7.4
1972	19.1	7.7	5.2	11.4
1973	8.6	4.8	9.7	15.9
1974	13.1	8.2	1.4	11.0
1975	36.2	24.2	8.2	8.7
1976	23.3	6.4	5.9	4.6
1977	8.2	3.1	2.8	2.1
1978	2.1	16.8	11.8	5.2
1979	11.0	8.9	8.9	6.1
1980	13.5	16.8	21.0	8.5
1981	11.8	9.9	0.4	8.3
1982	4.6	9.3	18.5	37.8
1983	15.7	17.8	6.3	10.7
1984	5.9	4.6	14.1	9.7
1985	11.7	7.1	9.5	19.7
1986	31.1	18.8	9.2	11.4
1987	30.6	13.6	22.9	5.9
1988	18.1	13.5	11.2	9.8
1989	15.1	12.9	16.1	5.7
1990	8.8	14.5	12.4	8.6
1991	21.8	11.2	6.6	9.3
1992	14.9	6.4	3.7	3.3
1993	8.9	7.7	6.3	7.3
1994	9.7	5.2	9.1	5.0
1995	13.6	19.3	11.3	13.9
1996	19.2	7.5	8.7	17.3
1997	17.6	6.5		
Totals	**467.4%**	**343.6%**	**311.8%**	**333.4%**
Average	**13.7%**	**10.1%**	**9.4%**	**10.1%**

JULY

MONDAY

  6

*Only buy stocks when the market declines
10% from that date a year ago, which
happens once or twice a decade.*
— Eugene D. Brody, Oppenheimer Capital

TUESDAY

  7

*Sell stocks whenever the market
is 30% higher over a year ago.*
— Eugene D. Brody, Oppenheimer Capital

WEDNESDAY

  8

*You have to figure out how the consensus
is wrong to be valuable to the client.*
— Edward Yardeni, Prudential Bache

THURSDAY

9

*Never will a man penetrate deeper into
error than when he is continuing on a road
that has led him to great success.*
— Friedrich von Hayek, *Counterrevolution of Science*

FRIDAY

 10

*Never overpay for a stock. More money
is lost than in any other way by projecting
above-average growth and paying
an extra multiple for it.*
— Charles Neuhauser, Bear, Stearns

SATURDAY

11

SUNDAY

12

MARKET REACTIONS TO CAPITAL GAINS TAX CUTS

We could be getting a capital gains tax cut one of these days. Good news for the stock market, right? Wrong!—at least for the short term—if history is any guide. In the past, capital gains tax cuts were a signal to many investors it was time to take profits.

The Revenue Act of 1978, lowering the capital gains tax rate to 28% from 35%, was passed on October 12, 1978. This sparked the October Massacre of 1978 when the Dow dropped over 100 points or 11%. As you can see from the chart, the Dow stayed down for a year and a half.

Now for the good news. Two years later the market had moved much higher—7% from the passage of the Act and 15% from the low 17 months following the cut.

Again in August of 1981, the capital gains tax rate was lowered to 20% with the passage of the Economic Recovery Tax Act. This time the market's reaction was even more drastic. The Dow was already giving back some of its gains in 1981 but fell 65 points in August, almost 7%. It was down 10% after three months and 15% after twelve months. But two years later in the early stage of this extended bull market, the Dow tacked on 237 points for a 25% gain from the time of the tax cut and 379 points from the low for a 47% gain.

AT PRESSTIME: A 7% drop in seven days began one day after President Clinton signed a bill cutting the capital gains tax from 28% to 20%. Expect more than normal tax selling near year end.

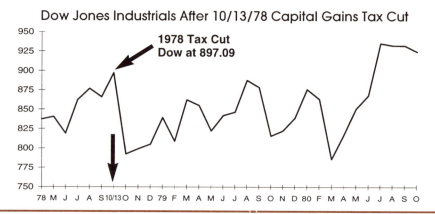

Dow Jones Industrials After 10/13/78 Capital Gains Tax Cut

1978 Tax Cut
Dow at 897.09

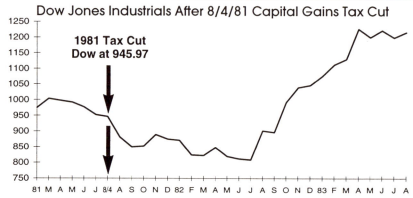

Dow Jones Industrials After 8/4/81 Capital Gains Tax Cut

1981 Tax Cut
Dow at 945.97

74

JULY

MONDAY
13

*I invest in people, not ideas; I want to see
fire in the belly and intellect.*
— Arthur Rock

TUESDAY
14

*Unless you've interpreted changes
before they've occurred, you'll be
decimated trying to follow them.*
— Robert J. Nurock

WEDNESDAY
15

*There's nothing wrong with cash.
It gives you time to think.*
— Robert Prechter, Jr., *Elliott Wave Theorist*

THURSDAY
16

*The big guys are the status quo,
not the innovators.*
— Kenneth L. Fisher

FRIDAY
  17

*A bull market tends to bail you out of all
your mistakes. Conversely, bear markets
make you PAY for your mistakes.*
— Richard Russell

SATURDAY
18

SUNDAY
19

DOW COULD GAIN WELL OVER 2000 POINTS FROM ITS 1998 LOW TO ITS HIGH IN 1999

Normally, major corrections occur sometime in the first or second years following presidential elections. In the last nine midterm election years, bear markets began or were in progress six times in a row before the onset in 1982 of our current biggest bull cycle in Wall Street history. Since then, we experienced a bull year in 1986, a Saddam Hussein-induced bear in 1990 and a flat year in 1994. Now, seven years without a sizeable correction makes it appear that an important low is likely in 1998.

The puniest advance, 14.5% from the 1946 low, was during the industrial contraction after World War II. The next four smallest advances with the major depressant in parentheses were: 1978 (OPEC–Iran) 20.9%, 1930 (economic collapse) 23.4%, 1966 (Vietnam) 26.7%, and 1990 (Persian Gulf War) 34.0%.

% CHANGE IN DOW JONES INDUSTRIALS BETWEEN THE MIDTERM YEAR LOW AND THE HIGH IN THE FOLLOWING YEAR

| Midterm Year Low | | Pre-Election Year High | | |
Date of Low	Dow	Date of High	Dow	% Gain
Jul 30 1914	71.42	Dec 8 1915	134.00	87.6%
Jan 15 1918	73.38	Nov 3 1919	119.62	63.0
Jan 10 1922	78.59	Mar 20 1923	105.38	34.1
Mar 30 1926	135.20	Dec 31 1927	202.40	49.7
Dec 31 1930	157.51	Feb 24 1931	194.36	23.4
Jul 26 1934	85.51	Nov 19 1935	148.44	73.6
Mar 31 1938	98.95	Sep 12 1939	155.92	57.6
Apr 28 1942	92.92	Jul 14 1943	145.82	56.9
Oct 9 1946	163.12	Jul 24 1947	186.85	14.5
Jan 13 1950	196.81	Sep 13 1951	276.37	40.4
Jan 11 1954	279.87	Dec 30 1955	488.40	74.5
Feb 25 1958	436.89	Dec 31 1959	679.36	55.5
Jun 26 1962	535.74	Dec 18 1963	767.21	43.2
Oct 7 1966	744.32	Sep 25 1967	943.08	26.7
May 26 1970	631.16	Apr 28 1971	950.82	50.6
Dec 6 1974	577.60	Jul 16 1975	881.81	52.7
Feb 28 1978	742.12	Oct 5 1979	897.61	20.9
Aug 12 1982	776.92	Nov 29 1983	1287.20	65.7
Jan 22 1986	1502.29	Aug 25 1987	2722.42	81.2
Oct 11 1990	2365.10	Dec 31 1991	3168.84	34.0
Apr 4 1994	3593.35	Dec 13 1995	5216.47	45.2
1998				
			Average Gain	**50.0%**

A hypothetical portfolio of stocks bought at midterm election-year lows since 1914 has gained 50.0% on average when the stock market reached its subsequent highs in the following pre-election years. A swing of such magnitude is equivalent to a move from 7000 to 10500 or from 8000 to 12000. With an advance of approaching 6000 Dow points since the 2365.10 bottom on October 11, 1990, I would gladly settle for a 2000-point move between 1998's low and the high of 1999.

Pretty impressive seasonality! And American politics being what it is, chances are the quadrennial Presidential Election/Stock Market Cycle will continue. Page 139 shows how effectively presidents have managed to have much stronger economies in the third and fourth years of their terms than in their first two.

JULY

MONDAY
20

*To turn $100 into $110 is work. To turn
$100 million into $110 million
is inevitable.*
— Edgar Bronfman, Seagrams, in *Newsweek*, 1985

TUESDAY
21

*Almost any insider purchase is worth
investigating for a possible lead to a
superior speculation. But very few
insider sales justify concern.*
— William Chidester

WEDNESDAY
22

*If the models are telling you to sell,
sell, sell, but only buyers are out
there, don't be a jerk. Buy!*
— William Silber, Ph.D. (N.Y.U.), in *Newsweek,* 1986

THURSDAY
23

*The higher a people's intelligence and
moral strength, the lower will be
the prevailing rate of interest.*
— Eugen von Bohm-Bawerk, 1910

FRIDAY
24

*When everybody starts looking really
smart, and not realizing that a lot of it
was luck, I get scared.*
— Raphael Yavneh, *Forbes*

SATURDAY
25

SUNDAY
26

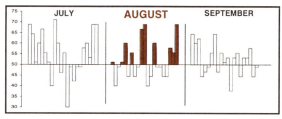

AUGUST ALMANAC

AUGUST						
S	M	T	W	T	F	S
					1	2
3	4	5	6	7	8	9
10	11	12	13	14	15	16
17	18	19	20	21	22	23
24	25	26	27	28	29	30
31						

SEPTEMBER						
S	M	T	W	T	F	S
	1	2	3	4	5	6
7	8	9	10	11	12	13
14	15	16	17	18	19	20
21	22	23	24	25	26	27
28	29	30				

See Market Probability Chart on page 125.

❑ Ignore articles extolling August bullishness since 1900, as August was up 80% of the time in the first half century but barely half the time thereafter ❑ Chance for weakness greatest in latter part of month ❑ Last 3 days before Labor Day up 26 times in 36 years (page 86), first three days now better ❑ As many declines as rallies have begun here ❑ RECORD: S&P 26 up, 21 down. Average gain 0.4% ❑ Tends to get clobbered during bear markets, except when July is hammered earlier.

AUGUST DAILY POINT CHANGES DOW JONES INDUSTRIALS

Previous Month Close	1987	1988	1989	1990	1991	1992	1993	1994	1995	1996
	2572.07	2128.73	2660.66	2905.20	3024.82	3393.78	3539.47	3764.50	4708.47	5528.91
1	—	1.78	−19.54	− 5.94	− 7.15	—	—	33.67	− 8.10	65.84
2	—	0.71	16.32	−34.66	−11.41	—	21.52	− 1.95	−10.22	85.08
3	−14.99	2.85	4.17	−54.95	—	1.62	0.28	− 3.56	11.27	—
4	−10.36	− 7.47	− 8.16	—	—	−11.08	− 9.22	−26.87	−17.96	—
5	19.93	− 7.47	—	—	−17.22	−19.18	− 3.08	−18.77	—	− 5.55
6	27.58	—	—	−93.31	38.24	−24.58	11.46	—	—	21.83
7	− 2.23	—	—	− 5.70	− 0.67	− 8.38	—	—	9.86	22.56
8	—	−11.73	4.18	24.26	−12.75	—	—	6.79	N/C	− 5.18
9	—	−28.27	−13.09	24.01	−17.66	—	15.65	1.95	−21.83	−32.18
10	43.84	−44.99	26.55	−42.33	—	5.40	− 3.35	11.00	−27.83	—
11	44.64	5.16	−28.64	—	—	− 6.48	10.62	−15.86	−25.36	—
12	−11.16	− 1.78	—	—	5.14	−10.27	−14.26	17.81	—	23.67
13	22.17	—	—	30.20	7.38	− 7.56	0.56	—	—	−57.70
14	− 6.06	—	− 6.07	0.99	− 3.35	15.67	—	—	41.56	19.60
15	—	−33.25	9.86	0.50	− 6.94	—	—	− 8.42	−19.02	− 1.10
16	—	17.24	5.51	−66.83	−30.41	—	9.50	24.28	− 1.76	23.67
17	15.14	4.45	−13.66	−36.64	—	− 4.05	7.83	− 8.09	− 8.45	—
18	−45.91	1.07	8.34	—	—	4.59	17.88	−21.05	−13.03	—
19	11.16	−11.03	—	—	−69.99	−22.42	7.27	− 0.32	—	9.99
20	40.97	—	—	11.64	15.66	− 2.17	3.35	—	—	21.82
21	2.71	—	−40.97	−52.48	88.10	−50.79	—	—	− 2.82	−31.44
22	—	−25.78	3.99	−43.81	5.59	—	—	− 3.89	5.64	43.65
23	—	− 0.89	27.12	−76.73	32.87	—	− 9.50	24.61	−35.57	−10.73
24	−12.43	37.34	56.53	49.50	—	−25.93	32.98	70.90	− 4.23	—
25	25.35	−15.82	− 2.28	—	—	4.05	13.13	−16.84	20.78	—
26	−20.57	6.58	—	—	− 0.89	14.59	− 3.91	51.16	—	−28.85
27	−26.79	—	—	78.71	−13.20	7.83	− 7.55	—	—	17.38
28	−35.71	—	11.00	3.22	29.07	12.97	—	—	− 7.40	1.11
29	—	24.00	−16.73	17.58	− 5.59	—	—	17.80	14.44	−64.73
30	—	− 3.20	1.52	−39.11	− 6.04	—	3.36	18.45	− 3.87	−31.44
31	23.60	− 6.58	9.12	21.04	—	−10.26	7.26	− 3.88	5.99	—
Close	2662.95	2031.65	2737.27	2614.36	3043.60	3257.35	3651.25	3913.42	4610.56	5616.21
Change	90.88	−97.08	76.61	−290.84	18.78	−136.43	111.78	148.92	−97.91	87.30

MONDAY
27

*Methodology is the last refuge
of a sterile mind.*
— Marianne L. Simmel

TUESDAY
28

Don't put all your eggs in one basket.
— Market maxim

WEDNESDAY
29

*Put your eggs in one basket
and watch the basket.*
— An alternate strategy

THURSDAY
 # 30

*Brazil is the country of the future
and always will be.*
— Brazilian joke

FRIDAY
 # 31

*Don't give up on yourself!
There's nothing you can't do!*
—Jacques D'Amboise

SATURDAY
1

SUNDAY
2

MARKET BEHAVIOR ON DAYS BEFORE AND AFTER HOLIDAYS AND END-OF-MONTH BUYING STRATEGIES

Throughout this year's calendar pages little "happy bulls" appear signifying a string of very favorable market days. These mostly include the best days of the month (see pages 64, 66, 134) and days around certain holidays.

Holiday market behavior shows the average basis point change (%) since 1980 for both the S&P 500 and the Zweig Unweighted Price Index (ZUPI). The January Effect for small stocks is dramatically visible in ZUPI starting in the day before New Year's Day. This would even be true going back over the past 68 years to 1928. Bullishness the day before other holidays and bearishness for a few days after is also evident except after Memorial Day (see Memorial Day Week on page 60). Third days after holidays are super.

HOLIDAYS: 3 DAYS BEFORE, 3 DAYS AFTER (Avg. Basis Point Change 1980–1997)

	−3	−2	−1		+1	+2	+3
S&P	−0.18	0.30	−0.10	New Year's	0.01	0.45	0.00
ZUPI	−0.05	0.24	0.54	Day	0.42	0.58	0.34
S&P	0.22	−0.18	−0.13	Presidents'	−0.25	−0.08	0.08
ZUPI	0.17	−0.04	0.05	Day	−0.32	−0.10	0.02
S&P	0.07	0.17	0.05	Good	−0.45	0.32	−0.04
ZUPI	−0.02	0.15	0.10	Friday	−0.34	0.17	0.04
S&P	0.00	−0.04	0.13	Memorial	0.45	0.34	0.14
ZUPI	−0.09	0.06	0.21	Day	0.17	0.24	0.19
S&P	0.01	−0.01	−0.04	Independence	−0.42	0.05	0.27
ZUPI	0.06	0.12	0.06	Day	−0.25	−0.05	0.13
S&P	0.04	−0.29	0.26	Labor	−0.11	0.14	0.12
ZUPI	0.08	0.00	0.25	Day	−0.12	0.09	0.30
S&P	−0.22	0.23	0.22	Thanksgiving	0.15	−0.26	0.48
ZUPI	−0.21	−0.09	0.19		0.33	−0.29	0.27
S&P	0.28	−0.11	0.19	Christmas	0.22	−0.18	0.34
ZUPI	0.13	0.11	0.35		0.10	−0.05	0.27
S&P	**0.03**	**0.03**	**0.07**	**Average**	**−0.05**	**0.10**	**0.17**
ZUPI	**0.01**	**0.07**	**0.28**	**All Listings**	**−0.00**	**0.08**	**0.19**

Being invested in small company stocks or no-load funds for five or seven days each month then switching to money market funds the rest of the month has produced annual returns of 15% or more over the years.

END-OF-MONTH BUY STRATEGIES (Average Basis Point Change Over 4 Time Spans)

		Strategy I Last Plus First 4 Days					Strategy II Same, Plus Additional Day Before and Day After (if not first day of week)			
	Since	1928	1980	1985	1990		Since	1928	1980	1985	1990
S&P		0.57	0.49	0.43	0.29	S&P		0.73	0.58	0.64	0.41
ZUPI		0.67	0.70	0.66	0.63	ZUPI		0.84	0.84	0.86	0.76

Data and ZUPI (Zweig Unweighted Price Index) courtesy of Martin Zweig/Catherine Nolan

AUGUST

MONDAY

*In a rising market, the tendency to look
beyond the simple fact of increasing
value to the reasons on which it
depends greatly diminishes.*
— John Kenneth Galbraith

TUESDAY

*Man's mind, once stretched by a new idea,
never regains its original dimensions.*
—Oliver Wendell Holmes

WEDNESDAY

*To pull off a great investment coup it
is best to be the only buyer of a stock
that you're building a position in.*
— Warren Buffet

THURSDAY

*Buy a stock the way you would buy
a house. Understand and like it
such that you'd be content to own
it in the absence of any market.*
— Warren Buffet

FRIDAY

*The market is a voting machine, whereon
countless individuals register choices
which are the product partly of
reason and partly of emotion.*
— Graham & Dodd

SATURDAY
8

SUNDAY
9

TWO BOOKS FOR YOUR INVESTMENT LIBRARY

In his book, *What Works On Wall Street*, chosen as Best Investment Book of 1996, James P. O'Shaughnessy's groundbreaking research provides one of the most thorough studies of what really works in the stock market. It shows how you could have beaten the market and almost all Wall Street pros by a wide margin using relatively simple strategies. And these strategies have worked over such a long period that there's every reason to believe they will continue to perform.

And what did he discover? What strategies really work? In brief, very small stocks turned in the best performance, though it's hard to capture those gains because the stocks are very volatile and the large average gain is accounted for by huge advances in just a few stocks. At the other end of the spectrum, large-cap stocks tend to lag the rest of the universe by a bit, but they can be safe and rewarding when a few selection criteria are applied. Mid-cap stocks, though favored by some market players, just don't cut it. These companies lack the flexibility of the small fry and the market clout and staying power of the big boys.

This landmark opus is sure to help you achieve superior stock market performance. This research enabled O'Shaughnessy, who now manages several hundred million dollars, to construct portfolios that would have beaten Value Line stocks rated #1 for timeliness two to one over the next 30 years.

Cyber Investing: Cracking Wall Street With Your Personal Computer, 1997's choice for Best Investment Book, was written by David L. Brown and Kassandra Bentley. It details how the computer revolution of the past dozen years has shattered the barriers between Wall Street and Main Street.

The stock market is one of the few place where an ordinary person can legitimately accumulate money. *Cyber Investing* teaches both beginning and seasoned investors alike how to screen available databases of over 10,000 stocks using their personal computers to spot extraordinary opportunities while streamlining their investment decisions. Investing without these tools is akin to an accountant not using a spreadsheet or a journalist not using a word processor.

This book will take you step-by-step through a cyber-investing process that will simplify and unify your whole approach to stock investing and turn you into a pro.

> To order either book, just call 800-477-3400. Have your credit card handy. *What Works On Wall Street* is $34.95 including shipping. *Cyber Investing* (softbound) including shipping is $29.95. These are two books that should be a part of every serious investor's permanent investment library.

AUGUST

MONDAY
10

*Your emotions are often a reverse
indicator of what you ought to be doing.*
— John F. Hindelong, Dillon, Reed

TUESDAY
11

*When the S&P Index Future premium
over "Cash" gets too high, I sell the
future and buy the stocks. If the
premium disappears, well, buy the future
and sell the stocks.*
— Neil Elliott, Fahnestock

WEDNESDAY
12

*To me, the "tape" is the final arbiter
of any investment decision. I have
a cardinal rule: Never fight the tape!*
— Martin Zweig

THURSDAY
13

*Stocks are super attractive when the Fed
is loosening and interest rates are falling.
In sum: Don't fight the Fed!*
— Martin Zweig

FRIDAY
14

*Every successful enterprise requires
three people— a dreamer, a businessman,
and a son-of-a-bitch.*
— Peter McArthur, 1904

SATURDAY
15

SUNDAY
16

BEST STOCK MARKET SEASONAL TRADES
LAST 15 YEARS (1982-1997) USING S&P FUTURES

Here is an interesting table showing trades that exhibit a high degree of accuracy. Just remember: nothing is cast in concrete; and that patterns do change; and when everybody knows about a seasonal trade that "always" works, it stops working. These trades are for experienced S&P futures traders only. The rationale for each seasonal trade follows:

- **Long December 10/27 to 11/03**
  November's performance as third best month coupled with "5-Day Bulge" (see page 134).

- **Long March 11/20 to 01/20**
  December is the strongest month of the year on average. Government's first fiscal quarter, when most new government funds are spent, ends in December.

- **Long March 12/15 to 12/30**
  Holiday cheer coupled with "thin" markets provide a strong tendency to rally the S&P 500 from mid-month to the start of the new year.

- **Long March 01/12 to 01/16**
  January is the second strongest month of the year.

- **Long March 01/23 to 02/12**
  February's tendency is often to correct January's excesses. Mid-February is a time for quick profit taking by traders and short-term investors. Do not overstay your welcome in this trade, it tends to fall apart rather quickly after the 12th.

- **Long March 01/29 to 02/09**
  Same reasons as above, but shortened to take advantage of the last plus first four days of the month (see page 66), with a few days for good measure.

- **Long June 04/30 to 06/01**
  In the last 10 years May has tended to be a very strong month. Federal income taxes have been paid, the Treasury Department is flush and has lower borrowing requirements. This equates with lower interest rates as the supply of Treasury Bonds is directly proportional to the government's borrowing needs.

- **Long June 05/18 to 06/01**
  The last half of May since 1985 has gained 2.2% on average. Only January's last half comes close (see page 46).

15 Years Seasonal S&P Futures Trades (1982-1997)

In Points

CONTRACT	Entry Date	Exit Date	Gains	Losses	Gain Percent	Total Gain	Average Gain	Worst Trade
Dec Long	27 Oct	3 Nov	13	2	87%	66.50	4.43	-3.70
Mar Long	20 Nov	20 Jan	13	2	87	174.40	11.63	-3.15
Mar Long	15 Dec	30 Dec	13	2	87	79.25	5.28	-6.20
Mar Long	12 Jan	16 Jan	14	1	93	52.30	3.49	-0.05
Mar Long	23 Jan	12 Feb	13	2	87	168.50	11.23	-9.85
MarLong	29 Jan	9 Feb	12	3	80	97.90	6.53	-9.30
Jun Long	30 Apr	1 Jun	13	2	87	176.95	11.80	-8.10
Jun Long	18 May	1 Jun	12	3	80	108.35	7.22	-4.55

In dollars (1 point equals $500)

CONTRACT	Entry Date	Exit Date	Gains	Losses	Gain Percent	Total Gain	Average Gain	Worst Trade
Dec Long	27 Oct	3 Nov	13	2	87%	$33,250	$2,217	$(1,850)
Mar Long	20 Nov	20 Jan	13	2	87	87,200	5,813	(1,575)
Mar Long	15 Dec	30 Dec	13	2	87	39,625	2,642	(3,100)
Mar Long	12 Jan	16 Jan	14	1	93	26,150	1,743	(25)
Mar Long	23 Jan	12 Feb	13	2	87	84,250	5,617	(4,925)
Mar Long	29 Jan	9 Feb	12	3	80	48,950	3,263	(4,650)
Jun Long	30 Apr	1 Jun	13	2	87	88,475	5,898	(4,050)
Jun Long	18 May	1 Jun	12	3	80	54,175	3,612	(2,275)

Research and data courtesy of Scott Barrie of Great Pacific Trading Company

MONDAY
17

*The public may boo me, but when I go
home and think of my money, I clap.*
— Horace, *Epistles*, c. 20 B.C.

TUESDAY
18

*Quality is never an accident; it
is always the result of
intelligent efforts.*
— John Ruskin

WEDNESDAY
19

*Edison has done more toward
abolishing poverty than all the
reformers and statesmen.*
— Henry Ford

THURSDAY
20

*I always keep these seasonal patterns in
the back of my mind. My antennae start
to purr at certain times of the year.*
— Kenneth Ward

FRIDAY
 # 21

*Don't compete. Create. Find out
what everyone else is doing
and then don't do it.*
— Joel Weldon

SATURDAY
22

SUNDAY
23

LAST THREE DAYS BEFORE LABOR DAY UP 17 IN A ROW NOW FIRST THREE DAYS OF WEEK ARE BEST

Summer is drawing to a close. Vacationers are returning home or taking one last fling. Spirits have been rejuvenated. A new business season and school year are about to begin. The air is filled with a sense of anticipation, optimism, and even euphoria. A happy setting indeed, and very likely the simple reason for seventeen straight years of rising markets during the three-day period prior to Labor Day, until 1978.

As you can see, these three "bullish" days wound up in the minus column in ten of the next nineteen years. However, to spotlight a brief three-day bullish bias is to doom it to subsequent failure. How could traders on stock and index future exchange floors have resisted more than a 1 percent gain on average for just three trading days? That's a return of 7 percent a month and over 100 percent a year compounded. Besides, they don't pay commissions and can trade on very low margins. The first three days of Labor Day week now appear to be better. Starting in 1982, of fifteen years, only four were losers: 1984, 1987, 1989 and 1996.

WEEK BEFORE LABOR DAY DAILY DOW POINT CHANGES

	MONDAY	TUESDAY	WEDNESDAY	THURSDAY	FRIDAY	WEEK'S CLOSE	CHANGE LAST 3 DAYS
1961	— 0.69	— 1.86	2.75	3.04	1.25	721.19	7.04
1962	— 1.17	— 7.32	— 2.01	— 0.92	6.86	609.18	3.93
1963	1.03	— 4.29	5.19	1.33	2.92	729.32	9.44
1964	— 0.61	5.52	1.08	0.94	2.29	848.31	4.31
1965	— 0.33	— 2.53	0.50	6.80	7.57	907.97	14.87
1966	—13.53	8.69	12.69	3.68	— 4.40	787.69	11.97
1967	0.64	0.05	— 1.04	7.57	— 0.11	901.18	6.42
1968	3.79	— 2.48	Closed	0.68	1.68	896.01	3.67
1969	— 5.81	— 7.92	1.26	3.63	8.31	836.72	13.20
1970	— 1.23	— 6.43	— 1.51	8.63	5.88	771.15	13.00
1971	— 6.72	— 3.36	0.95	1.61	12.12	912.75	14.68
1972	— 2.41	— 2.25	3.16	5.87	6.32	970.05	15.35
1973	7.22	1.36	11.36	— 0.90	5.04	887.57	15.50
1974	1.33	—16.59	— 4.93	— 9.77	21.74	678.58	7.04
1975	7.58	— 9.23	4.09	22.27	5.87	835.34	32.23
1976	4.99	4.82	12.21	— 1.16	4.32	989.11	15.37
1977	8.67	— 5.20	2.60	3.37	7.45	872.31	13.42
UP	8	5	12	13	15		17
DOWN	9	12	4	4	2		0
1978	—10.65	— 4.68	0.52	— 3.90	2.51	879.33	— 0.87
1979	5.21	— 0.77	0.26	— 1.20	3.93	887.63	2.99
1980	— 1.96	— 2.82	—10.32	—12.71	2.21	932.59	—20.82
1981	—10.75	1.24	1.52	—17.22	— 5.33	861.68	—21.03
1982	9.83	8.01	— 6.26	14.35	15.73	925.13	23.82
1983	2.04	1.93	20.12	— 9.35	8.64	1215.45	19.41
1984	— 8.61	4.19	— 5.19	— 3.64	1.10	1224.38	— 7.73
1985	— 0.67	4.82	8.62	4.04	— 1.12	1334.01	11.54
1986	—16.03	32.48	0.28	— 4.36	— 1.83	1898.34	— 5.91
1987	23.60	—51.98	— 8.93	— 2.55	—38.11	2561.38	—49.59
1988	24.00	— 3.20	— 6.58	—29.34	52.28	2054.59	16.36
1989	11.00	—16.73	1.52	9.12	14.82	2752.09	25.46
1990	78.71	3.22	17.58	—39.11	21.04	2614.36	— 0.49
1991	— 0.89	—13.20	29.07	— 5.59	— 6.04	3043.60	17.44
1992	—10.26	8.91	24.05	1.89	—10.27	3281.93	15.67
1993	3.36	7.26	— 6.15	—19.00	7.83	3633.93	—17.32
1994	17.80	18.45	— 3.88	—11.98	—15.86	3885.58	—31.72
1995	— 7.40	14.44	— 3.87	5.99	36.98	4647.54	39.10
1996	—28.85	17.38	1.11	—64.73	—31.44	5616.21	—95.06
UP	9	12	11	5	11		9
DOWN	10	7	8	14	8		10

MONDAY

24

*Averaging down in a bear market
is tantamount to taking a seat
on the down escalator at Macy's.*
— Richard Russell, *Dow Theory Letters*, 1984

TUESDAY

25

*Big money is made in the stock market
by being on the right side of major
moves. I don't believe in
swimming against the tide.*
— Martin Zweig

WEDNESDAY

26

*The possession of gold has ruined fewer
men than the lack of it.*
— Thomas Bailey Aldridge, 1903

THURSDAY

27

*A man will fight harder for his interests
than his rights.*
— Napoleon Bonaparte, 1815

FRIDAY

 # 28

*In all recorded history, there has not
been one economist who has had to
worry about where the next meal
would come from.*
— Peter Drucker

SATURDAY

29

SUNDAY

30

September Barometer works in reverse
Up in September, next year cursed

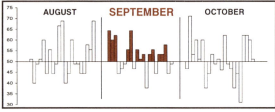

SEPTEMBER ALMANAC

See Market Probability Chart on page 125.

	SEPTEMBER				
S	M	T	W	T	F	S

SEPTEMBER
S	M	T	W	T	F	S
		1	2	3	4	5
6	7	8	9	10	11	12
13	14	15	16	17	18	19
20	21	22	23	24	25	26
27	28	29	30			

OCTOBER
S	M	T	W	T	F	S
					1	2	3
4	5	6	7	8	9	10
11	12	13	14	15	16	17
18	19	20	21	22	23	24
25	26	27	28	29	30	31

❑ First half tends to be stronger than second half ❑ September is a "reverse" barometer of the following year (page 90) ❑ RECORD: S&P up 19, down 27, flat 1 ❑ Average September loses 0.5% ❑ Dow up only 7 times in last 28 years: 1973, 1976, 1983, 1988, 1992, 1995 and 1996 ❑ Worst month of the year on both the Dow and S&P ❑ Midterm election year Septembers down nine times in a row.

SEPTEMBER DAILY POINT CHANGES DOW JONES INDUSTRIALS

	1987	1988	1989	1990	1991	1992	1993	1994	1995	1996
Previous Month Close	2662.95	2031.65	2737.27	2614.36	3043.60	3257.35	3651.25	3913.42	4610.56	5616.21
1	–51.98	–29.34	14.82	—	—	8.91	– 6.15	–11.98	36.98	—
2	– 8.93	52.28	—	—	H	24.05	–19.00	–15.86	—	H
3	– 2.55	—	—	H	–25.93	1.89	7.83	—	—	32.18
4	–38.11	—	H	– 0.99	– 9.17	–10.27	—	—	H	8.51
5	—	H	– 7.41	14.85	N/C	—	—	H	22.54	–49.94
6	—	10.67	–24.89	–31.93	3.13	—	H	13.12	13.73	52.90
7	H	0.53	–12.91	23.26	—	H	–26.83	–12.45	–14.09	—
8	–16.26	– 2.67	2.66	—	—	–21.34	–18.17	22.21	31.00	—
9	4.15	5.69	—	—	– 4.47	10.80	0.56	–33.65	—	73.98
10	26.78	—	—	– 3.96	–24.60	33.77	32.14	—	—	– 6.66
11	32.69	—	– 5.13	– 2.97	4.47	0.54	—	—	4.22	27.74
12	—	3.56	2.85	13.12	20.80	—	—	–14.47	42.27	17.02
13	—	10.67	–27.74	–43.07	–22.14	—	12.58	19.52	18.31	66.58
14	4.30	17.60	–14.63	–18.56	—	70.52	–18.45	15.47	36.28	—
15	–46.46	– 8.36	9.69	—	—	–48.90	17.89	58.55	– 4.23	—
16	–36.39	5.87	—	—	29.52	– 8.11	– 2.80	–20.53	—	50.68
17	– 2.29	—	—	3.22	– 2.02	– 3.51	–17.60	—	—	– 0.37
18	– 3.26	—	12.92	3.96	4.70	11.35	—	—	–17.16	–11.47
19	—	–17.07	– 0.19	–13.86	6.48	—	—	3.37	–13.37	– 9.62
20	—	6.40	– 3.42	–39.11	– 5.14	—	–37.45	–67.63	25.65	20.72
21	–31.82	3.02	– 3.61	– 5.94	—	– 6.22	–38.56	–17.49	–25.29	—
22	75.23	–10.49	1.33	—	—	–39.98	9.78	–14.47	– 3.25	—
23	17.62	10.67	—	—	– 8.72	– 2.16	– 7.27	– 5.38	—	6.28
24	–19.25	—	—	–59.41	18.56	9.18	3.36	—	—	–20.71
25	3.75	—	–22.42	32.67	– 8.05	–37.55	—	—	5.78	3.33
26	—	– 5.51	4.75	–25.99	– 3.80	—	—	17.49	– 4.33	– 8.51
27	—	– 2.84	9.12	–32.17	–11.18	—	24.59	13.80	– 3.25	4.07
28	31.33	3.20	21.85	25.00	—	25.94	– 1.68	15.14	25.29	—
29	–10.93	33.78	– 2.09	—	—	– 9.46	0.28	–23.55	1.44	—
30	5.71	– 6.40	—	—	10.73	4.86	–11.18	–11.44	—	9.25
Close	2596.28	2112.91	2692.82	2452.48	3016.77	3271.66	3555.12	3843.19	4789.08	5882.17
Change	–66.67	81.26	–44.45	–161.88	–26.83	14.31	–96.13	–70.23	178.52	265.96

MONDAY
 31

*The less a man knows about the past
and the present the more insecure must
be his judgment of the future.*
— Sigmund Freud

TUESDAY
 1

*Marx's great achievement was to place the
system of capitalism on the defensive.*
— Charles A. Madison, 1977

WEDNESDAY
 2

*The word "crisis" in Chinese
is composed of two characters:
the first, the symbol of danger;
the second, opportunity.*
— Anonymous

THURSDAY
 3

*In the course of evolution and a higher
civilization we might be able to get
along comfortably without Congress,
but without Wall Street, never.*
— Henry Clews, 1900

FRIDAY
 4

*Let us have the courage to stop
borrowing to meet the continuing
deficits. Stop the deficits.*
— Franklin D. Roosevelt, 1932

SATURDAY
 5

SUNDAY
 6

THE SEPTEMBER REVERSE BAROMETER

During the first sixty years of this century, the stock market in the final quarter of the year often took its cue from its own behavior in September, the start of a new business year and followed a similar course two-thirds of the time. As a result, September market activity was naturally regarded as a useful barometer and became folklore.

However, starting with 1960, an incredible transformation occurred. September became a **reverse barometer**. Bearish Septembers tended to be followed by bullish fourth quarters, and vice versa. In the last 37 years, 25 Septembers were losers or gained less than 1.0%. They preceded average fourth quarter gains of 3.8%. The other twelve Septembers were up and preceded fourth quarters gaining 2.4% on average.

AS SEPTEMBER GOES, BE CONTRARY!

	September % Change	4th Quarter % Change	Next Year's % Change
1960	− 6.0%	8.6%	23.1%
1961	− 2.0	7.2	−11.8
1962	− 4.8	12.1	18.9
1963	− 1.1	4.6	13.0
1964	2.9	0.7	9.1
1965	3.2	2.7	−13.1
1966	− 0.7	4.9	20.1
1967	3.3	− 0.2	7.7
1968	3.9	1.2	−11.4
1969	− 2.5	− 1.1	0.1
1970	3.4	9.3	10.8
1971	− 0.7	3.8	15.6
1972	− 0.5	6.8	−17.4
1973	4.0	−10.0	−29.7
1974	−11.9	7.9	31.5
1975	− 3.5	7.5	19.1
1976	2.3	2.1	−11.5
1977	− 0.2	− 1.5	1.1
1978	− 0.7	− 6.3	12.3
1979	0.0	− 1.3	25.8
1980	2.5	8.2	− 9.7
1981	− 5.4	5.5	14.8
1982	0.8	16.8	17.3
1983	1.0	− 0.7	1.4
1984	− 0.3	0.7	26.3
1985	− 3.5	16.0	14.6
1986	− 8.5	4.7	2.0
1987	− 2.4	−23.2	12.4
1988	4.0	2.1	27.3
1989	− 0.7	1.2	− 6.6
1990	− 5.1	7.9	26.3
1991	− 1.9	7.5	4.5
1992	0.9	4.3	7.1
1993	− 1.0	1.6	− 1.5
1994	− 2.7	− 0.7	34.1
1995	4.0	5.4	20.3
1996	5.4	7.8	??

Based on S&P composite index

Previous Bullish Septembers Ranked		
September % Change	4th Quarter % Change	Next Year's % Change
1996 5.4%	7.8%	??
1995 4.0	5.4	20.3
1973 4.0	−10.0	−29.7
1988 4.0	2.1	27.3
1968 3.9	1.2	−11.4
1970 3.4	9.3	10.8
1967 3.3	−0.2	7.7
1965 3.2	2.7	−13.1
1964 2.9	0.7	9.1
1980 2.5	8.2	− 9.7
1976 2.3	2.1	−11.5
1983 1.0	−0.7	1.4
Averages 2.4%		0.1%
Previous Bearish Septembers Ranked		
1992 0.9	4.3	7.1
1982 0.8	16.8	17.3
1979 0.0	− 1.3	25.8
1977 − 0.2	− 1.5	1.1
1984 − 0.3	0.7	26.3
1972 − 0.5	6.8	−17.4
1989 − 0.7	1.2	− 6.6
1971 − 0.7	3.8	15.6
1966 − 0.7	4.9	20.1
1978 − 0.7	− 6.3	12.3
1993 − 1.0	1.6	− 1.5
1963 − 1.1	4.6	13.0
1991 − 1.9	7.5	4.5
1961 − 2.0	7.2	−11.8
1987 − 2.4	−23.2	12.4
1969 − 2.5	− 1.1	0.1
1994 − 2.7	− 0.7	34.1
1975 − 3.5	7.5	19.1
1985 − 3.5	16.0	14.6
1962 − 4.8	12.1	18.9
1990 − 5.1	7.9	26.3
1981 − 5.4	5.5	14.8
1960 − 6.0	8.6	23.1
1986 − 8.5	4.7	2.0
1974 −11.9	7.9	31.5
Averages 3.8%		12.1%

Even more incredible is September's record as a reverse barometer giving us advance notice of what the market will do in the following year. Six of the eleven Septembers with gains of 1.0% or more, were followed by bear market years (1966, 1969, 1974, 1977, 1981, and 1984 through August). Twenty-five other Septembers were down, flat or slightly up and their following years gained 12.1% on average. Four losing years were not induced by recessions: 1962 (Kennedy stare-down with Big Steel and Cuban Missile Crisis), 1973 (OPEC oil embargo), 1990 (Persian Gulf Crisis) and 1994 (rising interest rates).

SEPTEMBER

MONDAY
7

No nation ought to be without debt.
A national debt is a national blessing.
— Thomas Paine, 1776

TUESDAY
8

If I had my life to live over again, I
would elect to be a trader of goods
rather than a student of science. I
think barter is a noble thing.
— Albert Einstein, 1934

WEDNESDAY
9

You must automate, emigrate,
or evaporate.
— James A. Baker, General Electric

THURSDAY
10

If you don't know who you are, the stock
market is an expensive place to find out.
— George Goodman, 1959

FRIDAY
11

The worst trades are generally when
people freeze and start to pray and
hope rather than take some action.
— Robert Mnuchin, Goldman, Sachs

SATURDAY
12

SUNDAY
13

BEST INVESTMENT BOOK OF THE YEAR

Many investors forget that the most basic force affecting stock prices is the law of supply and demand. The Point and Figure method of charting was developed as a logical, organized way of recording supply and demand. If there are more buyers in a particular security than there are sellers willing to sell, the price will rise. On the other hand, if there are more sellers in a particular security than there are buyers willing to buy, then the price will decline. If buying and selling are equal, the price will remain the same. This is the irrefutable law of supply and demand.

Whether it is from school or reading newspapers or magazines, investors are familiar with charts of some kind or other. Point and Figure charts were developed over 100 years ago and have stood the test of time.

In his book, *Point & Figure Charting: The Essential Application for Forecasting and Tracking Market Prices*, Thomas J. Dorsey shows you, step-by-step, how to create, maintain, and interpret your own Point and Figure charts. He explains how you can use your findings to track and forecast market prices and develop an overall investment strategy. Dorsey demonstrates how you can easily track the history of any particular stock or group and help you recognize promising trends early enough to take advantage of them.

Point and Figure charting adherents are only a small minority even among market technicians. But devotees claim that P&F charting presents unambiguous signals while bar charts are often a muddle. Today's leading advocate of Point and Figure probably is Tom Dorsey of Dorsey, Wright & Associates. He and his partner have built a major investment advisory firm based entirely on Point and Figure charting. The firm serves institutional investors and stockbrokers, charging a minimum of several thousand dollars a year for its various services. Dorsey says that 250 brokerage firms subscribe, plus fund managers and other institutions. That means at least several thousand professional investors read the firm's voluminous daily market letters and other reports and presumably act on the information.

On a consulting basis, Dorsey, Wright serves as the primary or supplementary technical research department for a number of firms, including a few of the largest brokerage houses. This may represent a major shift in thinking on Wall Street, where technical analysis once was relegated to a guy in a distant corner who spent all his time marking up graph paper—if technical analysis was tolerated at all.

Dorsey, Wright's analysts update some 2,000 charts daily by hand—to maintain their feel for the market, even though the firm's computers also maintain charts and make them available to subscribers on the Internet. It's an amazing operation considering that most investors have never heard of Point and Figure analysis and most of the rest probably think it's a forgotten art.

As far as we know, it was almost forgotten for a while, but was kept alive in the 1950s and '60s, notably by A. W. Cohen. He's the author of a classic book on the subject (long since out of print) and the founder of Chartcraft, a pub-

(continued on page 94)

SEPTEMBER

MONDAY
14

*A good trader has to have three things:
a chronic inability to accept things at
face value, to feel continuously
unsettled, and to have humility.*
— Michael Steinhardt

TUESDAY
15

*The pursuit of gain is the only way
in which people can serve the needs of
others whom they do not know.*
— Friedrich von Hayek, *Counterrevolution of Science*

WEDNESDAY
16

*Cheapening the cost of necessities and
conveniences of life is the most powerful
agent of civilization and progress.*
— Thomas Elliott Perkins, 1888

THURSDAY
17

*In the market, yesterday is a memory and
tomorrow is a vision. And looking back
is a lot easier than looking ahead.*
— Frankie Joe

FRIDAY

18

*The American system of ours gives
everyone of us a great opportunity if we
only seize it with both hands.*
— Al Capone, 1929

SATURDAY
19

SUNDAY
20

(continued from page 92)

lishing company whose chart books and the newsletter *Investors Intelligence* are still put out by Cohen's disciple Michael Burke. (For further information, contact Chartcraft at 914-632-0422.) Point and Figure actually goes back to the last century, well before bar charts were in general use. Charles Dow, founder of Dow Theory and *The Wall Street Journal.* is said to have used a version of the technique. Starting even earlier, James Keene, one of the most successful stock manipulators in history, employed "figure charts" in his operations. Jesse Livermore, perhaps the most famous trader of all time, used what could be called a variety of Point and Figure technique in the first two decades of this century. A book published in 1898, *The Game in Wall Street and How to Play It Successfully,* seems to have been the first text on the subject. There are other books, but not a lot—and we doubt that most of them are in print.

Point and Figure may look complicated if you're used to studying standard bar charts, but actually the technique is a simplification. The idea is to boil the price information down to its essentials in order to clarify the picture. Thus P&F charts are updated only when there is a significant move. That might be one point in the same direction or three points if the trend reverses, depending on the scale being used. Volume is ignored. While volume can be revealing, it is often confusing as well. P&F technicians would argue that what matters is simply the balance between supply and demand. If a stock turns up, then the buyers are more anxious than the sellers, whether the turn comes on 10,000 shares or 10 million.

How It's Done

The current standard versions of P&F charting reduces price action to columns filled with "Xs" or "Os." X represents an uptick and O a downtick. We'll talk only about a three point reversal chart for the purpose of simplicity. You start in the first column, and if the stock has moved up a point you place an X in the box corresponding to the current price on a vertical scale. If the stock moves up a full point, you place another X in the next higher box in the same column. A reversal requires that the stock fall at least three points. If it does, then move to the right and place an O in the next column, one box below the last X. With a low-priced stock, you would want to use less than one point per box, but we are trying to keep this explanation simple.

You wind up with a sheet containing columns that show moves up and moves down—supply and demand at work. A buy signal is given when a column of Xs tops the previous column of Xs, or even better, several such columns. A sell signal is the reverse. P&F zeros in on supply and demand, and issues clear signals. Not only that, but counting the number of Xs in a column up from a bottom, and applying a formula, will give a projection for the top of the ultimate upmove.

Michael Burke and Tom Dorsey have taken P&F well beyond analyzing stocks, applying the method to market averages, indicators and industry

(continued on page 95)

groups. The same advantages of simplicity and clear signals apply in these applications.

Both these experts say their most important indicator is the New York Stock Exchange Bullish Percent. This is simply the percentage of listed stocks in bull trends, as defined by their last Point and Figure signal. The indicator, in turn, is kept as a P&F chart and gives the usual sort of signals. The simple interpretation is that if at least 50% of stocks are in bull trends, the market is favorable. But if an overwhelming majority of stocks are favorable, watch out for any reversal, as it could be the start of a dangerous decline. Reversals that come from very overbought or oversold levels tend to be more violent than others.

A lot of emphasis is placed on sector analysis—how strong is each industry group, and which are attracting new money? As you might guess, a sector is rated by keeping track of the charts of all stocks in the group, just as is done for the market as a whole. Dorsey notes that most stocks are more influenced by market and industry group trends than fundamental developments at the company. But he advocates keeping track of fundamentals as well. He's not the sealed-room sort of technician—the type that doesn't want to know anything except the patterns on his charts. Instead he advocates using all available information, though he relies on others for fundamental analysis.

If you're the type who prefers to let others do the grunt work, take a look at Dorsey's internet site www.dorseywright.com. You can even get a free two-week trial.

See all the companies in each industry arranged across a bell curve to easily identify those stocks that are overbought or oversold.

Their Breakout Report separates breakouts (to the upside or downside) by sector. This way when a large number of stocks start to breakout in one sector, this obvious signal will jump out at you, if you're inclined to jump on the bandwagon early in the game.

As stocks tend to bounce off their moving averages, they'll show you all stocks an eighth point from their 50-day moving average, on a buy signal and with their 50-day moving average above their 200-day moving average.

There is much more. If you're a broker, an avid stock trader or want to be, you'll love this site.

I was impressed with how Point and Figure charts were explained in this book. *Point and Figure Charting* shows you step-by-step how to create, maintain, and interpret your own Point and Figure charts. This age-old method clearly illustrates who's winning the battle of supply vs. demand. This is an invaluable tool when making buy and sell decisions.

Just call us at 800-477-3400 and have your credit card handy, or use the enclosed post-paid order card. The cost, including shipping is $60.00 hardbound.

FALL PORTFOLIO REVIEW

NO. OF SHARES	SECURITY	A ORIGINAL COST	B CURRENT VALUE	C GAIN (B – A) OR LOSS (A – B)	D % CHANGE (C ÷ A)	E MONTHS HELD	F CHANGE PER MO. (D ÷ E)	G ANNUAL RETURN (F × 12)
200	Sample Corp.	$10,000	$10,400	$400	4.0%	8	0.5%	6.0%
TOTALS								

Stocks which have achieved their potential
1
2
3

Candidates for addition to portfolio
1
2
3

Stocks which have been disappointments
1
2
3

Investment decisions
1
2
3

BEST INVESTMENT BOOKS 1997 & 1998

As a special service to Almanac readers, we offer the opportunity to purchase CYBER INVESTING and POINT AND FIGURE CHARTING, the 1997 and 1998 Best Investment Books (see pages 82 and 92). To place an order or receive any information, contact The Hirsch Organization at 201-767-4100 or fax 201-767-7337. E-mail jahirsch@ix.netcom.com

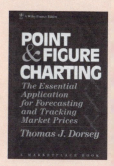

RESERVE YOUR 1999 STOCK TRADER'S ALMANAC NOW!

❑ Please reserve_____ copies of next year's Thirty-Second Edition, The 1999 STOCK TRADER'S ALMANAC. $29.95 for single copies plus $4.95 shipping and handling. *($15.00 shipping and handling for all foreign countries including Canada and Mexico.)* Quantity prices available on request.

❑ $_____ payment enclosed *(US funds only)*

Charge Credit Card (check one)

❑ VISA ❑ MasterCard ❑ AmEx

Name

Address

Account #

City

Expiration Date

State   Zip

Signature

❑ Please rush a copy of POINT & FIGURE CHARTING, $55.00 plus $4.95 shipping and handling. *($15.00 shipping and handling for all foreign countries including Canada and Mexico).*

❑ Please rush a copy of CYBER INVESTING, $24.95, softbound, plus $4.95 shipping and handling. *($15.00 shipping and handling for all foreign countries including Canada and Mexico).*

❑ Send_____ additional copies of the 1998 STOCK TRADER'S ALMANAC $29.95 for single copies plus $4.95 shipping and handling. *($15.00 shipping and handling for all foreign countries including Canada and Mexico.)* Quantity prices available on request.

❑ $_____ payment enclosed *(US funds only)*

Charge Credit Card (check one)

❑ VISA ❑ MasterCard ❑ AmEx

Name

Address

Account #

City

Expiration Date

State   Zip

Signature

THIRTY-SECONDANNUAL**EDITION**

of the 1999 Stock Trader's Almanac will be published in the Fall of 1998. Mail the postpaid card below to reserve your copy of this Edition.

SEPTEMBER

Rosh Hashanah

MONDAY

21

*If you don't profit from your investment
mistakes, someone else will.*
— Yale Hirsch

TUESDAY

22

*Major bottoms are usually made when
analysts cut their earnings estimates
and companies report earnings
which are below expectations.*
— Edward Babbitt, Jr., Avatar Associates

WEDNESDAY

23

*The worst bankrupt in the world is the person
who has lost his enthusiasm.*
—H.W. Arnold

THURSDAY

24

*Italians come to ruin most generally in three ways:
women, gambling and farming.
My family chose the slowest one.*
— Pope John XXIII, 1961

FRIDAY

25

*It's no coincidence that three of the top
five stock option traders in a recent
trading contest were all ex-Marines.*
—Robert Prechter, Jr., *Elliott Wave Theorist*

SATURDAY

26

SUNDAY

27

October, October don't show your face
Meltdown Monday '87 was a total disgrace

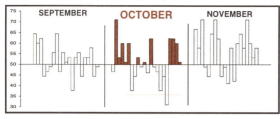

See Market Probability Chart on page 125.

OCTOBER ALMANAC

❑ Curse of October 1929 was receding—then came 1987 and a 602-point Dow loss ❑ Memory of back-to-back "massacres" in 1978 and 1979, a "meltdown" in 1987 and Friday the Thirteenth in 1989 could affect bullish spirits in forthcoming Octobers ❑ October is known as a "bear-killer," turning the tide in 8 major bear markets: 1946, 1957, 1960, 1962, 1966, 1974, 1987, and 1990 ❑ RECORD: S&P 27 up, 20 down since 1950 ❑ Big percentage moves: 1987 off 21.8%, 1974 up 16.3% and 1982 up 11.0%.

OCTOBER DAILY POINT CHANGES DOW JONES INDUSTRIALS

Previous Month Close	1987 2596.28	1988 2112.91	1989 2692.82	1990 2452.48	1991 3016.77	1992 3271.66	1993 3555.12	1994 3843.19	1995 4789.08	1996 5882.17
1	42.92	—	—	63.36	1.57	−17.29	25.99	—	—	22.73
2	1.79	—	20.90	−10.64	− 5.82	−53.76	—	—	−27.82	29.07
3	—	− 7.65	40.84	−15.84	−27.73	—	—	3.70	−11.56	− 1.12
4	—	− 3.20	16.53	27.47	−23.03	—	− 3.35	−45.76	− 9.03	60.01
5	− 0.81	4.45	2.47	− 6.19	—	−21.61	9.50	−13.79	22.04	—
6	− 91.55	1.24	11.96	—	—	− 0.81	11.73	−11.78	6.50	—
7	2.45	42.50	—	—	−19.01	−25.94	−15.36	21.87	—	−13.05
8	− 34.44	—	—	13.12	21.02	23.78	1.11	—	—	−13.04
9	− 34.43	—	5.89	−78.22	−17.44	−39.45	—	—	−42.99	−36.15
10	—	8.71	− 6.08	−37.62	30.19	—	—	23.89	− 5.42	− 8.95
11	—	− 2.49	−11.97	−42.82	7.16	—	8.67	55.51	14.45	47.71
12	− 10.77	−30.23	− 13.52	32.92	—	37.83	− 0.28	− 1.68	29.63	—
13	36.72	7.12	−190.58	—	—	27.01	10.06	14.80	28.90	—
14	− 95.46	− 0.18	—	—	35.77	− 5.94	18.44	20.52	—	40.62
15	− 57.61	—	—	18.32	21.92	−20.80	8.10	—	—	− 5.22
16	−108.35	—	88.12	−35.15	20.35	− 0.27	—	—	− 9.40	16.03
17	—	7.29	− 18.65	6.68	− 8.72	—	—	13.46	11.56	38.39
18	—	19.38	4.92	64.85	24.15	—	12.58	− 6.39	−18.42	35.03
19	−508.00	−22.58	39.55	68.07	—	14.04	− 6.99	18.50	24.93	—
20	102.27	43.92	5.94	—	—	− 2.43	9.78	−24.89	− 7.59	—
21	186.84	2.31	—	—	−16.77	1.08	− 8.94	−19.85	—	− 3.36
22	− 77.42	—	—	− 4.70	−20.58	13.78	13.14	—	—	−29.07
23	0.33	—	− 26.23	−22.03	1.12	6.76	—	—	−39.38	−25.34
24	—	−13.16	− 3.69	10.15	−24.60	—	—	−36.00	28.18	−43.98
25	—	3.02	− 5.94	−20.05	−11.40	—	24.31	− 4.71	−29.98	14.54
26	−156.83	− 8.18	− 39.55	−48.02	—	36.47	− 1.12	− 2.36	−49.86	—
27	52.56	−24.35	− 17.01	—	—	− 8.38	− 7.83	26.92	37.93	—
28	0.33	9.06	—	—	40.70	15.67	23.20	55.51	—	−34.29
29	91.51	—	—	− 5.94	16.32	− 5.13	− 7.27	—	—	34.29
30	55.20	—	6.76	17.82	9.84	−19.99	—	—	14.82	−13.79
31	—	− 1.24	41.60	− 5.69	− 2.68	—	—	−22.54	− 1.09	36.15
Close	1993.53	2148.65	2645.08	2442.33	3069.10	3226.28	3680.59	3908.12	4755.48	6029.38
Change	−602.75	35.74	−47.74	−10.15	52.33	−45.38	125.47	64.93	−33.60	147.21

SEPTEMBER/OCTOBER

MONDAY
28

*In nature there are no rewards or
punishments; there are consequences.*
— Horace Annesley Vachell, *The Force of Clay*

TUESDAY
 # 29

*A loss never bothers me after I take it.
I forget it overnight. But being wrong—
not taking the loss— that is what does
damage to the pocketbook and to the soul.*
— Jesse Livermore

Yom Kippur   ## WEDNESDAY
 # 30

*The facts are unimportant! It's what they
are perceived to be that determines the
course of events.*
— R. Earl Hadady

THURSDAY
 # 1

*The commodity futures game is a
money game— not a game involving
the supply-demand of the actual
commodity as commonly depicted.*
— R. Earl Hadady

FRIDAY
 # 2

*Regulatory agencies within five
years become controlled by industries they
were set up to regulate.*
— Gabriel Kolko

SATURDAY
3

SUNDAY
4

A CORRECTION FOR ALL SEASONS

While there's a rally for every season (page 72), almost always there's a decline or correction, too. Fortunately, corrections tend to be smaller than rallies, and that's what gives the stock market its long-term upward bias. In each season the average bounce outdoes the average setback. On average the net gain between the rally (page 72) and the correction is smallest in the summer and the fall.

The summer setback tends to be slightly outdone by the average correction in the fall. Tax selling and portfolio cleaning are the usual explanations—individuals sell to register a tax loss and institutions like to get rid of their losers before preparing year-end statements. The October jinx also plays a major part. Since 1964, there have been 10 fall declines of over 10%, and in six of them (1966, 1974, 1978, 1979, 1987, and 1990) the worst damage was done in October, where many bear markets end.

Most often, it has paid to buy after fourth quarter "waterfall declines" for a rally that may continue into January or even beyond.

SEASONAL LOSSES IN DOW JONES INDUSTRIALS

	WINTER CORRECTION Nov/Dec High to 1 Q. Low	SPRING CORRECTION Feb/Mar High to 2 Q. Low	SUMMER CORRECTION May/Jun High to 3 Q. Low	FALL CORRECTION Aug/Sep High to 4 Q. Low
1964	− 0.15%	− 2.43%	− 0.97%	− 2.09%
1965	− 2.46	− 7.25	− 8.29	− 0.88
1966	− 6.00	−13.16	−17.70	−12.68
1967	− 4.20	− 3.91	− 5.50	− 9.92
1968	− 8.84	− 0.27	− 5.46	+ 0.43
1969	− 8.67	− 8.71	−17.23	− 8.10
1970	−13.79	−20.21	− 8.76	− 2.53
1971	− 1.36	− 4.77	−10.67	−13.35
1972	− 0.50	− 2.64	− 6.26	− 5.33
1973	−10.96	−12.80	−10.94	−17.30
1974	−15.27	−10.80	−29.79	−27.58
1975	− 6.33	− 5.55	− 9.93	− 6.66
1976	− 0.23	− 5.07	− 4.67	− 8.94
1977	− 8.51	− 7.16	−11.52	−10.20
1978	−12.27	− 4.04	− 7.01	−13.49
1979	− 2.51	− 5.76	− 3.74	−10.88
1980	−10.02	−16.01	− 1.72	− 6.78
1981	− 6.86	− 5.10	−18.58	−12.86
1982	−10.89	− 7.50	−10.62	− 3.34
1983	− 4.06	− 2.83	− 6.83	− 3.64
1984	−11.89	−10.46	− 8.43	− 6.17
1985	− 4.76	− 4.41	− 2.81	− 2.31
1986	− 3.27	− 4.73	− 7.27	− 7.58
1987	− 1.45	− 6.61	− 1.68	−36.13
1988	− 6.70	− 6.99	− 7.57	− 4.47
1989	− 1.74	− 2.35	− 3.12	− 6.64
1990	− 7.89	− 4.01	−17.32	−18.42
1991	− 6.33	− 3.63	− 4.52	− 6.26
1992	+ 0.11	− 3.31	− 5.42	− 7.62
1993	− 2.74	− 3.09	− 2.95	− 2.04
1994	− 4.42	− 9.61	− 4.41	− 7.06
1995	− 0.81	− 0.10	− 0.20	− 2.04
1996	− 3.52	− 4.62	− 7.47	+ 0.17
1997	− 1.80	− 9.79		
Totals	**−191.09%**	**−219.67%**	**−269.35%**	**−282.69%**
Average	**− 5.62%**	**− 6.46%**	**− 8.16%**	**− 8.57%**

OCTOBER

MONDAY
 5

*Charts not only tell what was, they tell
what is; and a trend from was to is
(projected linearly into the will be)
contains better percentages
than clumsy guessing.*
— R.A. Levy

TUESDAY
 6

*If a battered stock refuses to sink any
lower no matter how many negative
articles appear in the papers, that
stock is worth a close look.*
— James L. Fraser, *Contrary Investor*

WEDNESDAY
 7

*I know but one sure tip from a
broker...your margin call.*
— Jesse Livermore

THURSDAY
8

*The business world worships mediocrity.
Officially we revere free enterprise,
initiative, and individuality.
Unofficially, we fear it.*
— George Lois, *Art of Advertising*, 1977

FRIDAY
9

*When a falling stock becomes a screaming
buy because it cannot conceivably drop
further, try to buy it 30 percent lower.*
— Al Rizzo, 1986

SATURDAY
10

SUNDAY
11

YEAR'S TOP INVESTMENT BOOKS

1. Point And Figure Charting: The Essential Application For Forecasting And Tracking Market Prices, Thomas J. Dorsey, John Wiley & Sons, $55.00. Many investors tend to forget that the most basic force affecting securities prices is the law of supply and demand. Point and Figure charting is a time-tested, proven method of tracking fluctuations in supply and demand and recognizing promising trends early enough to take advantage of them. (See page 92.)

2. Bloomberg By Bloomberg, Michael Bloomberg and Matthew Winkler, John Wiley & Sons, $24.95. Head of the world's fastest-growing media empire, Bloomberg has been hailed as the new standard for what it takes to win in the Information Age. A combination of personal reminiscence with insight into the worldwide demand for fast, accurate financial information.

3. Against The Gods: The Remarkable Story Of Risk, Peter L. Bernstein, John Wiley & Sons, $27.95. Without the instruments of risk management, decision making would be impossible, because no one could determine the likelihood of successful outcomes. The ability to define what may happen in the future and to choose among alternatives lies at the heart of contemporary societies. Extraordinary!

4. The Way Of The Warrior-Trader: The Financial Risk-Taker's Guide To Samurai Courage, Confidence And Discipline, Dr. Richard D. McCall, McGraw-Hill, $24.95. Applies time-honored precepts of the samurai discipline to modern trading. How to use centuries-old methods for victory in today's trading markets.

5. Direct Public Offerings: The New Method For Taking Your Company Public, Drew Field, Sourcebooks, $19.95. Explains how businesses can raise capital by marketing shares directly to their customers and how investors can profit from this hot new trend in corporate growth.

6. Technical Analysis Of Stock Trends, Robert D. Edwards and John Magee, AMACOM, $59.95. Now in its seventh edition, this completely updated version of the universally acclaimed investors' classic is the definitive reference on analyzing trends in stock performance through technical analysis.

7. The Financial Times Global Guide To Investing: The Secrets Of The World's Leading Investment Gurus, James Morton, Pitman Publishing, $75.00. Profit from the street smarts and anecdotal experience of the top investment performers of the 1990's. Contains advice from over 120 of the most successful investors and institutions from over 41 countries.

8. Going Global With Equities, Paul Melton, Pitman Publishing, $50.00. Provides practical advice on gathering information, finding the world's bargain equities, choosing countries and building a successful global portfolio. Going global could increase your profits and limit your risks.

9. Take Charge Of Your Financial Future, Marvin B. Roffman with Michael J. Schwager, Carol Publishing Group, $18.95. A guide to individual investing and personal money management. In twenty five no-nonsense chapters, practical advice is given that anyone can follow to set financial goals and reach them.

 (continued on page 104)

OCTOBER

MONDAY
12

*A great pleasure in life is doing what most people
say you cannot do.*
—Walter Bagehot

TUESDAY
13

*The "whole" or "cash-value" life
policy is certainly in its time one of
the most cleverly designed financial
products (from the insurance
industry's viewpoint) of all time.*
— Chris Welles

WEDNESDAY
14

*Wall Street's graveyards are filled with
men who were right too soon.*
— William Hamilton

THURSDAY
15

*Look for an impending crash in the
economy when the best seller lists are
filled with books on business strategies
and quick-fix management ideas.*
— Peter Drucker

FRIDAY
 # 16

*The stock market is that creation of
man which humbles him the most.*
— Anonymous

SATURDAY
17

SUNDAY
18

(continued from page 102)

10. The Art Of Short Selling, Kathryn F. Staley, John Wiley & Sons, $34.95. Packed with cutting-edge examples and up-to-the-minute guidelines. A timely and comprehensive reference that arms you with the necessary tools to make a prepared and confident entrance onto the short selling playing field.

11. McMillan On Options, Lawrence G. McMillan, John Wiley & Sons, $65.00. All the information you need to stay on top in the continually evolving marketplace of options. Packed with thorough coverage of pricing strategies, hedging techniques, options philosophy, volatility and risk control.

12. The (Almost) Perfect Investment System, Robert Harper, Halifax Publishing Co., $19.95. Shows how you can invest in no load, low expense index mutual funds and by following simple historic timing patterns achieve fantastic results. These limited timing strategies are virtually the ultimate in simplicity.

13. The Education Of A Speculator, Victor Niederhoffer, John Wiley & Sons, $29.95. In the world according to Victor Niederhoffer, life is speculation and we are all speculators, except when we lose—then we are gamblers. A trip from Brighton Beach to Wall Street with insights into his varied life.

14. The Great Wave: Price Revolutions And The Rhythm Of History, David Hackett Fischer, Oxford University Press, $30.00. The history of prices is a history of change. Price-inflation has been a continuing problem, but it has not been constant in its rhythm, rate, or timing. Prices tended to rise but most of the increases happened in four great waves of inflation—the price revolutions of the thirteenth, sixteenth, eighteenth, and twentieth centuries. Repeated long patterns of rising prices, followed by long periods of stability are evident.

15. Hit And Run Trading: The Short-Term Stock Traders' Bible, Jeff Cooper, M. Gordon Publishing Group, $100.00. Cooper's strategy features higher-priced trending stocks that have the ability to move quickly once a setup occurs. His main criteria for stock selection are trend and price, and the minor criteria are sponsorship and liquidity.

16. More Than L.I.P. Service: A Lifetime Investing Plan, Alvin H. Danenberg, PennWell Books, $49.95. Prepare for retirement with a value-driven asset allocation plan for wealth accumulation that uses monthly and annual monitoring techniques and no-load mutual funds as investment vehicles.

AMACOM
American Management Assoc.
1601 Broadway
New York NY 10019

Carol Publishing Group
120 Enterprise Avenue
Secaucus NJ 07094

M. Gordon Publishing Group
23805 Stuart Ranch Road
Suite 245
Malibu CA 90265

Halifax Publishing Co., Inc.
P O Box 2598-55
Chapel Hill NC 27515

Oxford University Press
198 Madison Avenue
New York NY 10016

PennWell Publishing Company
1421 South Sheridan
P O Box 1260
Tulsa OK 74101

Pitman Publishing
4720A Boston Way
Lanham MD 20706

Sourcebooks, Inc.
P O Box 372
Naperville IL 60566

John Wiley & Sons
605 Third Avenue
New York NY 10158

OCTOBER

MONDAY
19

*We pay the debts of the last generation
by issuing bonds payable by
the next generation.*
— Lawrence J. Peter

TUESDAY
20

*Fortune 500 companies have shrunk by
over one million workers while non-
manufacturing sectors dominated by small
entrepreneurial companies have added
more than 9 million workers in the 1980s.*
— John Rutledge

WEDNESDAY
21

*Small business has been the first rung
on the ladder upward for every minority
group in the nation's history.*
— S. I. Hayakawa, 1947

THURSDAY
22

*The inherent vice of capitalism is the
unequal sharing of blessings;
the inherent virtue of socialism
is the equal sharing of miseries.*
— Winston Churchill

FRIDAY
23

*It's not what you say.
It's what they hear.*
— A sign in an advertising office.

SATURDAY
24

SUNDAY
25

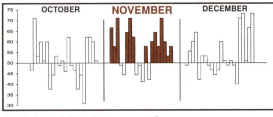

NOVEMBER ALMANAC

NOVEMBER							DECEMBER						
S	M	T	W	T	F	S	S	M	T	W	T	F	S
						1		1	2	3	4	5	6
2	3	4	5	6	7	8	7	8	9	10	11	12	13
9	10	11	12	13	14	15	14	15	16	17	18	19	20
16	17	18	19	20	21	22	21	22	23	24	25	26	27
23	24	25	26	27	28	29	28	29	30	31			
30													

See Market Probability Chart on page 125.

❑ Third best percentage gainer in 47 years based on S&P, up an average 1.6% per year ❑ Up 30 times, down 17 ❑ Flat on balance in recent years due to hefty losses in 1987, 1991, and 1994 but big Dow gains in 1995 and 1996, up 319.01 and 492.32 ❑ Day before and day after Thanksgiving combined 21 years without a loss until 1987 (page 114) ❑ Anticipators pushed up preceding Tuesday 7 years in a row until 1990 ❑ November, December, and January comprise Best 3 Months of the Year ❑ November begins the Best 6 Months of the Year (page 54).

NOVEMBER DAILY POINT CHANGES DOW JONES INDUSTRIALS

Previous Month Close	1987 1993.53	1988 2148.65	1989 2645.08	1990 2442.33	1991 3069.10	1992 3226.28	1993 3680.59	1994 3908.12	1995 4755.48	1996 6029.38
1	—	2.31	0.82	12.62	– 12.75	—	12.02	–44.75	11.20	– 7.45
2	20.56	5.87	–14.34	35.89	—	35.93	5.03	–26.24	41.91	—
3	–50.56	13.51	– 2.05	—	—	– 9.73	–35.77	8.75	16.98	—
4	–18.24	–24.54	—	—	– 10.73	–29.44	–36.89	–38.36	—	19.75
5	40.12	—	—	11.39	– 14.31	20.80	18.45	—	—	39.50
6	–26.36	—	–47.34	–17.08	7.15	– 3.78	—	—	–11.56	96.53
7	—	–21.16	14.96	–44.31	15.65	—	—	1.35	–16.98	28.33
8	—	2.85	26.23	2.97	– 8.49	—	4.47	21.87	55.64	13.78
9	–58.85	– 9.25	–19.67	44.8	—	0.81	– 7.83	1.01	11.56	—
10	–22.05	– 3.55	21.92	—	—	–15.40	23.48	– 9.76	6.14	—
11	21.05	–47.66	—	—	– 3.36	14.86	– 1.12	–20.52	—	35.78
12	61.01	—	—	51.74	11.85	– 0.54	22.08	—	—	10.44
13	– 25.2	—	0.82	– 4.95	11.19	– 6.76	—	—	2.53	8.20
14	—	– 1.95	–16.18	24.25	– 1.79	—	—	28.26	– 1.09	38.76
15	—	12.09	22.33	–14.60	–120.31	—	– 6.99	– 3.37	50.94	35.03
16	14.09	–38.59	3.08	5.20	—	–27.29	33.25	18.84	46.61	—
17	–26.85	13.87	17.00	—	—	–12.42	– 6.42	–17.15	20.59	—
18	16.91	9.96	—	—	29.52	14.05	–19.01	–12.79	—	– 1.12
19	–43.77	—	—	15.10	– 41.15	2.16	8.67	—	—	50.69
20	18.24	—	–20.62	–35.15	– 1.56	17.83	—	—	– 6.86	32.42
21	—	3.56	7.25	9.16	2.68	—	—	–45.75	40.46	–11.55
22	—	11.73	17.49	H	– 29.96	—	–23.76	–91.52	18.06	53.29
23	9.45	14.58	H	–12.13	—	– 4.32	3.92	– 3.36	H	—
24	40.45	H	18.77	—	—	25.66	13.41	H	7.23*	—
25	–16.58	–17.60	—	—	– 0.67	17.56	H	33.64	—	76.03
26	H	—	—	5.94	14.08	H	– 3.63	—	—	–19.38
27	–36.47	—	19.42	10.64	– 16.10	15.94	—	—	22.04	–29.07
28	—	6.76	7.04	– 8.66	H	—	—	31.29	7.22	H
29	—	20.09	–13.23	–16.34	– 5.36	—	– 6.15	– 1.01	27.46	22.36*
30	–76.93	12.98	17.49	40.84	—	22.96	6.15	0.68	–31.07	—
Close	1833.55	2114.51	2706.27	2559.65	2894.68	3305.16	3683.95	3739.23	5074.49	6521.70
Change	–159.98	–34.14	61.19	117.32	–174.42	78.88	3.36	–168.89	319.01	492.32

* Post-Thanksgiving shortened trading day.

OCTOBER/NOVEMBER

MONDAY

26

I believe in the exceptional man— the entrepreneur who is always out of money, not the bureaucrat who generates cash flow and pays dividends.
— Armand Erpf

TUESDAY

27

History is a collection of agreed upon lies.
— Voltaire

WEDNESDAY

28

When I have to depend upon hope in a trade, I get out of it.
— Jesse Livermore

THURSDAY

 # 29

Statements by high officials are practically always misleading when they are designed to bolster a falling market.
— Gerald M. Loeb

FRIDAY

 # 30

Companies which do well generally tend to report (their quarterly earnings) earlier than those which do poorly.
— Alan Abelson, *Barron's*

Halloween

SATURDAY

31

SUNDAY

1

PROSPERITY MORE THAN PEACE DETERMINES OUTCOME OF CONGRESSIONAL RACES

Though the stock market in Presidential election years is usually able to predict if the party in power will retain or lose the White House, the outcome of congressional races in mid-term years is another matter entirely. Typically, the President's party will invariably lose a number of House seats in these elections (1934 was a lone exception). It is considered a victory for the President when his party loses a small number of seats and a repudiation when a large percentage of seats are lost.

The table below would seem to indicate that there is no relationship between the stock market's behavior in the ten months prior to the election and the magnitude of Congressional seat losses. (Mid-term years are arranged by size of seat loss by the President's party.) During Eisenhower's term, the mid-term elections in 1954 and 1958 were both preceded by roaring bull markets; however, the Republicans lost few seats in one, and a huge number in the other. The Democrats gained seats in 1934 when the market was dull, but were clobbered while the market was rising sharply in 1938.

If the market does not offer a clue to the outcome of Congressional races, does anything? Yes! In the twenty mid-terms below, no war or recession began in the two years prior to the elections in 1934, 1962, 1986, 1926, and 1978 and Congressional victories resulted. In 1990, 1970, and 1954, moderate House losses followed mild recessions. The next group includes four Democrats who suffered sizable losses in their party's Congressional seats. What *they* all had in common was that a major war broke out between their reelections and the following mid-term elections. The seven worst repudiations of a President are at the bottom of the list. Their mid-term Congressional elections were preceded by severe economic setbacks, with the exception of Clinton's. **Obviously, prosperity is of greater importance than peace!** This premise will be put to the test in 1998.

LAST 20 MID-TERM ELECTIONS RANKED BY % LOSS OF SEATS BY PRESIDENT'S PARTY

	% Seats Gained/Lost	Year	President	Dow Jones Industrials New Year to Election Day	Election Day to Year End
1.	2.9%	1934	D: Roosevelt	— 3.8%	8.3%
2.	— 1.9	1962	D: Kennedy	—16.5	6.8
3.	— 2.3	1986	R: Reagan	22.5	0.1
4.	— 4.0	1926	R: Coolidge	— 3.9	4.4
5.	— 5.1	1978	D: Carter	— 3.7	0.6
6.	— 5.7	1990	R: Bush	— 9.1	5.3
7.	— 6.3	1970	R: Nixon	— 5.3	10.7
8.	— 8.1	1954	R: Eisenhower	26.0	14.2
9.	—11.0	1950	D: Truman (Korea)	11.2	— 5.8
10.	—12.0	1918	D: Wilson (World War I)	15.2	— 4.1
11.	—14.1	1982	R: Reagan	14.9	4.1
12.	—15.9	1966	D: Johnson (Vietnam)	—17.2	— 2.1
13.	—18.7	1942	D: Roosevelt (World War II)	3.4	4.1
14.	—19.9	1930	R: Hoover	—25.4	—11.2
15.	—21.1	1938	D: Roosevelt	28.2	— 0.1
16.	—22.3	1946	D: Truman	— 9.6	1.6
17.	—23.0	1994	D: Clinton	1.5	0.7
18.	—23.5	1958	R: Eisenhower	25.1	7.1
19.	—24.4	1974	R: Ford	—22.8	— 6.2
20.	—25.2	1922	R: Harding	21.4	0.3

NOVEMBER

MONDAY

2

*No profession requires more hard
work, intelligence, patience, and mental
discipline than successful speculation.*
— Robert Rhea

Election Day

TUESDAY

3

*Live beyond your means; then you're
forced to work hard, you have to succeed.*
— Edward G. Robinson

WEDNESDAY

4

*I have a simple philosophy.
Fill what's empty. Empty what's full.
And scratch where it itches.*
— Alice Roosevelt Longworth

THURSDAY

5

Lack of money is the root of all evil.
— George Bernard Shaw

FRIDAY

6

*A statistician is someone who can draw
a straight line from an unwarranted
assumption to a foregone conclusion.*
— Anonymous

SATURDAY
7

SUNDAY
8

"JANUARY EFFECT" FAVORS SMALL STOCKS

My research on the January Effect since 1953 using the S&P Low-Priced stock index as a proxy for small stocks vs. the blue-chip S&P 500 is shown in the table.

Simply stated, the January Effect is the tendency for small stocks to outperform large stocks in January. Hundreds have studied this effect. Two professors, Robert A. Haugen and Josef Lakonichok, analyzed all the research and wrote *The Incredible January Effect* (Irwin Professional Publishing).

Some of their conclusions:

• Average returns to the stocks of small companies in January are typically larger than those of the biggest companies.

• In January buying the Value Line index futures contract while selling the S&P 500 contract is a profitable hedge strategy.

• Low-grade bonds beat higher-grade bonds and non-dividend paying stocks outperform the dividend payers in January.

• The January Effect has been in operation since the introduction of the income tax and it's even more prevalent in foreign countries.

Low-priced stocks had double-digit gains and a better "batting average" than the S&P 500 in 1961, 1968, 1971, 1972, 1974, 1975, 1976, 1979, 1991 and 1992. These were Januarys following bear markets or when the stock market was clobbered late in the year.

Though the low-priced stock index outperformed the S&P 500 in 40 out of the past 45 Januarys by 5.4 percentage points on average, note that the margin between the two has been smaller in recent years until 1991 and 1992.

January losses for low-priced stocks resulted in 1969, 1973, 1978, 1982, and 1990 when bear markets began or were in progress, at least for the smaller capitalization issues.

Surprisingly quick military victories in Kuwait in mid-January 1991 and a one-point discount rate reduction prior to January 1992 led to the best two consecutive January Effects since 1975 and 1976.

The January Effect failed to materialize two years in a row in 1996 and 1997 as blue chips outperformed small caps. This was the only back-to-back occurrence in 45 years..

Prospects for January 1998 will be excellent if small stocks are in the doldrums during 1997's fourth quarter, or if there has been a sizeable correction.

JANUARY % CHANGES
(Based on Monthly Averages)

	Daily S&P 500 Index	Weekly Low–Priced Index	Difference
1953	0.5%	4.6%	4.1
1954	2.5	7.6	5.1
1955	1.8	7.8	6.0
1956	— 2.7	0.9	3.6
1957	— 2.2	4.0	6.2
1958	2.0	8.7	6.7
1959	4.0	6.9	2.9
1960	— 1.7	3.1	4.8
1961	5.1	10.0	4.9
1962	— 3.7	2.2	5.9
1963	3.9	4.8	0.9
1964	3.1	5.7	2.6
1965	2.6	6.1	3.5
1966	1.7	3.2	1.5
1967	3.8	7.1	3.3
1968	— 0.3	15.1	15.4
1969	— 4.2	— 4.7	— 0.5
1970	— 8.7	3.7	12.4
1971	3.3	14.4	11.1
1972	4.2	13.1	8.9
1973	0.8	— 3.6	— 4.4
1974	1.4	14.7	13.3
1975	8.2	28.5	20.3
1976	9.2	16.8	7.6
1977	— 0.9	6.3	7.2
1978	— 3.8	— 1.4	2.4
1979	3.7	11.9	8.2
1980	3.5	7.3	3.8
1981	— 0.4	2.9	3.3
1982	— 5.3	— 0.3	5.0
1983	3.5	6.1	2.6
1984	1.2	4.7	3.5
1985	4.3	9.0	4.7
1986	0.4	1.9	1.5
1987	6.4	8.4	2.0
1988	4.0	7.1	3.1
1989	3.2	7.4	4.2
1990	— 2.5	— 3.8	— 1.3
1991	4.2*	21.0*	16.8
1992	— 2.0	14.3	16.3
1993	0.7	8.5	7.8
1994	3.2	3.8	0.6
1995	2.4	6.3	3.9
1996	3.3	2.2	— 1.1
1997	6.1	2.8	— 3.3
45 year Average	**1.6%**	**6.8%**	**5.4**

*Month–end prices now available

NOVEMBER

MONDAY
9

*In investing, the return you want
should depend on whether you
want to eat well or sleep well.*
— J. Kenfield Morley

TUESDAY
10

*Those who are of the opinion that money
will do everything may very well be
suspected to do everything for money.*
— Sir George Savile

Veteran's Day

WEDNESDAY
11

*All you need is to look over the earnings
forecasts publicly made a year ago to
see how much care you need to give
those being made now for next year.*
— Gerald M. Loeb

THURSDAY
12

*The miracle, or the power, that elevates the few is
to be found in their perseverance under the
promptings of a brave, determined spirit.*
—Mark Twain

FRIDAY
13

*When a company reports higher earnings
for its first quarter (over its previous
year's first quarter), chances are almost
five to one it will also have increased
earnings in its second quarter.*
— Niederhoffer, Cross & Zeckhauser

SATURDAY
14

SUNDAY
15

LOOKING AHEAD TO THE YEAR 2000
WHY YOU SHOULD STILL STAY BULLISH

For the average investor nothing beats common stocks. And those who continually make big money always share two traits; a long term perspective and a bullish philosophy. Five years ago in the *1993 Stock Trader's Almanac* I wrote a similar article about the year 2000 and gave reasons why the 1990s could provide returns even better than the norm. This has proven to be so, as we are in the biggest bull market of all time which should continue for the next few years, despite an occasional 10% correction. Some reasons to stay bullish:

Collapse of communism. Vast new markets are opening among the East European countries (100 million people) and those of the former Soviet Union (300 million people). The end of the Cold War is also freeing resources previously devoted to the military. Capitalism is at work!

Booming capitalism. While China is still under communist control the government has embraced capitalism and the country's billion people are experiencing one of the highest growth rates in the world. Capitalism is also flexing its muscles for the two other billion people in India and Southeast Asia. And it's A-OK in the USA too!

Low inflation. We may not have licked inflation for good, but it appears to be well under control and may not raise its ugly head for a few more years.

Low interest rates. Compared to the 1980s interest rates have been rather low in recent years. This makes for a hospitable climate for businesses and consumers. And as the US deficit shrinks, rates are under less pressure from government borrowing.

Cheap energy. If you've driven up to a pump lately, its quite obvious that oil prices are very reasonable and will not likely cause massive inflation again.

Less cyclical economy. Due to modern inventory management and the shift to a service and information-based economy, recessions have been less frequent and less severe. Hence, market corrections have been the same. Further, with less recession risk, stocks logically should sell at higher multiples.

Merger mania. Some $600 billion of common stock disappeared in the 1980s due to mergers and buy-ins. In this decade, shares are vanishing before our eyes at an even higher rate in many sectors such as: banking, entertainment, technology telecommunications, health, securities, etc. Thinning supply in periods of great demand will move stock prices higher, to perhaps Dow 10000 in the year 2000.

Baby boomers come of (savings) age. Record investment inflows from boomers entering their fifties while total shares shrink equals even higher stock prices.

Leaner, meaner companies. We went through a painful industrial restructuring enabling US corporations to far better cope with foreign competition. This is doing wonders for the bottom line as profit margins greatly improve.

Information superhighway, telecommunications revolution. Dramatic events are taking place. The Internet (World Wide Web), cellular phones, computerization of the world, rapidly increasing longevity, software, telecommunications—you name it. Will the wonders never cease? And in all these fields American companies are the leaders.

There is always an air of excitement near the start of a new decade. Also thrilling is the anticipation of a new century. Combine these two with the approach of a new millennium, add a world at peace among major powers and add approximately one and a half billion exuberant new capitalists. What a glorious bullish feeling! Don't sell America short yet!

MONDAY
16

*I'm a great believer in luck, and I find the
harder I work the more I have of it.*
— Thomas Jefferson

TUESDAY
17

*The price of a stock varies inversely with
the thickness of its research file.*
— Martin Sosnoff

WEDNESDAY
18

*Money makes money. And the money that
money makes makes more money.*
— Benjamin Franklin

THURSDAY
19

*The fewer analysts who follow a situation,
the more pregnant its possibilities…if
Wall Street hates a stock, buy it.*
— Martin T. Sosnoff

FRIDAY
 # 20

*A bank is a place where they lend you an
umbrella in fair weather and ask for it
back again when it begins to rain.*
— Robert Frost

SATURDAY
21

SUNDAY
22

THANKSGIVING MARKET—NO TURKEY!
SURE WAY TO WIN THE TURKEY SHOOT

Easy! Be invested on the day before and after Thanksgiving. These two days combined gained about nine Dow points on average for 21 straight years without a loss until 1987's crash. In 45 years there were only six losses. Thanksgiving strength may be attributed to the "holiday spirit," but November has been a top performer since 1950. Notice in recent years Tuesdays were up thanks to anticipators and seven of the last twelve Fridays were down because of too many "game" players. I would go long prior to the Tuesday before Thanksgiving and exit sometime the following Monday.

WHAT DOW JONES INDUSTRIALS DID ON
THE DAY BEFORE AND AFTER THANKSGIVING

	2 Days Before	Day Before	Day After	Total Gain Dow Points	Dow Close	Next Monday
1952	— 0.18	1.54	1.22	2.76	283.66	0.04
1953	1.71	0.65	2.45	3.10	280.23	1.14
1954	3.27	1.89	3.16	5.05	387.79	0.72
1955	4.61	0.71	0.26	0.97	482.88	— 1.92
1956	— 4.49	— 2.16	4.65	2.49	472.56	— 2.27
1957	— 9.04	10.69	3.84	14.53	449.87	— 2.96
1958	— 4.37	8.63	8.31	16.94	557.46	2.61
1959	2.94	1.41	1.42	2.83	652.52	6.66
1960	— 3.44	1.37	4.00	5.37	606.47	— 1.04
1961	— 0.77	1.10	2.18	3.28	732.60	— 0.61
1962	6.73	4.31	7.62	11.93	644.87	— 2.81
1963	32.03	— 2.52	9.52	7.00	750.52	1.39
1964	— 1.68	— 5.21	— 0.28	— 5.49	882.12	— 6.69
1965	2.56	0.00	— 0.78	— 0.78	948.16	— 1.23
1966	— 3.18	1.84	6.52	8.36	803.34	— 2.18
1967	13.17	3.07	3.58	6.65	877.60	4.51
1968	8.14	— 3.17	8.76	5.59	985.08	— 1.74
1969	— 5.61	3.23	1.78	5.01	812.30	— 7.26
1970	5.21	1.98	6.64	8.62	781.35	12.74
1971	— 5.18	0.66	17.96	18.62	816.59	13.14
1972	8.21	7.29	4.67	11.96	1025.21	— 7.45
1973	—17.76	10.08	— 0.98	9.10	854.00	—29.05
1974	5.32	2.03	— 0.63	1.40	618.66	—15.64
1975	9.76	3.15	2.12	5.27	860.67	— 4.33
1976	— 6.57	1.66	5.66	7.32	956.62	— 6.57
1977	6.41	0.78	1.12	1.90	844.42	— 4.85
1978	— 1.56	2.95	3.12	6.07	810.12	3.72
1979	— 6.05	— 1.80	4.35	2.55	811.77	16.98
1980	3.93	7.00	3.66	10.66	993.34	—23.89
1981	18.45	7.90	7.80	15.70	885.94	3.04
1982	— 9.01	9.01	7.36	16.37	1007.36	— 4.51
1983	7.01	— 0.20	1.83	1.63	1277.44	— 7.62
1984	9.83	6.40	18.78	25.18	1220.30	— 7.95
1985	0.12	18.92	— 3.56	15.36	1472.13	—14.22
1986	6.05	4.64	— 2.53	2.11	1914.23	— 1.55
1987	40.45	—16.58	—36.47	—53.05	1910.48	—76.93
1988	11.73	14.58	—17.60	— 3.02	2074.68	6.76
1989	7.25	17.49	18.77	36.26	2675.55	19.42
1990	—35.15	9.16	—12.13	— 2.97	2527.23	5.94
1991	14.08	—16.10	— 5.36	—21.46	2894.68	40.70
1992	25.66	17.56	15.94	33.50	3282.20	22.96
1993	3.92	13.41	— 3.63	9.78	3683.95	— 6.15
1994	—91.52	— 3.36	33.64	30.28	3708.27	31.29
1995	40.46	18.06	7.23	25.29	5048.84	22.04
1996	—19.38	—29.07	22.36	— 6.71	6521.70	N/C

NOVEMBER

MONDAY

23

Contribute to SJ Pret Capital Campaign

If you destroy a free market you create a black market. If you have ten thousand regulations you destroy all respect for the law.
— Winston Churchill

TUESDAY

24

My son, my son, if you knew with what little wisdom the world is ruled.
— Oxenstierna (Thirty Years' War)

WEDNESDAY

 # 25

If buying equities seem the most hazardous and foolish thing you could possibly do, then you are near the bottom that will end the bear market.
— Joseph E. Granville

**Thanksgiving
(Market Closed)**

THURSDAY

26

If a man can see both sides of a problem, you know that none of his money is tied up in it.
— Verda Ross

FRIDAY

  # 27

Knowledge born from actual experience is the answer to why one profits; lack of it is the reason one loses.
— Gerald M. Loeb

SATURDAY

28

SUNDAY

29

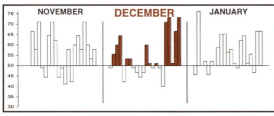

DECEMBER ALMANAC

DECEMBER								JANUARY						
S	M	T	W	T	F	S		S	M	T	W	T	F	S
	1	2	3	4	5	6							1	2	3
7	8	9	10	11	12	13		4	5	6	7	8	9	10
14	15	16	17	18	19	20		11	12	13	14	15	16	17
21	22	23	24	25	26	27		18	19	20	21	22	23	24
28	29	30	31					25	26	27	28	29	30	31

See Market Probability Chart on page 125.

❑ Inferior Decembers often precede bear market years or are hit by tax loss selling after bear markets have ended ❑ "Free lunch" served on Wall Street at mid-month (page 118) ❑ Low-priced stocks usually beat high quality in January ❑ RECORD: S&P up 35, down 12 times ❑ December is best month, with average 1.7% S&P gain and ranks third in Dow with total gain of 1055.07 points since 1950 ❑ For January Effect see page 110 ❑ SEC changing from 5-day to 3-day settlement date after trades may be affecting month-end seasonality.

DECEMBER DAILY POINT CHANGES DOW JONES INDUSTRIALS

Previous Month Close	1987 1833.55	1988 2114.51	1989 2706.27	1990 2559.65	1991 2894.68	1992 3305.16	1993 3683.95	1994 3739.23	1995 5074.49	1996 6521.70
1	8.79	−12.63	41.38	—	—	−10.80	13.13	−38.36	12.64	—
2	6.63	− 9.60	—	—	40.70	− 8.11	5.03	44.75	—	N/C
3	−72.44	—	—	5.94	− 5.82	− 9.72	1.96	—	—	− 79.01
4	− 9.79	—	5.98	14.11	−17.89	12.15	—	—	52.39	− 19.75
5	—	31.48	−11.95	30.70	−22.58	—	—	− 3.70	37.93	14.16
6	—	25.60	− 4.91	− 7.92	− 2.69	—	6.14	4.03	21.68	− 55.16
7	45.43	4.27	−15.99	−12.38	—	18.65	8.67	−10.43	− 39.74	—
8	56.20	−11.92	10.66	—	—	14.85	15.65	−49.79	− 2.53	—
9	34.15	1.78	—	—	−14.75	1.63	− 4.75	5.38	—	82.00
10	−47.08	—	—	6.68	− 7.83	−11.62	10.89	—	—	9.31
11	11.60	—	− 3.20	−10.64	1.56	− 8.11	—	—	27.46	− 70.73
12	—	− 3.91	23.89	36.14	29.75	—	—	27.26	− 9.40	− 98.81
13	—	3.91	8.96	− 7.92	19.23	—	23.76	− 3.03	41.55	1.16
14	65.82	− 9.24	− 7.46	−20.55	—	−11.88	−21.80	30.95	− 34.32	—
15	8.62	− 1.25	−14.08	—	—	− 7.84	−25.71	19.18	− 5.42	—
16	32.99	17.71	—	—	4.69	−29.18	9.22	41.72	—	− 36.52
17	−50.07	—	—	− 0.49	−16.77	14.05	25.43	—	—	39.98
18	50.90	—	−42.02	33.41	5.81	44.04	—	—	−101.52	38.44
19	—	21.97	− 1.92	N/C	6.27	—	—	−16.49	34.68	126.87
20	—	− 6.61	− 7.68	2.73	20.12	—	3.64	−23.55	− 50.57	10.76
21	15.08	− 1.43	3.20	4.20	—	− 0.81	−10.06	34.65	37.21	—
22	−11.93	− 4.28	20.26	—	—	8.64	17.04	13.12	1.44	—
23	27.19	8.57	—	—	88.10	− 7.56	− 4.47	18.51	—	4.62
24	− 5.97	—	—	−12.37	28.40	12.70	—	—	—	33.83*
25	H	H	H	H	H	H	H	H	H	H
26	—	—	− 2.13	15.84	31.98	—	—	—	12.29	23.83
27	—	− 6.25	15.14	−11.63	18.56	—	35.21	28.26	− 4.34	14.23
28	−56.70	3.75	7.90	3.71	—	7.02	0.84	−22.20	− 10.12	—
29	−16.08	16.25	20.90	—	—	−22.42	0.56	− 6.06	21.32	—
30	23.21	−14.11	—	—	62.39	10.26	−18.45	1.01	—	− 11.54
31	−11.27	—	—	4.45	4.92	−19.99	−21.79	—	—	−101.10
Close	1938.83	2168.57	2753.20	2633.66	3168.83	3301.11	3754.09	3834.44	5117.12	6448.27
Change	105.28	54.06	46.93	74.01	274.15	−4.05	70.14	95.21	42.63	−73.43

* Pre-Christmas Shortened Trading Day

NOVEMBER/DECEMBER

MONDAY
 30

*Those companies that the market
expects will have the best futures, as
measured by the price/earnings ratios
they are accorded, have consistently
done worst subsequently.*
— David Dreman

TUESDAY
 1

*Small volume is usually accompanied
by a fall in price; large volume
by a rise in price.*
— Charles C. Ying (Computer Study)

WEDNESDAY
 2

*I do not rule Russia;
ten thousand clerks do.*
— Nicholas I (1795-1855)

THURSDAY
 3

*Under capitalism man exploits man:
under socialism the reverse is true.*
— Polish proverb

FRIDAY
 4

*A gold mine is a hole in the
ground with a liar on top.*
— Mark Twain

SATURDAY
5

SUNDAY
6

MID-DECEMBER NEW LOWS
THE ONLY FREE LUNCH ON WALL STREET

Several shrewd observers note that many depressed issues sell at "bargain" levels near the close of each year as investors rid their portfolios of these "losers" for tax purposes. Stocks hitting new lows for the year around December 15 tend to out-perform the market handsomely by February 15 in the following year.

BARGAIN STOCKS VS. THE MARKET

60-Day Period Dec 15 - Feb 15	New Lows Around Dec 15	% Change Around Feb 15	% Change NYSE Composite	Bargain Stocks Advantage
1966-67	45	18.0%	8.9%	9.1%
1967-68	45	7.4	— 4.7	12.1
1968-69	24	5.0	— 3.4	8.4
1974-75	112	48.9	22.1	26.8
1975-76	21	34.9	14.9	20.0
1976-77	2	1.3	— 3.3	4.6
1977-78	15	2.8	— 4.5	7.3
1978-79	43	11.8	3.9	7.9
1979-80	5	9.3	6.1	3.2
1980-81	14	7.1	— 2.0	9.1
1981-82	21	— 2.6	— 7.4	4.8
1982-83	4	33.0	9.7	23.3
1983-84	13	— 3.2	— 3.8	0.6
1984-85	32	19.0	12.1	6.9
1985-86	4	—22.5	3.9	—26.4
1986-87	22	9.3	12.5	— 3.2
1987-88	23	13.2	6.8	6.4
1988-89	14	30.0	6.4	23.6
1989-90	25	— 3.1	— 4.8	1.7
1990-91	18	18.8	12.6	6.2
1991-92	23	51.1	7.7	43.4
1992-93	9	8.7	0.6	8.1
1993-94	10	— 1.4	2.0	— 3.4
1994-95	25	14.6	5.7	8.9
1995-96	5	—11.3	5.5	—16.8
1996-97	16	8.4	9.7	1.3
26-Year Totals		**308.5%**	**117.2%**	**191.3%**
Average		**11.9%**	**4.5%**	**7.4%**

Remember this is a trading—not an investing—strategy. Select stocks that are making mid-December new lows by first eliminating preferred stocks and those at new lows because of splits. Then buy stocks that are down the most.

Understandably, lower quality stocks tend to bounce back even higher than their blue-chip brethren. Santa Claus seems to reward pre-Christmas "scavengers" on Wall Street. The biggest bull market of all time has favored the big blue chip Dow type stocks, leaving smalle, depressed issues behind.

Examination of December trades by NYSE members through the years shows they tend to buy on balance during this month contrary to other months. Perhaps they knew about the January Effect all these years (see page 110).

DECEMBER

MONDAY
7

"I never buy at the bottom and
I always sell too soon."
— Baron Rothchild's success formula

TUESDAY
8

I prefer to be a gold bug rather
than a paper worm.
— Nicholas Deak

WEDNESDAY
9

Next to being shot at and missed,
nothing is really quite as satisfying
as an income tax refund.
— F.J. Raymond

THURSDAY
10

Selling a soybean contract short is
worth two years at the
Harvard Business School.
— Robert Stovall

FRIDAY
11

History shows that once the United States
fully recognizes an economic problem
and thereby places all its
efforts on solving it, the problem is
about to be solved by natural forces.
— James L. Fraser

SATURDAY
12

SUNDAY
13

THE SANTA CLAUS RALLY

Santa Claus comes to Wall Street nearly every year and brings a short, sweet, respectable rally. In the past 45 years, he failed to appear only in 1955, 1966, 1968, 1977, 1979, 1981, 1984, 1990, 1992 and 1993. The rally occurs within the last five days of the year (four prior to 1968) and the first two in January and is good for an average 1.5% gain.

DAILY % CHANGE IN S&P COMPOSITE INDEX AT YEAR END

	Trading Days Before Year-End						First Days in Jan			Rally % Change
	6	5	4	3	2	1	1	2	3	
1952	—0.4	0.1	0.2	0.6	0.7	—0.1	—0.1	0.5	—0.7	1.7%
1953	—0.3	0.4	—0.4	—0.6	0.9	0.2	0.6	0.6	0.2	1.2
1954	0.1	—0.8	1.0	0.9	0.0	0.7	2.1	—0.9	—2.5	3.8
1955	0.2	0.2	—0.6	—0.4	0.2	0.7	—0.7	—0.4	—0.1	—1.1
1956	—0.8	0.7	0.0	—0.1	0.5	0.2	—1.0	0.9	0.1	0.5
1957	0.0	0.1	1.0	—0.4	—0.5	1.0	0.9	1.3	—0.5	3.4
1958	—0.7	—0.5	1.3	1.2	0.3	0.5	0.4	0.4	—0.1	4.2
1959	—0.3	0.1	0.0	0.5	0.8	0.2	0.0	0.8	—0.4	2.4
1960	—0.3	0.1	0.1	0.5	0.5	0.1	—0.9	1.4	0.4	1.6
1961	—0.4	0.1	0.2	0.9	0.1	—0.2	—0.8	0.2	—0.7	0.3
1962	—0.3	0.0	0.6	—0.1	0.05	0.2	—0.6	1.6	0.6	1.7
1963	—0.6	0.2	0.5	0.2	0.2	0.6	0.5	0.1	0.2	2.1
1964	—0.2	0.0	—0.1	—0.3	0.6	0.5	—0.6	0.5	0.3	0.6
1965	—0.1	—0.7	0.0	0.3	0.4	0.2	—0.3	0.1	0.6	0.8
1966	0.4	—0.3	—0.6	—0.5	—0.3	0.0	0.1	0.2	1.3	—1.1
1967	0.2	—0.2	0.1	0.7	0.0	0.6	—0.4	—0.5	—0.3	0.5
1968	—1.1	—0.2	0.1	—0.4	—0.9	0.1	0.1	0.1	—1.5	—1.0
1969	—0.4	1.1	0.8	—0.7	0.4	0.5	1.0	0.5	—0.7	3.6**
1970	0.1	0.6	0.5	1.1	0.2	—0.1	—1.1	0.7	0.6	1.9
1971	—0.4	0.2	1.0	0.3	0.4	0.3	—0.4	0.4	1.0	1.3
1972	—0.3	—0.7	0.6	0.4	0.5	1.0	0.9	0.4	—0.1	3.1
1973	—1.1	—0.7	3.1	2.1	—0.2	0.0	0.1	2.2	—0.9	6.7
1974	—1.4	1.4	0.8	—0.4	0.03	2.1	2.4	0.7	0.5	7.2
1975	0.7	0.8	0.9	—0.1	—0.4	0.5	0.8	1.8	1.0	4.3
1976	0.1	1.2	0.7	—0.4	0.5	0.5	—0.4	—1.2	—0.9	0.8
1977	0.8	0.9	0.0	0.1	0.2	0.2	—1.3	—0.3	—0.8	—0.3
1978	0.0	1.7	1.3	—0.9	—0.4	—0.2	0.6	1.1	0.8	3.3
1979	—0.6	0.1	0.1	0.2	—0.1	0.1	—2.0	—0.5	1.2	—2.2
1980	—0.4	0.4	0.5	—1.1	0.2	0.3	0.4	1.2	0.1	2.0
1981	—0.5	0.2	—0.2	—0.5	0.5	0.2	0.2	—2.2	—0.7	—1.8
1982	0.6	1.8	—1.0	0.3	—0.7	0.2	—1.6	2.2	0.4	1.2
1983	—0.2	0.0	0.9	0.3	0.2	0.0	—0.5	1.7	1.2	2.1
1984	—0.5	0.8	—0.2	—0.4	0.3	0.6	—1.1	—0.5	—0.5	—0.6
1985	—1.1	—0.7	0.2	0.9	0.5	0.3	—0.8	0.6	—0.1	1.1
1986	—1.0	0.2	0.1	—0.9	—0.5	—0.5	1.8	2.3	0.2	2.4
1987	1.3	—0.5	—2.6	—0.4	1.3	—0.3	3.6	1.1	0.1	2.2
1988	—0.2	0.3	—0.4	0.1	0.8	—0.6	—0.9	1.5	0.2	0.9
1989	0.6	0.8	—0.2	0.6	0.5	0.8	1.8	—0.3	—0.9	4.1
1990	0.5	—0.6	0.3	—0.8	0.1	0.5	—1.1	—1.4	—0.3	—3.0
1991	2.5	0.6	1.4	0.4	2.1	0.5	0.04	0.5	—0.3	5.7
1992	—0.3	0.2	—0.1	—0.3	0.2	—0.7	—0.1	—0.2	0.0	—1.1
1993	0.0	0.7	0.1	—0.1	—0.4	—0.5	—0.2	0.3	0.1	—0.1
1994	0.0	0.2	0.4	—0.3	0.1	—0.4	0.0	0.3	—0.1	0.2
1995	0.8	0.2	0.4	0.04	—0.1	0.3	0.8	0.1	—0.6	1.8
1996	—0.3	0.5	0.6	0.1	—0.4	—1.7	—0.5	1.5	—0.1	0.1
Avg	—0.11	0.39*	0.30	0.05	0.18	0.21	0.03	0.48	—0.05	1.5%

*From 1968 to date; **Seven days

Average 7-Day Gain 1.5%

28 years had substantial gains of 0.9% to 7.1% during this holiday period. Of the other 17 years, ten had losses and eight had substandard gains of less than 0.7%. The bear markets of 1957, 1962, 1966, 1969, and 1977 were not preceded by Santa Claus rallies. Seven other lackluster periods preceded years when stocks could have been purchased at much lower prices later in the year (1956, 1965, 1968, 1978, 1980, 1982 and 1994). Getting back into the seasonal spirit: **If Santa Claus should fail to call Bears may come to Broad & Wall**

DECEMBER

MONDAY
14

*A committee is a group of the
unprepared, appointed by the
unwilling, to do the unnecessary.*
— Fred Allen

TUESDAY
15

*Foreign Aid: taxing poor people
in rich countries for the benefit of
rich people in poor countries.*
— Bernard Rosenberg

WEDNESDAY
16

*If the aircraft industry had progressed as
rapidly as the semiconductor or computer
business in recent years, the Concorde
would now hold 10,000 passengers, travel
at 60,000 miles an hour and a ticket
would cost 1 cent.*
— New York Times

THURSDAY
17

*Don't try to buy at the bottom and sell
at the top. This can't be done,
except by liars.*
— Bernard Baruch

FRIDAY

18

*A fall in price is followed on the
average by a further fall in price; a rise
in price by a further rise in price.*
— Charles C. Ying (Computer Study)

SATURDAY
19

SUNDAY
20

DECEMBER

MONDAY
21

*The best minds are not in government. If
any were, business would hire them away.*
— Ronald Reagan

TUESDAY
22

*$1,000 left to earn interest at 8% a year
will grow to $43 quadrillion in 400 years,
but the first hundred years are the hardest.*
— Sidney Homer, Salomon Brothers

WEDNESDAY
23

Murphy & Murphy   4Hrs
Set Up $C Law

*I always worry when bargains get hard
to find because historically that has
meant the market is fully valued
and will soon drop.*
— W.J. Maeck

THURSDAY
24

*Luck is the preparation for, recognition
of, and proper seizure of opportunity.*
— Walter Heiby

FRIDAY
25

Christmas Day
(Market Closed)

The stock doesn't know you own it.
— George "Adam Smith" Goodman, *Money Game*

SATURDAY
26

SUNDAY
27

DECEMBER/JANUARY

MONDAY
 28

Nothing is as easy as it looks. Everything takes longer than you think. If anything can go wrong, it will.
— Murphy's Law

TUESDAY
 29

The punishment of wise men who refuse to take part in the affairs of government is to live under the government of unwise men.
— Plato

LOSCALZO SEMINAR
Best of A&A Forum

WEDNESDAY
 30

It is a socialist idea that making profits is a vice; I consider the real vice is making losses.
— Winston Churchill

THURSDAY
 31

The men who can manage men manage the men who manage only things, and the men who can manage money manage all.
— Will Durant

**New Year's Day
(Market Closed)**

FRIDAY
1

We make progress at night, while the politicians sleep.
— Brazilian peasant proverb

SATURDAY
2

SUNDAY
3

MARKET PROBABILITY CALENDAR 1998

The chance of the market rising on any trading day of the year*

(Based on the number of times the S&P 500 rose on a particular trading day during May 1952–April 1997)

Date	Jan	Feb	Mar	Apr	May	Jun	Jul	Aug	Sep	Oct	Nov	Dec
1	H	S	S	60.9	51.1	57.8	68.9	S	64.4	46.7	S	48.9
2	45.7	55.6	62.2	55.6	S	60.0	64.4	S	60.0	71.1	66.7	55.6
3	S	62.2	68.9	57.8	S	57.8	H	51.1	62.2	S	57.8	60.0
4	S	48.9	60.0	S	75.6	55.6	S	40.0	44.4	S	71.1	64.4
5	76.1	51.1	46.7	S	64.4	48.9	S	48.9	S	53.3	48.9	S
6	50.0	53.3	46.7	55.6	46.7	S	51.1	51.1	S	60.0	44.4	S
7	52.2	S	S	57.8	44.4	S	60.0	60.0	H	51.1	S	42.2
8	45.7	S	S	64.4	51.1	40.0	66.7	S	46.7	60.0	S	53.3
9	52.2	40.0	57.8	64.4	S	37.8	55.6	S	48.9	37.8	64.4	53.3
10	S	40.0	62.2	53.3	S	62.2	51.1	44.4	55.6	S	71.1	48.9
11	S	62.2	51.1	S	53.3	66.7	S	55.6	64.4	S	62.2	46.7
12	50.0	48.9	62.2	S	48.9	53.3	S	44.4	S	44.4	44.4	S
13	58.7	44.4	51.1	55.6	46.7	S	40.0	48.9	S	53.3	48.9	S
14	65.2	S	S	66.7	53.3	S	71.1	66.7	46.7	48.9	S	44.4
15	65.2	S	S	62.2	53.3	48.9	60.0	S	55.6	51.1	S	46.7
16	56.5	H	62.2	50.0	S	44.4	46.2	S	51.1	46.2	41.2	60.0
17	S	44.4	64.4	55.6	S	40.0	55.6	68.9	53.3	S	57.8	51.1
18	S	37.8	46.7	S	46.7	42.2	S	40.0	37.8	S	42.2	48.9
19	57.8	51.1	42.2	S	46.7	53.3	S	44.4	S	62.2	60.0	S
20	51.1	51.1	44.4	40.0	60.0	S	28.9	60.0	S	48.9	64.4	S
21	48.9	S	S	48.9	42.2	S	48.9	48.9	53.3	46.7	S	51.1
22	62.2	S	S	48.9	53.3	57.8	42.2	S	55.6	37.8	S	48.9
23	64.4	42.2	48.9	46.7	S	46.7	48.9	S	44.4	44.4	57.8	40.0
24	S	42.2	40.0	51.1	S	35.6	48.9	48.9	53.3	S	71.1	71.1
25	S	62.2	55.6	S	H	48.9	S	44.4	53.3	S	60.0	H
26	51.1	48.9	57.8	S	46.7	51.1	S	44.4	S	31.1	H	S
27	55.6	62.2	H	57.8	44.4	S	57.8	57.8	S	62.2	53.3	S
28	46.7	S	S	55.6	53.3	S	60.0	55.6	57.8	62.2	S	73.3
29	66.7		S	44.4	62.2	62.2	53.3	S	44.4	60.0	S	51.1
30	66.7		35.6	63.0	S	55.6	68.9	S	48.9	51.1	57.8	66.7
31	S		40.0		S		68.9	68.9		S		73.3

*See page 132 regarding Monday's new strength

MARKET PROBABILITY CHART

The chances of the market rising on any trading day of the year

(Based on the number of times the S&P 500 rose on a particular trading day during May 1952–April 1997)

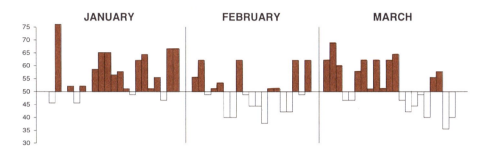

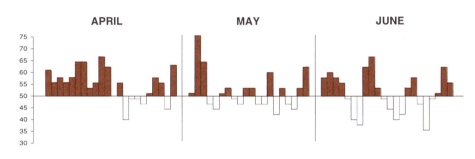

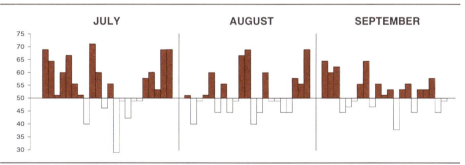

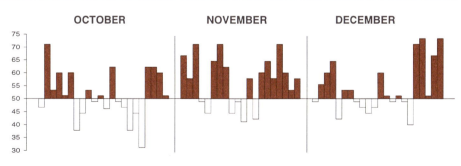

Shows the number of trading days in each month (Saturdays, Sundays, and holidays excluded) for 1998
Graphic representation of page 124

	MONDAY	TUESDAY	WEDNESDAY	THURSDAY	FRIDAY	SATURDAY	SUNDAY
JANUARY	28	29	30	31	1 JANUARY New Year's Day	2	3
	4	5	6	7	8	9	10
	11	12	13	14	(15)	16	17
	18 Martin Luther King Day	19	20	21	22	23	24
	25	26	27	28	29	30	31
FEBRUARY	1 FEBRUARY	2	3	4	5	6	7
	8	9	10	11	12	13	14 ♥
	15 Presidents' Day	16	17 Ash Wednesday	18	(19)	20	21
	22	23	24	25	26	27	28
MARCH	1 MARCH	2	3	4	5	6	7
	8	9	10	11	12	13	14
	15	16	17 ♣	18	(19)	20	21
	22	23	24	25	26	27	28
	29	30	31	1 APRIL Passover	2 Good Friday	3	4 Easter
APRIL	5	6	7	8	9	10	11
	12	13	14	15	(16)	17	18
	19	20	21	22	23	24	25
	26	27	28	29	30	1 MAY	2
MAY	3	4	5	6	7	8	9 Mother's Day
	10	11	12	13	14	15	16
	17	18	19	20	(21)	22	23
	24	25	26	27	28	29	30
	31 Memorial Day	1 JUNE	2	3	4	5	6
JUNE	7	8	9	10	11	12	13
	14	15	16	17	(18)	19	20 Father's Day
	21	22	23	24	25	26	27

1999 STRATEGY CALENDAR
(Option expiration dates encircled)

MONDAY	TUESDAY	WEDNESDAY	THURSDAY	FRIDAY	SATURDAY	SUNDAY	
28	29	30	1 JULY	2	3	4 *Independence Day*	JULY
5	6	7	8	9	10	11	
12	13	14	15	(16)	17	18	
19	20	21	22	23	24	25	
26	27	28	29	30	31	1 AUGUST	
2	3	4	5	6	7	8	AUGUST
9	10	11	12	13	14	15	
16	17	18	19	(20)	21	22	
23	24	25	26	27	28	29	
30	31	1 SEPTEMBER	2	3	4	5	SEPTEMBER
6 *Labor Day*	7	8	9	10	11 *Rosh Hashanah*	12	
13	14	15	16	(17)	18	19	
20 *Yom Kippur*	21	22	23	24	25	26	
27	28	29	30	1 OCTOBER	2	3	OCTOBER
4	5	6	7	8	9	10	
11 *Columbus Day*	12	13	14	(15)	16	17	
18	19	20	21	22	23	24	
25	26	27	28	29	30	31 *Boo!*	
1 NOVEMBER	2 *Election Day*	3	4	5	6	7	NOVEMBER
8	9	10	11 *Veteran's Day*	12	13	14	
15	16	17	18	(19)	20	21	
22	23	24	25 *Thanksgiving*	26	27	28	
29	30	1 DECEMBER	2	3	4 *Chanukah*	5	DECEMBER
6	7	8	9	10	11	12	
13	14	15	16	(17)	18	19	
20	21	22	23	24	25 *Christmas*	26	
27	28	29	30	31			

WINTER PORTFOLIO REVIEW

NO. OF SHARES	SECURITY	A ORIGINAL COST	B CURRENT VALUE	C GAIN (B – A) OR LOSS (A – B)	D % CHANGE (C ÷ A)	E MONTHS HELD	F CHANGE PER MO. (D ÷ E)	G ANNUAL RETURN (F × 12)
200	Sample Corp.	$10,000	$10,400	$400	4.0%	8	0.5%	6.0%
	TOTALS							

Stocks which have achieved their potential
1
2
3

Candidates for addition to portfolio
1
2
3

Stocks which have been disappointments
1
2
3

Investment decisions
1
2
3

DIRECTORY OF SEASONAL TRADING PATTERNS

CONTENTS

A TYPICAL DAY IN THE MARKET

Market movements on a half-hourly basis are shown here since January 1987. Compared to the typical day during 1963 to 1985, the major difference now is stronger openings and closings in a more bullish market dominated by professionals. Morning and afternoon weakness appears one hour earlier.

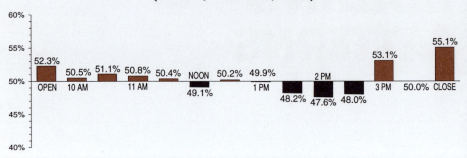

MARKET PERFORMANCE EACH HALF-HOUR OF THE DAY
(January 1987–May 1997)

Based on the number of times the Dow Jones industrial average increased over previous half-hour.

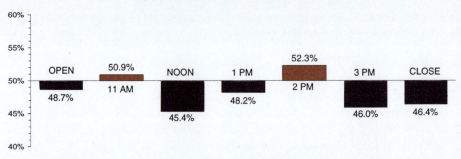

MARKET PERFORMANCE EACH HOUR OF THE DAY
(November 1963–May 1997)

Based on the number of times the Dow Jones industrial average increased over previous hour.

On the opposite page, half-hourly movements since January 1987 have been separated by day of the week. Visible proof of my discovery that Monday is the strongest comeback day of the week is evident. This is not surprising in as much as Monday used to be the most massacred trading day. In the last five years Mondays have been the strongest day of the week. (See page 56.) Other days tended to rise most often at the open. Tuesdays and Fridays after lunch were two of the weakest hours of the week.

THROUGH THE WEEK ON A HALF-HOURLY BASIS

From the chart showing the percentage of times the Dow Jones industrial average rose over the preceding half-hour (January 1987–May 1997*) the typical week unfolds.

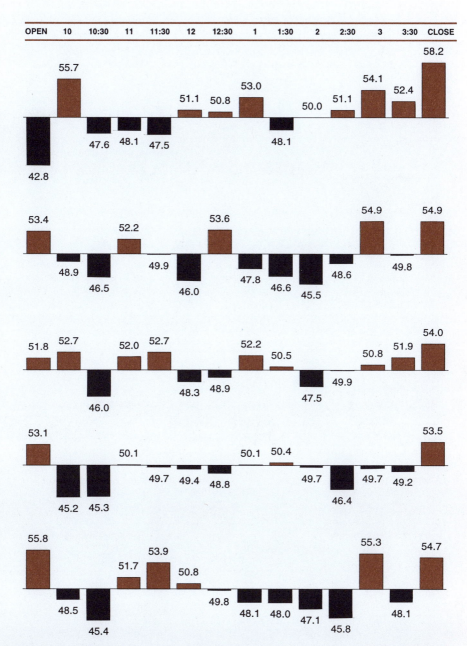

*Research indicates that where Tuesday is the first trading day of the week, it follows the Monday pattern. Therefore, all such Tuesdays were combined with the Mondays here. Thursdays that are the final trading day of a given week behave like Fridays, and were similarly grouped with Fridays.

131

MONDAY IS NOW WINNINGEST DAY OF WEEK

Between 1952 and 1989 Monday was the worst trading day of the week. The first trading day of the week (including Tuesday, when Monday is a holiday) rose only 44.9% of the time, while the other trading days of the week closed higher 54.2% of the time.

MARKET PERFORMANCE EACH DAY OF THE WEEK
(June 1952–December 1989)

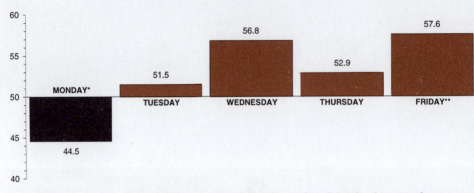

A dramatic reversal occurred starting in 1990. Since then Monday became the most powerful day of the week. Wednesday slipped to second place but Friday slipped to third place.

To see how the Dow Jones industrial average performed on different days of the week each year in points gained or lost, see page 56.

MARKET PERFORMANCE EACH DAY OF THE WEEK
(January 1990–December 1996)

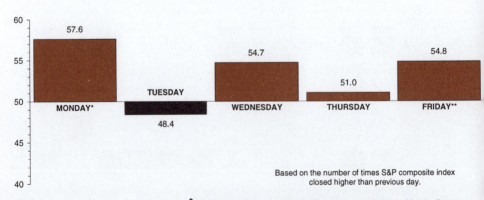

Based on the number of times S&P composite index closed higher than previous day.

*On Monday holidays, the following Tuesday is included in the Monday figure.
**On Friday holidays, the preceding Thursday is included in the Friday figure.

DAILY PERFORMANCE EACH YEAR SINCE 1952

To determine if market trend alters performance of different days of the week, I separated the fourteen bear years of 1953, '57, '60, '62, '66, '69, '70, '73, '74, '77, '81, '84, '90 and '94 from the 31 bull market years. While middle days—Tuesday, Wednesday and Thursday—did not vary much on average between bull and bear years, Mondays and Fridays were sharply affected. There was a swing of 11.5 percentage points in Monday's performance and 10.3 percentage points in Friday's. Mondays have been stronger in recent years.

PERCENTAGE OF TIMES MARKET
CLOSED HIGHER THAN PREVIOUS DAY

	Monday	Tuesday	Wednesday	Thursday	Friday
1952	48.4%	55.6%	58.1%	51.9%	66.7%
1953	34.6	52.1	54.9	59.6	54.7
1954	50.0	57.4	63.5	59.2	73.1
1955	50.0	45.7	63.5	60.0	78.8
1956	37.7	39.6	45.8	50.0	59.6
1957	26.9	54.0	66.7	48.9	44.2
1958	59.6	52.0	58.8	68.1	73.1
1959	40.4	53.1	55.8	48.9	69.8
1960	34.6	50.0	44.2	54.0	59.6
1961	53.8	52.2	64.0	56.0	63.5
1962	28.3	52.1	54.0	53.1	48.1
1963	46.2	63.3	51.0	57.4	69.2
1964	40.4	48.0	61.5	58.7	77.4
1965	46.2	57.4	55.8	51.0	71.2
1966	36.5	47.8	53.8	42.0	57.7
1967	38.5	50.0	60.8	64.0	69.2
1968*	49.1	55.3	63.0	40.4	55.8
1969	32.7	45.8	50.0	67.4	50.0
1970	40.4	44.0	65.4	46.8	52.8
1971	44.2	62.5	55.8	57.1	50.0
1972	38.5	60.9	57.7	51.0	67.3
1973	32.1	51.1	52.9	44.9	44.2
1974	32.7	57.1	51.0	36.7	30.8
1975	53.8	38.8	61.5	56.3	55.8
1976	55.8	55.3	55.8	40.8	58.5
1977	40.4	40.4	46.2	53.1	53.8
1978	51.9	43.5	59.6	54.0	48.1
1979	54.7	53.2	58.8	66.0	44.2
1980	55.8	56.3	69.8	35.4	55.8
1981	44.2	38.8	55.8	53.2	47.2
1982	46.2	39.6	44.2	44.9	50.0
1983	55.8	46.8	61.5	50.0	55.8
1984	39.6	63.8	31.4	46.0	44.2
1985	44.2	61.2	54.9	56.3	53.8
1986	51.9	44.9	67.3	58.3	55.8
1987	51.9	57.1	63.5	61.7	49.1
1988	51.9	61.7	51.9	48.0	59.6
1989	51.9	47.8	69.2	58.0	69.2
1990	67.9	53.2	52.9	40.0	51.9
1991	44.2	46.9	52.9	49.0	51.9
1992	51.9	49.0	53.8	56.3	45.3
1993	65.4	41.7	55.8	44.9	48.1
1994	55.8	46.8	52.9	48.0	59.6
1995	63.5	56.5	63.5	62.0	63.5
1996	54.7	44.9	51.0	57.1	63.5
1997**	70.6	75.0	41.2	37.5	58.8
Average	47.1%	51.5%	56.2%	52.3%	57.2%
31 Bull Years	50.0%	51.6%	58.4%	54.0%	60.4%
14 Bear Years	39.1%	49.8%	52.3%	49.5%	49.9%

*Excludes last six months of four-day market weeks.
**Four months only. Not included in averages.
Based on S&P composite index.

133

THE MONTHLY FIVE-DAY BULGE

The market rises more often (62.3%) on the second trading day of the month and a period of five consecutive trading days, the last, first, second, third, and fourth, distinctly outperforms the rest of the days of the month. In a 540-month study (May 1952–April 1997) the market was up 57.8% of the time on these five bullish days, as compared to an average of 52.0% for the remaining sixteen trading days of a typical month.

This occurs because individuals and institutions tend to operate on a monthly fiscal basis. Big cash inflows at banks, funds and insurance companies occur around the end or beginning of the month and often cause upward pressure. (See pages 64 and 66.)

Much of the market strength in these 45 years has centered around the last plus the first four trading days of the month. While the market has risen on average 53.4% of the time, the **prime five days** have risen 57.8%.

Sophisticated short-term traders, floor specialists, and portfolio managers could benefit immensely by studying this month-end/beginning upward bias. It would be difficult for long-term investors to take advantage of this phenomenon.

I have observed the market many times at month's end pausing during a sharp downturn, spurting after a resting or quiet phase, or accelerating its previously gradual rate of climb during a bull market.

Increasing publicity about this bullish pattern has led to many more investors playing the "game." In recent years, there has been added strength in the two days prior to the last day of the month and less bullishness on the third and fourth days of the month. The new SEC three-day settlement rule may be affecting patterns somewhat.

Several portfolios have been managed successfully by switching back and forth between no-load growth funds for each month's prime days and to a money market fund for the rest of the month's trading days.

MARKET PERFORMANCE EACH DAY OF THE MONTH
(May 1952–April 1997)

Based on the number of times the S&P composite closed higher than previous day

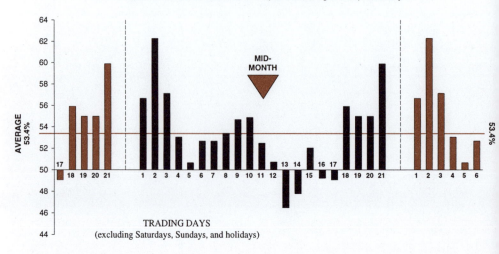

TRADING DAYS
(excluding Saturdays, Sundays, and holidays)

NOVEMBER, DECEMBER, AND JANUARY
YEAR'S BEST THREE-MONTH SPAN

The most important observation to be made from a chart showing the average monthly percent change in market prices since 1950 is that institutions (mutual funds, pension funds, banks, etc.) determine the trading patterns in today's

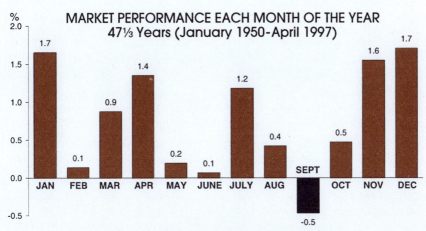

MARKET PERFORMANCE EACH MONTH OF THE YEAR
47⅓ Years (January 1950–April 1997)

Average month-to-month % change in Standard & Poor's composite index
(Based on monthly closing prices)

market. The "investment calendar" reflects the annual, semi-annual and quarterly operations of institutions during January, April and July. October, besides being a "tight money" month, and the last campaign month before elections, is also the time when most bear markets seem to end, as in 1946, 1957, 1960, 1966, 1974, 1987, and 1990. (August was most favored in 1982 and 1984.)

Unusual year-end strength comes from corporate and private pension funds producing a 5.0% gain on average between November 1 and January 31.

September's dismal performance makes it the worst month of the year and the only month with a loss. In the last thirteen years it has only been up five times. In midterm election years, Septembers have been down nine times in a row.

In the last ten years (see page 140) May was the best month while November was third from the bottom.

See page 50 for monthly performance tables for the S&P 500 and the Dow Jones industrials. See page 54 for unique six-month switching strategy.

20TH CENTURY BULL AND BEAR MARKETS

— Beginning —		— Ending —		Bull		Bear	
Date	DJIA	Date	DJIA	% Gain	Days	% Change	Days
09/24/00	52.96	06/17/01	78.26	47.8	266	−46.1	875
11/09/03	42.15	01/19/06	103.00	144.4	802	−48.5	665
11/15/07	53.00	11/19/09	100.53	89.7	735	−27.4	675
09/25/11	72.94	09/30/12	94.15	29.1	371	−43.5	668
12/24/14	53.17	11/21/16	110.15	107.2	698	−40.1	393
12/19/17	65.95	11/03/19	119.62	81.4	684	−46.6	660
08/24/21	63.90	03/20/23	105.38	64.9	573	−18.6	221
10/27/23	85.76	09/03/29	381.17	344.5	2138	−47.9	71
11/13/29	198.69	04/17/30	294.07	48.0	155	−86.0	813
07/08/32	41.22	09/07/32	79.93	93.9	61	−37.2	173
02/27/33	50.16	02/05/34	110.74	120.8	343	−22.8	171
07/26/34	85.51	03/10/37	194.40	127.3	958	−49.1	386
03/31/38	98.95	11/12/38	158.41	60.1	226	−23.3	147
04/08/39	121.44	09/12/39	155.92	28.4	157	−40.4	959
04/28/42	92.92	05/29/46	212.50	128.7	1492	−23.2	353
05/17/47	163.21	06/15/48	193.16	18.4	395	−16.3	363
06/13/49	161.60	01/05/53	293.79	81.8	1302	−13.0	252
09/14/53	255.49	04/06/56	521.05	103.9	935	−19.4	564
10/22/57	419.79	01/05/60	685.47	63.3	805	−17.4	294
10/25/60	566.05	12/31/61	734.91	29.8	414	−27.1	195
06/26/62	535.76	02/09/66	995.15	85.7	1324	−25.2	240
10/07/66	744.32	12/03/68	985.21	32.4	788	−35.9	539
05/26/70	631.16	04/28/71	950.82	50.6	337	−16.1	209
11/23/71	797.97	01/11/73	1051.70	31.8	415	−45.1	694
12/06/74	577.60	09/21/76	1014.79	75.7	655	−26.9	525
02/28/78	742.12	09/08/78	907.74	22.3	192	−16.4	591
04/21/80	759.13	04/27/81	1024.05	34.9	371	−24.1	472
08/12/82	776.92	11/29/83	1287.20	65.7	474	−15.6	238
07/24/84	1086.57	08/25/87	2722.42	150.6	1127	−36.1	55
10/19/87	1738.74	07/17/90	2999.75	72.5	1002	−21.2	86
10/11/90	2365.10						

Data: Ned Davis Research
Based on Dow Jones industrial average

Bear markets begin at the end of one bull market and end at the start of the next bull market (7/17/90 to 10/11/90 as an example). The high at Dow 3978.36 on January 31, 1994 was followed by a 9.7 percent correction. A 10.3 percent correction occurred between the May 22, 1996 closing high of 5778 and the intraday low on July 16, 1996. We are now in the seventh year of the longest bull market on record.

STOCK FRACTIONS IN DECIMALS AND CENTS

The table below is for investors who want to quickly convert stock price quotations into dollars and cents equivalents. One simple method to find an approximate price is to multiply the numerator by 3¢ for 32nds ($^{11}/_{32}$: 11 x 3¢ = 33¢). For 16ths, multiply the numerator by 6¢.

FRACTIONS	DECIMALS	CENTS	FRACTIONS	DECIMALS	CENTS
$^1/_{32}$	.03125	3⅛¢	$^{17}/_{32}$	.53125	53⅛¢
$^1/_{16}$	.0625	6¼¢	$^9/_{16}$	.5625	56¼¢
$^3/_{32}$	.09375	9⅜¢	$^{19}/_{32}$	.59375	59⅜¢
⅛	.125	12½¢	⅝	.625	62½¢
$^5/_{32}$	.15625	15⅝¢	$^{21}/_{32}$	.65625	65⅝¢
$^3/_{16}$	.1875	18¾¢	$^{11}/_{16}$	.6875	68¾¢
$^7/_{32}$	.21875	21⅞¢	$^{23}/_{32}$	.71875	71⅞¢
¼	.25	25¢	¾	.75	75¢
$^9/_{32}$	.28125	28⅛¢	$^{25}/_{32}$	.78125	78⅛¢
$^5/_{16}$	.3125	31¼¢	$^{13}/_{16}$	.8125	81¼¢
$^{11}/_{32}$	.34375	34⅜¢	$^{27}/_{32}$	.84375	84⅜¢
⅜	.375	37½¢	⅞	.875	87½¢
$^{13}/_{32}$	.40625	40⅝¢	$^{29}/_{32}$	.90625	90⅝¢
$^7/_{16}$	.4375	43¾¢	$^{15}/_{16}$	.9375	93¾¢
$^{15}/_{32}$	.46875	46⅞¢	$^{31}/_{32}$	.96875	96⅞¢
½	.50	50¢	1	1.0	100¢

DECENNIAL CYCLE: A MARKET PHENOMENON

By arranging each year's market gain or loss so the first years of a decade fall into the same column, certain interesting patterns emerge—strong fifth and eighth years, weak seventh and zero years.

This fascinating phenomenon was first presented by Edgar Lawrence Smith in *Common Stocks and Business Cycles* (William-Frederick Press). Anthony Gaubis co-pioneered the decennial pattern with Smith.

When Smith first cut graphs of market prices into ten-year segments and placed them above one another, he observed that each decade tended to have three bull market cycles and that the longest and strongest bull markets seem to favor the middle years of a decade.

It's difficult to place too much emphasis on the decennial cycle, other than the fifth and zero years, as the stock market obviously mirrors the quadrennnial presidential election cycle, shown on page 139.

As expected, 1995 turned out to be an addition to its perfect record of up "five" years. The "seventh" year, the worst year of the decade, is on its way to breaking the jinx. It could complete three consecutive major yearly gains for the first time this century.

THE TEN-YEAR STOCK MARKET CYCLE

Annual % change in Standard & Poor's Composite Index

DECADES	1st	2nd	3rd	4th	5th	6th	7th	8th	9th	10th
1881-1890	3	— 3	— 9	—19	20	9	— 7	— 2	3	—14
1891-1900	18	1	—20	— 3	1	— 2	13	19	7	14
1901-1910	16	1	—19	25	16	3	—33	37	14	—12
1911-1920	1	3	—14	— 9	32	3	—31	16	13	—24
1921-1930	7	20	— 3	19	23	5	26	36	—15	—29
1931-1940	—47	—18	48	— 2	39	28	—34	13	0	—12
1941-1950	—15	6	21	14	33	—10	— 2	— 2	11	20
1951-1960	15	7	— 3	39	23	4	—13	33	—11	— 4
1961-1970	27	—13	18	13	9	—11	17	12	—14	— 1
1971-1980	10	12	—19	—32	32	18	—10	2	11	26
1981-1990	— 7	13	18	0	26	20	— 3	15	26	— 6
1991-2000	18	12	7	— 2	35	20				
Up Years	9	9	5	5	12	9	3	9	7	3
Down Years	3	3	7	6	0	3	8	2	3	8
Total % Change	46%	41%	25%	43%	289%	87%	—77%	179%	45%	—42%

Based on average December prices.
Prior to 1918 based on Cowles indices.

PRESIDENTIAL ELECTION/STOCK MARKET CYCLE
THE 165-YEAR SAGA CONTINUES

It is no mere coincidence that the last two years (pre-election year and election year) of the 41 administrations since 1832 produced a total net market gain of 612%, dwarfing the 79% gain of the first two years of these administrations.

The presidential election every four years has a profound impact on the economy and the stock market. Wars, recessions and bear markets tend to start or occur in the first half of the term; prosperous times and bull markets, in the latter half.

The last cycle ran true to form with a net gain of 5% for 1993 and 1994 vs. a combined 55% for 1995 and 1996

STOCK MARKET ACTION SINCE 1832
Net change from year to year based on average December S&P prices

4-Year Cycle Beginning	Election Year	President Elected	Post-Election Year	Mid-Term	Pre-Election Year
1832	15%	Jackson (D)	— 3%	10%	2%
1836	— 8	Van Buren (D)	— 8	1	—13
1840*	5	W.H. Harrison (W)**	—14	—13	36
1844*	8	Polk (D)	6	—15	1
1848*	— 4	Taylor (W)**	0	19	— 3
1852*	20	Pierce (D)	—13	—30	1
1856	4	Buchanan (D)	—30	— 7	— 7
1860*	— 4	Lincoln (R)	— 4	43	30
1864	0	Lincoln (R)**	—14	— 3	— 6
1868	2	Grant (R)	— 7	— 4	7
1872	7	Grant (R)	—13	3	— 4
1876	—18	Hayes (R)	—10	6	43
1880	19	Garfield (R)**	3	— 3	— 9
1884*	—19	Cleveland (D)	20	9	— 7
1888*	— 2	B. Harrison (R)	3	—14	18
1892*	1	Cleveland (D)	—20	— 3	1
1896*	— 2	McKinley (R)	13	19	7
1900	14	McKinley (R)**	16	1	—19
1904	25	T. Roosevelt (R)	16	3	—33
1908	37	Taft (R)	14	—12	1
1912*	3	Wilson (D)	—14	— 9	32
1916	3	Wilson (D)	—31	16	13
1920*	—24	Harding (R)	7	20	— 3
1924	19	Coolidge (R)	23	5	26
1928	36	Hoover (R)	—15	—29	—47
1932*	—18	F. Roosevelt (D)	48	— 2	39
1936	28	F. Roosevelt (D)	—34	13	0
1940	—12	F. Roosevelt (D)	—15	6	21
1944	14	F. Roosevelt (D)**	33	—10	— 2
1948	— 2	Truman (D)	11	20	15
1952*	7	Eisenhower (R)	— 3	39	23
1956	4	Eisenhower (R)	—13	33	11
1960*	— 4	Kennedy (D)**	27	—13	18
1964	13	Johnson (D)	9	—11	17
1968*	12	Nixon (R)	—14	— 1	10
1972	12	Nixon (R)***	—19	—32	32
1976*	18	Carter (D)	—10	2	11
1980*	26	Reagan (R)	— 7	13	18
1984	0	Reagan (R)	26	20	— 3
1988	15	Bush (R)	26	— 6	18
1992*	12	Clinton (D)	7	— 2	35
1996	20	Clinton (D)			
	100%	1832-1911 Totals	—45%	10%	46%
	182%	1912-1996 Totals	42%	72%	284%
	282%	1832-1996 Totals	— 3%	82%	330%

*Party in power ousted **Death in office ***Resigned **D**—Democrat, **W**—Whig, **R**—Republican

Prior to 1892 based on Cowles and other indices

MONTHLY PERCENT CHANGES
IN STANDARD & POOR'S 500

	JAN	FEB	MAR	APR	MAY	JUN
1950	1.7%	1.0%	0.4%	4.5%	3.9%	— 5.8%
1951	6.1	0.6	— 1.8	4.8	— 4.1	— 2.6
1952	1.6	— 3.6	4.8	— 4.3	2.3	4.6
1953	— 0.7	— 1.8	— 2.4	— 2.6	— 0.3	— 1.6
1954	5.1	0.3	3.0	4.9	3.3	0.1
1955	1.8	0.4	— 0.5	3.8	— 0.1	8.2
1956	— 3.6	3.5	6.9	— 0.2	— 6.6	3.9
1957	— 4.2	— 3.3	2.0	3.7	3.7	— 0.1
1958	4.3	— 2.1	3.1	3.2	1.5	2.6
1959	0.4	0.0	0.1	3.9	1.9	— 0.4
1960	— 7.1	0.9	— 1.4	— 1.8	2.7	2.0
1961	6.3	2.7	2.6	0.4	1.9	— 2.9
1962	— 3.8	1.6	— 0.6	— 6.2	— 8.6	— 8.2
1963	4.9	— 2.9	3.5	4.9	1.4	— 2.0
1964	2.7	1.0	1.5	0.6	1.1	1.6
1965	3.3	— 0.1	— 1.5	3.4	— 0.8	— 4.9
1966	0.5	— 1.8	— 2.2	2.1	— 5.4	— 1.6
1967	7.8	0.2	3.9	4.2	— 5.2	1.8
1968	— 4.4	— 3.1	0.9	8.2	1.1	0.9
1969	— 0.8	— 4.7	3.4	2.1	— 0.2	— 5.6
1970	— 7.6	5.3	0.1	— 9.0	— 6.1	— 5.0
1971	4.0	0.9	3.7	3.6	— 4.2	0.1
1972	1.8	2.5	0.6	0.4	1.7	— 2.2
1973	— 1.7	— 3.7	— 0.1	— 4.1	— 1.9	— 0.7
1974	— 1.0	— 0.4	— 2.3	— 3.9	— 3.4	— 1.5
1975	12.3	6.0	2.2	4.7	4.4	4.4
1976	11.8	— 1.1	3.1	— 1.1	— 1.4	4.1
1977	— 5.1	— 2.2	— 1.4	0.02	— 2.4	4.5
1978	— 6.2	— 2.5	2.5	8.5	0.5	— 1.8
1979	4.0	— 3.7	5.5	0.2	— 2.6	3.9
1980	5.8	— 0.4	— 10.2	4.1	4.7	2.7
1981	— 4.6	1.3	3.6	— 2.3	— 0.2	— 1.0
1982	— 1.8	— 6.1	— 1.0	4.0	— 3.9	— 2.0
1983	3.3	1.9	3.3	7.5	— 1.2	3.5
1984	— 0.9	— 3.9	1.3	0.5	— 5.9	1.7
1985	7.4	0.9	— 0.3	— 0.5	5.4	1.2
1986	0.2	7.1	5.3	— 1.4	5.0	1.4
1987	13.2	3.7	2.6	— 1.1	0.6	4.8
1988	4.0	4.2	— 3.3	0.9	0.3	4.3
1989	7.1	— 2.9	2.1	5.0	3.5	— 0.8
1990	— 6.9	0.9	2.4	— 2.7	9.2	— 0.9
1991	4.2	6.7	2.2	0.03	3.9	— 4.8
1992	— 2.0	1.0	— 2.2	2.8	0.1	— 1.7
1993	0.7	1.0	1.9	— 2.5	2.3	0.1
1994	3.3	— 3.0	— 4.6	1.2	1.2	— 2.7
1995	2.4	3.6	2.7	2.8	3.6	2.1
1996	3.3	0.7	0.8	1.3	2.3	0.2
1997	6.1	0.6	— 4.3	5.8	5.9	4.3

MONTHLY PERCENT CHANGES IN STANDARD & POOR'S 500

JUL	AUG	SEP	OCT	NOV	DEC		Year's Change
0.8%	3.3%	5.6%	0.4%	— 0.1%	4.6%	1950	21.8%
6.9	3.9	— 0.1	— 1.4	— 0.3	3.9	1951	16.5
1.8	— 1.5	— 2.0	— 0.1	4.6	3.5	1952	11.8
2.5	— 5.8	0.1	5.1	0.9	0.2	1953	— 6.6
5.7	— 3.4	8.3	— 1.9	8.1	5.1	1954	45.0
6.1	— 0.8	1.1	— 3.0	7.5	— 0.1	1955	26.4
5.2	— 3.8	— 4.5	0.5	— 1.1	3.5	1956	2.6
1.1	— 5.6	— 6.2	— 3.2	0.5	— 3.1	1957	— 14.3
4.3	1.2	4.8	2.5	2.2	5.2	1958	38.1
3.5	— 1.5	— 4.6	1.1	1.3	2.8	1959	8.5
— 2.5	2.6	— 6.0	— 0.2	4.0	4.6	1960	— 3.0
3.3	2.0	— 2.0	2.8	3.9	0.3	1961	23.1
6.4	1.5	— 4.8	0.4	10.2	1.3	1962	— 11.8
— 0.3	4.9	— 1.1	3.2	— 1.1	2.4	1963	18.9
1.8	— 1.6	2.9	0.8	— 0.5	0.4	1964	13.0
1.3	2.3	3.2	2.7	— 0.9	0.9	1965	9.1
— 1.3	— 7.8	— 0.7	4.8	0.3	— 0.1	1966	— 13.1
4.5	— 1.2	3.3	— 2.9	0.1	2.6	1967	20.1
— 1.8	1.1	3.9	0.7	4.8	— 4.2	1968	7.7
— 6.0	4.0	— 2.5	4.4	— 3.5	— 1.9	1969	— 11.4
7.3	4.4	3.3	— 1.1	4.7	5.7	1970	0.1
— 4.1	3.6	— 0.7	— 4.2	— 0.3	8.6	1971	10.8
0.2	3.4	— 0.5	0.9	4.6	1.2	1972	15.6
3.8	— 3.7	4.0	— 0.1	— 11.4	1.7	1973	— 17.4
— 7.8	— 9.0	— 11.9	16.3	— 5.3	— 2.0	1974	— 29.7
— 6.8	— 2.1	— 3.5	6.2	2.5	— 1.2	1975	31.5
— 0.8	— 0.5	2.3	— 2.2	— 0.8	5.2	1976	19.1
— 1.6	— 2.1	— 0.2*	— 4.3	2.7	0.3	1977	— 11.5
5.4	2.6	— 0.7	— 9.2	1.7	1.5	1978	1.1
0.9	5.3	0.0	— 6.9	4.3	1.7	1979	12.3
6.5	0.6	2.5	1.6	10.2	— 3.4	1980	25.8
— 0.2	— 6.2	— 5.4	4.9	3.7	— 3.0	1981	— 9.7
— 2.3	11.6	0.8	11.0	3.6	1.5	1982	14.8
— 3.3	1.1	1.0	— 1.5	1.7	— 0.9	1983	17.3
— 1.6	10.6	— 0.3	— 0.01	— 1.5	2.2	1984	1.4
— 0.5	— 1.2	— 3.5	4.3	6.5	4.5	1985	26.3
— 5.9	7.1	— 8.5	5.5	2.1	— 2.8	1986	14.6
4.8	3.5	— 2.4	— 21.8	— 8.5	7.3	1987	2.0
— 0.5	— 3.9	4.0	2.6	— 1.9	1.5	1988	12.4
8.8	1.6	— 0.7	— 2.5	1.7	2.1	1989	27.3
— 0.5	— 9.4	— 5.1	— 0.7	6.0	2.5	1990	— 6.6
4.5	2.0	— 1.9	1.2	— 4.4	11.2	1991	26.3
3.9	— 2.4	0.9	0.2	3.0	1.0	1992	4.5
— 0.5	3.4	— 1.0	1.9	— 1.3	1.0	1993	7.1
3.1	3.8	— 2.7	2.1	— 4.0	1.2	1994	— 1.5
3.2	— 0.03	4.0	— 0.5	4.1	1.7	1995	34.1
— 4.6	1.9	5.4	2.6	7.3	— 2.2	1996	20.3
7.8						1997	

141

MONTHLY CLOSING PRICES
IN STANDARD & POOR'S 500

	JAN	FEB	MAR	APR	MAY	JUN
1950	17.05	17.22	17.29	18.07	18.78	17.69
1951	21.66	21.80	21.40	22.43	21.52	20.96
1952	24.14	23.26	24.37	23.32	23.86	24.96
1953	26.38	25.90	25.29	24.62	24.54	24.14
1954	26.08	26.15	26.94	28.26	29.19	29.21
1955	36.63	36.76	36.58	37.96	37.91	41.03
1956	43.82	45.34	48.48	48.38	45.20	46.97
1957	44.72	43.26	44.11	45.74	47.43	47.37
1958	41.70	40.84	42.10	43.44	44.09	45.24
1959	55.42	55.41	55.44	57.59	58.68	58.47
1960	55.61	56.12	55.34	54.37	55.83	56.92
1961	61.78	63.44	65.06	65.31	66.56	64.64
1962	68.84	69.96	69.55	65.24	59.63	54.75
1963	66.20	64.29	66.57	69.80	70.80	69.37
1964	77.04	77.80	78.98	79.46	80.37	81.69
1965	87.56	87.43	86.16	89.11	88.42	84.12
1966	92.88	91.22	89.23	91.06	86.13	84.74
1967	86.61	86.78	90.20	94.01	89.08	90.64
1968	92.24	89.36	90.20	97.59	98.68	99.58
1969	103.01	98.13	101.51	103.69	103.46	97.71
1970	85.02	89.50	89.63	81.52	76.55	72.72
1971	95.88	96.75	100.31	103.95	99.63	99.70
1972	103.94	106.57	107.20	107.67	109.53	107.14
1973	116.03	111.68	111.52	106.97	104.95	104.26
1974	96.57	96.22	93.98	90.31	87.28	86.00
1975	76.98	81.59	83.36	87.30	91.15	95.19
1976	100.86	99.71	102.77	101.64	100.18	104.28
1977	102.03	99.82	98.42	98.44	96.12	100.48
1978	89.25	87.04	89.21	96.83	97.29	95.53
1979	99.93	96.28	101.59	101.76	99.08	102.91
1980	114.16	113.66	102.09	106.29	111.24	114.24
1981	129.55	131.27	136.00	132.87	132.59	131.21
1982	120.40	113.11	111.96	116.44	111.88	109.61
1983	145.30	148.06	152.96	164.42	162.39	168.11
1984	163.41	157.06	159.18	160.05	150.55	153.18
1985	179.63	181.18	180.66	179.83	189.55	191.85
1986	211.78	226.92	238.90	235.52	247.35	250.84
1987	274.08	284.20	291.70	288.36	290.10	304.00
1988	257.07	267.82	258.89	261.33	262.16	273.50
1989	297.47	288.86	294.87	309.64	320.52	317.98
1990	329.08	331.89	339.94	330.80	361.23	358.02
1991	343.93	367.07	375.22	375.35	389.83	371.16
1992	408.79	412.70	403.69	414.95	415.35	408.14
1993	438.78	443.38	451.67	440.19	450.19	450.53
1994	481.61	467.14	445.77	450.91	456.50	444.27
1995	470.42	487.39	500.71	514.71	533.40	544.75
1996	636.02	640.43	645.50	654.17	669.12	670.63
1997	786.16	790.82	757.12	801.34	848.28	885.15

MONTHLY CLOSING PRICES
IN STANDARD & POOR'S 500

JUL	AUG	SEP	OCT	NOV	DEC	
17.84	18.42	19.45	19.53	19.51	20.41	**1950**
22.40	23.28	23.26	22.94	22.88	23.77	**1951**
25.40	25.03	24.54	24.52	25.66	26.57	**1952**
24.75	23.32	23.35	24.54	24.76	24.81	**1953**
30.88	29.83	32.31	31.68	34.24	35.98	**1954**
43.52	43.18	43.67	42.34	45.51	45.48	**1955**
49.39	47.51	45.35	45.58	45.08	46.67	**1956**
47.91	45.22	42.42	41.06	41.27	39.99	**1957**
47.19	47.75	50.06	51.33	52.48	55.21	**1958**
60.51	59.60	56.88	57.52	58.28	59.89	**1959**
55.51	56.96	53.52	53.39	55.54	58.11	**1960**
66.76	68.07	66.73	68.62	71.32	71.55	**1961**
58.23	59.12	56.27	56.52	62.26	63.10	**1962**
69.13	72.50	71.70	74.01	73.23	75.02	**1963**
83.18	81.83	84.18	84.86	84.42	84.75	**1964**
85.25	87.17	89.96	92.42	91.61	92.43	**1965**
83.60	77.10	76.56	80.20	80.45	80.33	**1966**
94.75	93.64	96.71	93.90	94.00	96.47	**1967**
97.74	98.86	102.67	103.41	108.37	103.86	**1968**
91.83	95.51	93.12	97.24	93.81	92.06	**1969**
78.05	81.52	84.21	83.25	87.20	92.15	**1970**
95.58	99.03	98.34	94.23	93.99	102.09	**1971**
107.39	111.09	110.55	111.58	116.67	118.05	**1972**
108.22	104.25	108.43	108.29	95.96	97.55	**1973**
79.31	72.15	63.54	73.90	69.97	68.56	**1974**
88.75	86.88	83.87	89.04	91.24	90.19	**1975**
103.44	102.91	105.24	102.90	102.10	107.46	**1976**
98.85	96.77	96.53	92.34	94.83	95.10	**1977**
100.68	103.29	102.54	93.15	94.70	96.11	**1978**
103.81	109.32	109.32	101.82	106.16	107.94	**1979**
121.67	122.38	125.46	127.47	140.52	135.76	**1980**
130.92	122.79	116.18	121.89	126.35	122.55	**1981**
107.09	119.51	120.42	133.71	138.54	140.64	**1982**
162.56	164.40	166.07	163.55	166.40	164.93	**1983**
150.66	166.68	166.10	166.09	163.58	167.24	**1984**
190.92	188.63	182.08	189.82	202.17	211.28	**1985**
236.12	252.93	231.32	243.98	249.22	242.17	**1986**
318.66	329.80	321.83	251.79	230.30	247.08	**1987**
272.02	261.52	271.91	278.97	273.70	277.72	**1988**
346.08	351.45	349.15	340.36	345.99	353.40	**1989**
356.15	322.56	306.05	304.00	322.22	330.22	**1990**
387.81	395.43	387.86	392.46	375.22	417.09	**1991**
424.21	414.03	417.80	418.68	431.35	435.71	**1992**
448.13	463.56	458.93	467.83	461.79	466.45	**1993**
458.26	475.49	462.69	472.35	453.69	459.27	**1994**
562.06	561.88	584.41	581.50	605.37	615.93	**1995**
639.95	651.99	687.33	705.27	757.02	740.74	**1996**
954.29						**1997**

MONTHLY PERCENT CHANGES
IN DOW JONES INDUSTRIALS

	JAN	FEB	MAR	APR	MAY	JUN
1950	0.8%	0.8%	1.3%	4.0%	4.2%	— 6.4%
1951	5.7	1.3	— 1.6	4.5	— 3.7	— 2.8
1952	0.5	— 3.9	3.6	— 4.4	2.1	4.3
1953	— 0.7	— 1.9	— 1.5	— 1.8	— 0.9	— 1.5
1954	4.1	0.7	3.0	5.2	2.6	1.8
1955	1.1	0.7	— 0.5	3.9	— 0.2	6.2
1956	— 3.6	2.7	5.8	0.8	— 7.4	3.1
1957	— 4.1	— 3.0	2.2	4.1	2.1	— 0.3
1958	3.3	— 2.2	1.6	2.0	1.5	3.3
1959	1.8	1.6	— 0.3	3.7	3.2	0.0
1960	— 8.4	1.2	— 2.1	— 2.4	4.0	2.4
1961	5.2	2.1	2.2	0.3	2.7	— 1.8
1962	— 4.3	1.1	— 0.2	— 5.9	— 7.8	— 8.5
1963	4.7	— 2.9	3.0	5.2	1.3	— 2.8
1964	2.9	1.9	1.6	— 0.3	1.2	1.3
1965	3.3	0.1	— 1.6	3.7	— 0.5	— 5.4
1966	1.5	— 3.2	— 2.8	1.0	— 5.3	— 1.6
1967	8.2	— 1.2	3.2	3.6	— 5.0	0.9
1968	— 5.5	— 1.7	0.0	8.5	— 1.4	— 0.1
1969	0.2	— 4.3	3.3	1.6	— 1.3	— 6.9
1970	— 7.0	4.5	1.0	— 6.3	— 4.8	— 2.4
1971	3.5	1.2	2.9	4.1	— 3.6	— 1.8
1972	1.3	2.9	1.4	1.4	0.7	— 3.3
1973	— 2.1	— 4.4	— 0.4	— 3.1	— 2.2	— 1.1
1974	0.6	0.6	— 1.6	— 1.2	— 4.1	0.0
1975	14.2	5.0	3.9	6.9	1.3	5.6
1976	14.4	— 0.3	2.8	— 0.3	— 2.2	2.8
1977	— 5.0	— 1.9	— 1.8	0.8	— 3.0	2.0
1978	— 7.4	— 3.6	2.1	10.6	0.4	— 2.6
1979	4.2	— 3.6	6.6	— 0.8	— 3.8	2.4
1980	4.4	— 1.5	— 9.0	4.0	4.1	2.0
1981	— 1.7	2.9	3.0	— 0.6	— 0.6	— 1.5
1982	— 0.4	— 5.4	— 0.2	3.1	— 3.4	— 0.9
1983	2.8	3.4	1.6	8.5	— 2.1	1.8
1984	— 3.0	— 5.4	0.9	0.5	— 5.6	2.5
1985	6.2	— 0.2	— 1.3	— 0.7	4.6	1.5
1986	1.6	8.8	6.4	— 1.9	5.2	0.9
1987	13.8	3.1	3.6	— 0.8	0.2	5.5
1988	1.0	5.8	— 4.0	2.2	— 0.1	5.4
1989	8.0	— 3.6	1.6	5.5	2.5	— 1.6
1990	— 5.9	1.4	3.0	— 1.9	8.3	0.1
1991	3.9	5.3	1.1	— 0.9	4.8	— 4.0
1992	1.7	1.4	— 1.0	3.8	1.1	— 2.3
1993	0.3	1.8	1.9	— 0.2	2.9	— 0.3
1994	6.0	— 3.7	— 5.1	1.3	2.1	— 3.5
1995	0.2	4.3	3.7	3.9	3.3	2.0
1996	5.4	1.7	1.9	— 0.3	1.3	0.2
1997	5.7	0.9	— 4.3	6.5	4.6	4.7

JUL	AUG	SEP	OCT	NOV	DEC		Year's Change
0.1%	3.6%	4.4%	— 0.6%	1.2%	3.4%	**1950**	17.6%
6.3	4.8	0.3	— 3.2	— 0.4	3.0	**1951**	14.4
1.9	— 1.6	— 1.6	— 0.5	5.4	2.9	**1952**	8.4
2.7	— 5.1	1.1	4.5	2.0	— 0.2	**1953**	— 3.8
4.3	— 3.5	7.3	— 2.3	9.8	4.6	**1954**	44.0
3.2	0.5	— 0.3	— 2.5	6.2	1.1	**1955**	20.8
5.1	— 3.0	— 5.3	1.0	— 1.5	5.6	**1956**	2.3
1.0	— 4.8	— 5.8	— 3.3	2.0	— 3.2	**1957**	— 12.8
5.2	1.1	4.6	2.1	2.6	4.7	**1958**	34.0
4.9	— 1.6	— 4.9	2.4	1.9	3.1	**1959**	16.4
— 3.7	1.5	— 7.3	0.0	2.9	3.1	**1960**	— 9.3
3.1	2.1	— 2.6	0.4	2.5	1.3	**1961**	18.7
6.5	1.9	— 5.0	1.9	10.1	0.4	**1962**	— 10.8
— 1.6	4.9	0.5	3.1	— 0.6	1.7	**1963**	17.0
1.2	— 0.3	4.4	— 0.3	0.3	— 0.1	**1964**	14.6
1.6	1.3	4.2	3.2	— 1.5	2.4	**1965**	10.9
— 2.6	— 7.0	— 1.8	4.2	— 1.9	— 0.7	**1966**	— 18.9
5.1	— 0.3	2.8	— 5.1	— 0.4	3.3	**1967**	15.2
— 1.6	1.5	4.4	1.8	3.4	— 4.2	**1968**	4.3
— 6.6	2.6	— 2.8	5.3	— 5.1	— 1.5	**1969**	— 15.2
7.4	4.1	— 0.5	— 0.7	5.1	5.6	**1970**	4.8
— 3.7	4.6	— 1.2	— 5.4	— 0.9	7.1	**1971**	6.1
— 0.5	4.2	— 1.1	0.2	6.6	0.2	**1972**	14.6
3.9	— 4.2	6.7	1.0	— 14.0	3.5	**1973**	— 16.6
— 5.6	— 10.4	— 10.4	9.5	— 7.0	— 0.4	**1974**	— 27.6
— 5.4	0.5	— 5.0	5.3	2.9	— 1.0	**1975**	38.3
— 1.8	— 1.1	1.7	— 2.6	— 1.8	6.1	**1976**	17.9
— 2.9	— 3.2	— 1.7	— 3.4	1.4	0.2	**1977**	— 17.3
5.3	1.7	— 1.3	— 8.5	0.8	0.7	**1978**	— 3.1
0.5	4.9	— 1.0	— 7.2	0.8	2.0	**1979**	4.2
7.8	— 0.3	0.0	— 0.9	7.4	— 3.0	**1980**	14.9
— 2.5	— 7.4	— 3.6	0.3	4.3	— 1.6	**1981**	— 9.2
— 0.4	11.5	— 0.6	10.7	4.8	0.7	**1982**	19.6
— 1.9	1.4	1.4	— 0.6	4.1	— 1.4	**1983**	20.3
— 1.5	9.8	— 1.4	0.1	— 1.5	1.9	**1984**	— 3.7
0.9	— 1.0	— 0.4	3.4	7.1	5.1	**1985**	27.7
— 6.2	6.9	— 6.9	6.2	1.9	— 1.0	**1986**	22.6
6.3	3.5	— 2.5	— 23.2	— 8.0	5.7	**1987**	2.3
— 0.6	— 4.6	4.0	1.7	— 1.6	2.6	**1988**	11.8
9.0	2.9	— 1.6	— 1.8	2.3	1.7	**1989**	27.0
0.9	— 10.0	— 6.2	— 0.4	4.8	2.9	**1990**	— 4.3
4.1	0.6	— 0.9	1.7	— 5.7	9.5	**1991**	20.3
2.3	— 4.0	0.4	— 1.4	2.4	— 0.1	**1992**	4.2
0.7	3.2	— 2.6	3.5	0.1	1.9	**1993**	13.7
3.8	4.0	— 1.8	1.7	— 4.3	2.5	**1994**	2.1
3.3	— 2.1	3.9	— 0.7	6.7	0.8	**1995**	33.5
— 2.2	1.6	4.7	2.5	8.2	— 1.1	**1996**	26.0
7.2						**1997**	

MONTHLY POINT CHANGES IN DOW JONES INDUSTRIALS

	JAN	FEB	MAR	APR	MAY	JUN
1950	1.66	1.65	2.61	8.28	9.09	— 14.31
1951	13.42	3.22	— 4.11	11.19	— 9.48	— 7.01
1952	1.46	— 10.61	9.38	— 11.83	5.31	11.32
1953	— 2.13	— 5.50	— 4.40	— 5.12	— 2.47	— 4.02
1954	11.49	2.15	8.97	15.82	8.16	6.04
1955	4.44	3.04	— 2.17	15.95	— 0.79	26.52
1956	— 17.66	12.91	28.14	4.33	— 38.07	14.73
1957	— 20.31	— 14.54	10.19	19.55	10.57	— 1.64
1958	14.33	— 10.10	6.84	9.10	6.84	15.48
1959	10.31	9.54	— 1.79	22.04	20.04	— 0.19
1960	— 56.74	7.50	— 13.53	— 14.89	23.80	15.12
1961	32.31	13.88	14.55	2.08	18.01	— 12.76
1962	— 31.14	8.05	— 1.10	— 41.62	— 51.97	— 52.08
1963	30.75	— 19.91	19.58	35.18	9.26	— 20.08
1964	22.39	14.80	13.15	— 2.52	9.79	10.94
1965	28.73	0.62	— 14.43	33.26	— 4.27	— 50.01
1966	14.25	— 31.62	— 27.12	8.91	— 49.61	— 13.97
1967	64.20	— 10.52	26.61	31.07	— 44.49	7.70
1968	— 49.64	— 14.97	0.17	71.55	— 13.22	1.20
1969	2.30	— 40.84	30.27	14.70	— 12.62	— 64.37
1970	— 56.30	33.53	7.98	— 49.50	— 35.63	— 16.91
1971	29.58	10.33	25.54	37.38	— 33.94	— 16.67
1972	11.97	25.96	12.57	13.47	6.55	— 31.69
1973	— 21.00	— 43.95	— 4.06	— 29.58	— 20.02	— 9.70
1974	4.69	4.98	— 13.85	— 9.93	— 34.58	0.24
1975	87.45	35.36	29.10	53.19	10.95	46.70
1976	122.87	— 2.67	26.84	— 2.60	— 21.62	27.55
1977	— 50.28	— 17.95	— 17.29	7.77	— 28.24	17.64
1978	— 61.25	— 27.80	15.24	79.96	3.29	— 21.66
1979	34.21	— 30.40	53.36	— 7.28	— 32.57	19.65
1980	37.11	— 12.71	— 77.39	31.31	33.79	17.07
1981	— 16.72	27.31	29.29	— 6.12	— 6.00	— 14.87
1982	— 3.90	— 46.71	— 1.62	25.59	— 28.82	— 7.61
1983	29.16	36.92	17.41	96.17	— 26.22	21.98
1984	— 38.06	— 65.95	10.26	5.86	— 65.90	27.55
1985	75.20	— 2.76	— 17.23	— 8.72	57.35	20.05
1986	24.32	138.07	109.55	— 34.63	92.73	16.01
1987	262.09	65.95	80.70	— 18.33	5.21	126.96
1988	19.39	113.40	— 83.56	44.27	— 1.21	110.59
1989	173.75	— 83.93	35.23	125.18	61.35	— 40.09
1990	—162.66	36.71	79.96	— 50.45	219.90	4.03
1991	102.73	145.79	31.68	— 25.99	139.63	—120.75
1992	54.56	44.28	— 32.20	123.65	37.76	— 78.36
1993	8.92	60.78	64.30	— 7.56	99.88	— 11.35
1994	224.27	—146.34	—196.06	45.73	76.68	—133.41
1995	9.42	167.19	146.64	163.58	143.87	90.96
1996	278.18	90.32	101.52	— 18.06	74.10	11.45
1997	364.82	64.65	—294.26	425.51	322.05	341.75
UP	34	28	30	30	26	24
DOWN	14	20	18	18	22	24
TOTALS	1618.94	539.11	241.46	1236.90	944.22	263.32

146

MONTHLY POINT CHANGES IN DOW JONES INDUSTRIALS

JUL	AUG	SEP	OCT	NOV	DEC	Year's Close	
0.29	7.47	9.49	− 1.35	2.59	7.81	**235.41**	1950
15.22	12.39	0.91	− 8.81	− 1.08	7.96	**269.23**	1951
5.30	− 4.52	− 4.43	− 1.38	14.43	8.24	**291.90**	1952
7.12	− 14.16	2.82	11.77	5.56	− 0.47	**280.90**	1953
14.39	− 12.12	24.66	− 8.32	34.63	17.62	**404.39**	1954
14.47	2.33	− 1.56	− 11.75	28.39	5.14	**488.40**	1955
25.03	− 15.77	− 26.79	4.60	− 7.07	26.69	**499.47**	1956
5.23	− 24.17	− 28.05	− 15.26	8.83	− 14.18	**435.69**	1957
24.81	5.64	23.46	11.13	14.24	26.19	**583.65**	1958
31.28	− 10.47	− 32.73	14.92	12.58	20.18	**679.36**	1959
− 23.89	9.26	− 45.85	0.22	16.86	18.67	**615.89**	1960
21.41	14.57	− 18.73	2.71	17.68	9.54	**731.14**	1961
36.65	11.25	− 30.20	10.79	59.53	2.80	**652.10**	1962
− 11.45	33.89	3.47	22.44	− 4.71	12.43	**762.95**	1963
9.60	− 2.62	36.89	− 2.29	2.35	− 1.30	**874.13**	1964
13.71	11.36	37.48	30.24	− 14.11	22.55	**969.26**	1965
− 22.72	− 58.97	− 14.19	32.85	− 15.48	− 5.90	**785.69**	1966
43.98	− 2.95	25.37	− 46.92	− 3.93	29.30	**905.11**	1967
− 14.80	13.01	39.78	16.60	32.69	− 41.33	**943.75**	1968
− 57.72	21.25	− 23.63	42.90	− 43.69	− 11.94	**800.36**	1969
50.59	30.46	− 3.90	− 5.07	38.48	44.83	**838.92**	1970
− 32.71	39.64	− 10.88	− 48.19	− 7.66	58.86	**890.20**	1971
− 4.29	38.99	− 10.46	2.25	62.69	1.81	**1020.02**	1972
34.69	− 38.83	59.53	9.48	−134.33	28.61	**850.86**	1973
− 44.98	− 78.85	− 70.71	57.65	− 46.86	− 2.42	**616.24**	1974
− 47.48	3.83	− 41.46	42.16	24.63	− 8.26	**852.41**	1975
− 18.14	− 10.90	16.45	− 25.26	− 17.71	57.43	**1004.65**	1976
− 26.23	− 28.58	− 14.38	− 28.76	11.35	1.47	**831.17**	1977
43.32	14.55	− 11.00	− 73.37	6.58	5.98	**805.01**	1978
4.44	41.21	− 9.05	− 62.88	6.65	16.39	**838.74**	1979
67.40	− 2.73	− 0.17	− 7.93	68.85	− 29.35	**963.99**	1980
− 24.54	− 70.87	− 31.49	2.57	36.43	− 13.98	**875.00**	1981
− 3.33	92.71	− 5.06	95.47	47.56	7.26	**1046.54**	1982
− 22.74	16.94	16.97	− 7.93	50.82	− 17.38	**1258.64**	1983
− 17.12	109.10	− 17.67	0.67	− 18.44	22.63	**1211.57**	1984
11.99	− 13.44	− 5.38	45.68	97.82	74.54	**1546.67**	1985
−117.41	123.03	−130.76	110.23	36.42	− 18.28	**1895.95**	1986
153.54	90.88	− 66.67	−602.75	−159.98	105.28	**1938.83**	1987
− 12.98	− 97.08	81.26	35.74	− 34.14	54.06	**2168.57**	1988
220.60	76.61	− 44.45	− 47.74	61.19	46.93	**2753.20**	1989
24.51	−290.84	−161.88	− 10.15	117.32	74.01	**2633.66**	1990
118.07	18.78	− 26.83	52.33	−174.42	274.15	**3168.83**	1991
75.26	−136.43	14.31	− 45.38	78.88	− 4.05	**3301.11**	1992
23.39	111.78	− 96.13	125.47	3.36	70.14	**3754.09**	1993
139.54	148.92	− 70.23	64.93	−168.89	95.21	**3834.44**	1994
152.37	− 97.91	178.52	− 33.60	319.01	42.63	**5117.12**	1995
−125.72	87.30	265.96	147.21	492.32	− 73.43	**6448.27**	1996
549.82*							1997
29	27	17	26	31	33		
18	20	30	21	16	14		
759.95	174.94	−217.39	−102.08	958.22	1055.07		

*Not included in totals

147

MONTHLY CLOSING PRICES
IN DOW JONES INDUSTRIALS

	JAN	FEB	MAR	APR	MAY	JUN
1950	201.79	203.44	206.05	214.33	223.42	209.11
1951	248.83	252.05	247.94	259.13	249.65	242.64
1952	270.69	260.08	269.46	257.63	262.94	274.26
1953	289.77	284.27	279.87	274.75	272.28	268.26
1954	292.39	294.54	303.51	319.33	327.49	333.53
1955	408.83	411.87	409.70	425.65	424.86	451.38
1956	470.74	483.65	511.79	516.12	478.05	492.78
1957	479.16	464.62	474.81	494.36	504.93	503.29
1958	450.02	439.92	446.76	455.86	462.70	478.18
1959	593.96	603.50	601.71	623.75	643.79	643.60
1960	622.62	630.12	616.59	601.70	625.50	640.62
1961	648.20	662.08	676.63	678.71	696.72	683.96
1962	700.00	708.05	706.95	665.33	613.36	561.28
1963	682.85	662.94	682.52	717.70	726.96	706.88
1964	785.34	800.14	813.29	810.77	820.56	831.50
1965	902.86	903.48	889.05	922.31	918.04	868.03
1966	983.51	951.89	924.77	933.68	884.07	870.10
1967	849.89	839.37	865.98	897.05	852.56	860.26
1968	855.47	840.50	840.67	912.22	899.00	897.80
1969	946.05	905.21	935.48	950.18	937.56	873.19
1970	744.06	777.59	785.57	736.07	700.44	683.53
1971	868.50	878.83	904.37	941.75	907.81	891.14
1972	902.17	928.13	940.70	954.17	960.72	929.03
1973	999.02	955.07	951.01	921.43	901.41	891.71
1974	855.55	860.53	846.68	836.75	802.17	802.41
1975	703.69	739.05	768.15	821.34	832.29	878.99
1976	975.28	972.61	999.45	996.85	975.23	1002.78
1977	954.37	936.42	919.13	926.90	898.66	916.30
1978	769.92	742.12	757.36	837.32	840.61	818.95
1979	839.22	808.82	862.18	854.90	822.33	841.98
1980	875.85	863.14	785.75	817.06	850.85	867.92
1981	947.27	974.58	1003.87	997.75	991.75	976.88
1982	871.10	824.39	822.77	848.36	819.54	811.93
1983	1075.70	1112.62	1130.03	1226.20	1199.98	1221.96
1984	1220.58	1154.63	1164.89	1170.75	1104.85	1132.40
1985	1286.77	1284.01	1266.78	1258.06	1315.41	1335.46
1986	1570.99	1709.06	1818.61	1783.98	1876.71	1892.72
1987	2158.04	2223.99	2304.69	2286.36	2291.57	2418.53
1988	1958.22	2071.62	1988.06	2032.33	2031.12	2141.71
1989	2342.32	2258.39	2293.62	2418.80	2480.15	2440.06
1990	2590.54	2627.25	2707.21	2656.76	2876.66	2880.69
1991	2736.39	2882.18	2913.86	2887.87	3027.50	2906.75
1992	3223.39	3267.67	3235.47	3359.12	3396.88	3318.52
1993	3310.03	3370.81	3435.11	3427.55	3527.43	3516.08
1994	3978.36	3832.02	3635.96	3681.69	3758.37	3624.96
1995	3843.86	4011.05	4157.69	4321.27	4465.14	4556.10
1996	5395.30	5485.62	5587.14	5569.08	5643.18	5654.63
1997	6813.09	6877.74	6583.48	7008.99	7331.04	7672.79

MONTHLY CLOSING PRICES
IN DOW JONES INDUSTRIALS

JUL	AUG	SEP	OCT	NOV	DEC	
209.40	216.87	226.36	225.01	227.60	235.41	**1950**
257.86	270.25	271.16	262.35	261.27	269.23	**1951**
279.56	275.04	270.61	269.23	283.66	291.90	**1952**
275.38	261.22	264.04	275.81	281.37	280.90	**1953**
347.92	335.80	360.46	352.14	386.77	404.39	**1954**
465.85	468.18	466.62	454.87	483.26	488.40	**1955**
517.81	502.04	475.25	479.85	472.78	499.47	**1956**
508.52	484.35	456.30	441.04	449.87	435.69	**1957**
502.99	508.63	532.09	543.22	557.46	583.65	**1958**
674.88	664.41	631.68	646.60	659.18	679.36	**1959**
616.73	625.99	580.14	580.36	597.22	615.89	**1960**
705.37	719.94	701.21	703.92	721.60	731.14	**1961**
597.93	609.18	578.98	589.77	649.30	652.10	**1962**
695.43	729.32	732.79	755.23	750.52	762.95	**1963**
841.10	838.48	875.37	873.08	875.43	874.13	**1964**
881.74	893.10	930.58	960.82	946.71	969.26	**1965**
847.38	788.41	774.22	807.07	791.59	785.69	**1966**
904.24	901.29	926.66	879.74	875.81	905.11	**1967**
883.00	896.01	935.79	952.39	985.08	943.75	**1968**
815.47	836.72	813.09	855.99	812.30	800.36	**1969**
734.12	764.58	760.68	755.61	794.09	838.92	**1970**
858.43	898.07	887.19	839.00	831.34	890.20	**1971**
924.74	963.73	953.27	955.52	1018.21	1020.02	**1972**
926.40	887.57	947.10	956.58	822.25	850.86	**1973**
757.43	678.58	607.87	665.52	618.66	616.24	**1974**
831.51	835.34	793.88	836.04	860.67	852.41	**1975**
984.64	973.74	990.19	964.93	947.22	1004.65	**1976**
890.07	861.49	847.11	818.35	829.70	831.17	**1977**
862.27	876.82	865.82	792.45	799.03	805.01	**1978**
846.42	887.63	878.58	815.70	822.35	838.74	**1979**
935.32	932.59	932.42	924.49	993.34	963.99	**1980**
952.34	881.47	849.98	852.55	888.98	875.00	**1981**
808.60	901.31	896.25	991.72	1039.28	1046.54	**1982**
1199.22	1216.16	1233.13	1225.20	1276.02	1258.64	**1983**
1115.28	1224.38	1206.71	1207.38	1188.94	1211.57	**1984**
1347.45	1334.01	1328.63	1374.31	1472.13	1546.67	**1985**
1775.31	1898.34	1767.58	1877.81	1914.23	1895.95	**1986**
2572.07	2662.95	2596.28	1993.53	1833.55	1938.83	**1987**
2128.73	2031.65	2112.91	2148.65	2114.51	2168.57	**1988**
2660.66	2737.27	2692.82	2645.08	2706.27	2753.20	**1989**
2905.20	2614.36	2452.48	2442.33	2559.65	2633.66	**1990**
3024.82	3043.60	3016.77	3069.10	2894.68	3168.83	**1991**
3393.78	3257.35	3271.66	3226.28	3305.16	3301.11	**1992**
3539.47	3651.25	3555.12	3680.59	3683.95	3754.09	**1993**
3764.50	3913.42	3843.19	3908.12	3739.23	3834.44	**1994**
4708.47	4610.56	4789.08	4755.48	5074.49	5117.12	**1995**
5528.91	5616.21	5882.17	6029.38	6521.70	6448.27	**1996**
8222.61						**1997**

INDIVIDUAL RETIREMENT ACCOUNTS
MOST AWESOME INVESTMENT INCENTIVE EVER DEVISED

IRA INVESTMENTS OF $2,000 A YEAR
COMPOUNDING AT VARIOUS RATES OF RETURN
FOR DIFFERENT PERIODS

Annual Rate	5 Yrs	10 Yrs	15 Yrs	20 Yrs	25 Yrs
1%	$10,304	$21,134	$ 32,516	$ 44,478	$ 57,050
2%	10,616	22,337	35,279	49,567	65,342
3%	10,937	23,616	38,314	55,353	75,106
4%	11,266	24,973	41,649	61,938	86,623
5%	11,604	26,414	45,315	69,439	100,227
6%	11,951	27,943	49,345	77,985	116,313
7%	12,307	29,567	53,776	87,730	135,353
8%	12,672	31,291	58,649	98,846	157,909
9%	13,047	33,121	64,007	111,529	184,648
10%	13,431	35,062	69,899	126,005	216,364
11%	13,826	37,123	76,380	142,530	253,998
12%	14,230	39,309	83,507	161,397	298,668
13%	14,645	41,629	91,343	182,940	351,700
14%	15,071	44,089	99,961	207,537	414,665
15%	15,508	46,699	109,435	235,620	489,424
16%	15,955	49,466	119,850	267,681	578,177
17%	16,414	52,400	131,298	304,277	683,525
18%	16,884	55,510	143,878	346,042	808,544
19%	17,366	58,807	157,700	393,695	956,861
20%	17,860	62,301	172,884	448,051	1,132,755

IRA INVESTMENTS OF $2,000 A YEAR
COMPOUNDING AT VARIOUS RATES OF RETURN
FOR DIFFERENT PERIODS

Annual Rate	30 Yrs	35 Yrs	40 Yrs	45 Yrs	50 Yrs
1%	$ 70,265	$ 84,154	$ 98,750	$ 114,092	$ 130,216
2%	82,759	101,989	123,220	146,661	172,542
3%	98,005	124,552	155,327	191,003	232,362
4%	116,657	153,197	197,653	251,741	317,548
5%	139,522	189,673	253,680	335,370	439,631
6%	167,603	236,242	328,095	451,016	615,512
7%	202,146	295,827	427,219	611,504	869,972
8%	244,692	372,204	559,562	834,852	1,239,344
9%	297,150	470,249	736,584	1,146,372	1,776,882
10%	361,887	596,254	973,704	1,581,591	2,560,599
11%	441,826	758,329	1,291,654	2,190,338	3,704,672
12%	540,585	966,926	1,718,285	3,042,435	5,376,041
13%	662,630	1,235,499	2,290,972	4,235,612	7,818,486
14%	813,474	1,581,346	3,059,817	5,906,488	11,387,509
15%	999,914	2,026,691	4,091,908	8,245,795	16,600,747
16%	1,230,323	2,600,054	5,476,957	11,519,435	24,210,705
17%	1,515,008	3,337,989	7,334,781	16,097,540	35,309,434
18%	1,866,637	4,287,298	9,825,183	22,494,522	51,478,901
19%	2,300,775	5,507,829	13,160,993	31,424,150	75,006,500
20%	2,836,516	7,076,019	17,625,259	43,875,144	109,193,258

G.M. LOEB'S "BATTLE PLAN" FOR INVESTMENT SURVIVAL

LIFE IS CHANGE: Nothing can ever be the same a minute from now as it was a minute ago. Everything you own is changing in price and value. You can find that last price of an active security on the stock ticker, but you cannot find the *next* price anywhere. The value of your money is changing. Even the value of your home is changing, though no one walks in front of it with a sandwich board consistently posting the changes.

RECOGNIZE CHANGE: Your basic objective should be to profit from change. The art of investing is being able to recognize change and to adjust investment goals accordingly.

WRITE THINGS DOWN: You will score more investment success and avoid more investment failures if you write things down. Very few investors have the drive and inclination to do this.

KEEP A CHECKLIST: If you aim to improve your investment results, try to get into the habit of keeping a checklist on every issue you consider buying. Before making a commitment, it will pay you to write down the answers to at least some of the basic questions—How much am I investing in this company? How much do I think I can make? How much do I have to risk? How long do I expect to take to reach my goal?

HAVE A SINGLE RULING REASON: Above all, writing things down is the best way to find "the ruling reason." When all is said and done, there is invariably a single reason that stands out above all others why a particular security transaction can be expected to show a profit. All too often many relatively unimportant statistics are allowed to obscure this single important point.

Any one of a dozen factors may be the point of a particular purchase or sale. It could be a technical reason—a coming increase in earnings or dividend not yet discounted in the market price—a change of management—a promising new product—an expected improvement in the market's valuation of earnings—or many others. But, in any given case, one of these factors will almost certainly be more important than all the rest put together.

CLOSING OUT A COMMITMENT: If you have a loss in your stocks, the solution is automatic, provided you decide what to do at the time you buy. Otherwise, the question divides itself into two parts. Are we in a bull or bear market? Few of us really know until it is too late. For the sake of the record, if you think it is a bear market, just put that consideration first and sell as much as your conviction suggests and your nature allows.

If you think it is a bull market, or at least a market where some stocks move up, some mark time and only a few decline, do not sell unless:

✓ You see a bear market ahead.

✓ You see trouble for a particular company in which you own shares.

✓ Time and circumstances have turned up a new and seemingly far better buy than the issue you like least in your list.

✓ Your shares stop going up and start going down.

A subsidiary question is, which stock to sell first? Two further observations may help here:

✓ Do not sell solely because you think a stock is "overvalued."

✓ If you want to sell some of your stocks and not all, in most cases it is better to go against your emotional inclinations and sell first the issues with losses, small profits or none at all, the weakest, the most disappointing, etc.

Mr. Loeb is the author of *The Battle for Investment Survival*, Fraser Publishing, Box 494, Burlington VT 05402.

G.M. LOEB'S INVESTMENT SURVIVAL CHECKLIST

Objectives and Risks

Security		Price	Shares	Date

"Ruling reason" for commitment	Amount of commitment
	$ _____
	% of my investment capital
	_____ %

Price objective	Est. time to achieve it	I will risk _____ points	Which would be $ _____

Technical Position

Price action of stock:	Dow Jones Industrial Average
☐ hitting new highs ☐ in a trading range	
☐ pausing in an uptrend ☐ moving up from low ground	**Trend of Market**
☐ acting stronger than market ☐ _____	

Selected Yardsticks

	Price Range		Earnings Per Share Actual or Projected	Price/Earnings Ratio Actual or Projected
	High	Low		
Current Year				
Previous Year				

Merger Possibilities	Years for earnings to double in past
Comment on Future	Years for market price to double in past

Periodic Re-checks

Date	Stock Price	D.J.I.A.	Comment	Action taken, if any

Completed Transactions

Date Closed	Period of time held	Profit or loss

Reason for profit or loss

LARGEST ONE–DAY DOW GAINS AND LOSSES SINCE OCTOBER 1928 BY POINTS AND PERCENT

Top Twenty Gains Since 1928 By Points

Day	DJIA Close	Points Change	% Change
10/21/87	2027.85	186.84	10.1%
4/29/97	6962.03	179.01	2.6
4/22/97	6833.59	173.38	2.6
7/22/97	8061.65	154.93	2.0
6/24/97	7758.06	153.80	2.0
5/5/97	7214.49	143.29	2.0
6/12/97	7711.47	135.64	1.8
4/15/97	6587.16	135.26	2.1
6/6/97	7435.78	130.49	1.8
12/19/96	6473.64	126.87	2.0
5/12/97	7292.75	123.22	1.7
8/19/97	7918.10	114.74	1.5
1/17/91	2623.51	114.60	4.6
3/11/96	5581.00	110.55	2.0
8/18/97	7803.36	108.70	1.4
7/8/97	7962.31	103.82	1.3
2/12/97	6961.63	103.52	1.5
8/20/97	8021.23	103.13	1.3
10/20/87	1841.01	102.27	5.9
1/3/97	6544.09	101.60	1.6

Top Twenty Losses Since 1928 By Points

Day	DJIA Close	Points Change	% Change
10/19/87	1738.74	− 508.00	−22.6%
8/15/97	7694.66	− 247.37	− 3.1
6/23/97	7604.26	− 192.25	− 2.5
10/13/89	2569.26	− 190.58	− 6.9
3/8/96	5470.45	− 171.24	− 3.0
7/15/96	5349.51	− 161.05	− 2.9
3/13/97	6878.89	− 160.48	− 2.3
3/31/97	6583.48	− 157.11	− 2.3
10/26/87	1793.93	− 156.83	− 8.0
8/8/97	8031.22	− 156.78	− 1.9
4/11/97	6391.69	− 148.36	− 2.3
1/8/88	1911.31	− 140.58	− 6.9
3/27/97	6740.59	− 140.11	− 2.0
5/7/97	7085.65	− 139.67	− 1.9
5/16/97	7194.67	− 138.88	− 1.9
7/18/97	7890.46	− 130.31	− 1.6
8/21/97	7893.95	− 127.28	− 1.6
11/15/91	2943.20	− 120.31	− 3.9
7/9/97	7842.43	− 119.88	− 1.5
7/5/96	5588.14	− 114.88	− 2.0

Top Twenty Gains Since 1950 By %

Day	DJIA Close	Points Change	% Change
10/21/87	2027.85	186.84	10.1%
10/20/87	1841.01	102.27	5.9
5/27/70	663.20	32.04	5.1
10/29/87	1938.33	91.51	5.0
8/17/82	831.24	38.81	4.9
10/9/74	631.02	28.39	4.7
5/29/62	603.96	27.03	4.7
1/17/91	2623.51	114.60	4.6
11/26/63	743.52	32.03	4.5
11/1/78	827.79	35.34	4.5
11/3/82	1065.49	43.41	4.2
10/23/57	437.13	17.34	4.1
10/6/82	944.26	37.07	4.1
4/22/80	789.85	30.72	4.0
10/29/74	659.34	25.50	4.0
1/4/88	2015.25	76.42	3.9
10/7/74	607.56	23.00	3.9
1/27/75	692.66	26.05	3.9
8/16/71	888.95	32.93	3.8
5/31/88	2031.12	74.68	3.8

Top Twenty Losses Since 1950 By %

Day	DJIA Close	Points Change	% Change
10/19/87	1738.74	− 508.00	−22.6%
10/26/87	1793.93	− 156.83	− 8.0
10/13/89	2569.26	− 190.58	− 6.9
1/8/88	1911.31	− 140.58	− 6.9
9/26/55	455.56	− 31.89	− 6.5
5/28/62	576.93	− 34.95	− 5.7
4/14/88	2005.64	− 101.46	− 4.8
6/26/50	213.91	− 10.44	− 4.7
9/11/86	1792.89	− 86.61	− 4.6
10/16/87	2246.74	− 108.35	− 4.6
11/30/87	1833.55	− 76.93	− 4.0
11/15/91	2943.20	− 120.31	− 3.9
12/3/87	1776.53	− 72.44	− 3.9
10/22/87	1950.43	− 77.42	− 3.8
10/14/87	2412.70	− 95.46	− 3.8
6/29/50	206.72	− 7.96	− 3.7
10/25/82	995.13	− 36.33	− 3.5
11/18/74	624.92	− 22.69	− 3.5
10/6/87	2548.63	− 91.55	− 3.5
11/26/73	824.95	− 29.05	− 3.4

Top Ten Gains 1928–1950 By %

Day	DJIA Close	Points Change	% Change
3/15/33	62.10	8.26	15.3%
10/6/31	99.34	12.86	14.9
10/30/29	258.47	28.40	12.3
6/22/31	145.82	15.51	11.9
9/21/32	75.16	7.67	11.4
8/3/32	58.22	5.06	9.5
9/5/39	148.12	12.87	9.5
2/11/32	78.60	6.80	9.5
11/14/29	217.28	18.59	9.4
12/18/31	80.69	6.90	9.4

Top Ten Losses 1928–1950 By %

Day	DJIA Close	Points Change	% Change
10/28/29	260.64	− 40.58	−13.5%
10/29/29	230.07	− 30.57	−11.7
10/5/31	86.48	− 10.40	−10.7
11/6/29	232.13	− 25.55	− 9.9
8/12/32	63.11	− 5.79	− 8.4
1/4/32	71.59	− 6.31	− 8.1
6/16/30	230.05	− 19.64	− 7.9
7/21/33	88.71	− 7.55	− 7.8
10/18/37	125.73	− 9.75	− 7.2
10/5/32	66.07	− 5.09	− 7.2

LARGEST WEEKLY DOW GAINS AND LOSSES SINCE OCTOBER 1928 BY POINTS AND PERCENT

Top Twenty Gains Since 1928 By Points

Week Ending	DJIA Close	Points Change	% Change
6/13/97	7782.04	346.26	4.7%
5/2/97	7071.20	332.33	4.9
4/18/97	6703.55	311.86	4.9
7/25/97	8113.44	222.98	2.8
7/3/97	7895.81	208.09	2.7
8/2/96	5679.83	206.77	3.8
11/8/96	6219.82	197.89	3.3
8/22/97	7887.91	193.25	2.5
12/20/96	6484.40	179.53	2.8
9/13/96	5838.52	178.66	3.2
5/17/96	5687.50	169.36	3.1
2/9/96	5541.62	167.63	3.1
12/27/96	3101.52	167.04	5.7
1/10/97	6703.79	159.70	2.4
5/23/97	7345.91	151.24	2.1
7/7/95	4702.73	146.63	3.2
1/18/91	2646.78	145.29	5.8
2/14/97	6988.96	133.16	1.9
2/5/93	3442.14	132.11	4.0
1/17/97	6833.10	129.31	1.9

Top Twenty Losses Since 1928 By Points

Week Ending	DJIA Close	Points Change	% Change
8/15/97	7694.66	−337.16	− 4.2%
10/23/87	1950.76	−295.98	−13.2
10/16/87	2246.74	−235.47	− 9.5
10/13/89	2569.26	−216.26	− 7.8
4/4/97	6526.07	−214.52	− 3.2
8/8/97	8031.22	−162.82	− 2.0
10/9/87	2482.21	−158.78	− 6.0
4/12/96	5532.59	−150.29	− 2.6
12/4/87	1766.74	−143.74	− 7.5
9/12/86	1758.72	−141.03	− 7.4
6/24/94	3636.94	−139.84	− 3.7
12/6/96	6381.94	−139.76	− 2.1
3/31/94	3635.96	−138.77	− 3.7
1/24/97	6696.48	−136.62	− 2.0
4/11/97	6391.69	−134.38	− 2.1
3/21/97	6804.79	−130.67	− 1.9
11/4/94	3807.52	−123.14	− 3.1
3/25/94	3774.73	−120.92	− 3.1
1/12/96	5061.12	−120.31	− 2.3
5/31/96	5643.18	−119.68	− 2.1

Top Twenty Gains Since 1950 By %

Week Ending	DJIA Close	Points Change	% Change
10/11/74	658.17	73.61	12.6%
8/20/82	869.29	81.24	10.3
10/8/82	986.85	79.11	8.7
8/3/84	1202.08	87.46	7.8
9/20/74	670.76	43.57	6.9
6/7/74	853.72	51.55	6.4
11/2/62	604.58	35.56	6.2
1/9/76	911.13	52.42	6.1
11/5/82	1051.78	60.06	6.1
6/3/88	2071.30	114.86	5.9
1/18/91	2646.78	145.29	5.8
12/18/87	1975.30	108.26	5.8
11/14/80	986.35	53.93	5.8
5/29/70	700.44	38.27	5.8
12/27/91	3101.52	167.04	5.7
12/11/87	1867.04	100.30	5.7
4/11/75	789.50	42.24	5.7
1/31/75	703.69	37.08	5.6
11/29/63	750.52	39.03	5.5
3/14/86	1792.74	92.91	5.5

Top Twenty Losses Since 1950 By %

Week Ending	DJIA Close	Points Change	% Change
10/23/87	1950.76	−295.98	−13.2%
10/16/87	2246.74	−235.47	− 9.5
10/13/89	2569.26	−216.26	− 7.8
12/4/87	1766.74	−143.74	− 7.5
9/13/74	627.19	− 50.69	− 7.5
9/12/86	1758.72	−141.03	− 7.4
9/27/74	621.95	− 48.81	− 7.3
6/30/50	209.11	− 15.24	− 6.8
6/22/62	539.19	− 38.99	− 6.7
12/6/74	577.60	− 41.06	− 6.6
10/20/78	838.01	− 59.08	− 6.6
10/12/79	838.99	− 58.62	− 6.5
8/23/74	686.80	− 44.74	− 6.1
10/9/87	2482.21	−158.78	− 6.0
10/4/74	584.56	− 37.39	− 6.0
5/25/62	611.88	− 38.82	− 6.0
8/16/74	731.54	− 45.76	− 5.9
5/22/70	662.17	− 40.05	− 5.7
11/2/73	935.28	− 51.78	− 5.2
3/25/88	1978.95	−108.42	− 5.2

Top Ten Gains 1928–1950 By %

Week Ending	DJIA Close	Points Change	% Change
6/26/31	154.04	23.73	18.2%
8/5/32	62.60	8.71	16.2
6/24/38	129.06	16.00	14.2
7/29/32	53.89	6.20	13.0
3/17/33	60.73	6.89	12.8
8/26/32	74.43	7.59	11.4
4/21/33	69.78	7.09	11.3
9/8/39	150.04	14.79	10.9
11/11/32	68.03	6.50	10.6
7/15/32	45.47	4.25	10.3

Top Ten Losses 1928–1950 By %

Week Ending	DJIA Close	Points Change	% Change
7/21/33	88.71	−16.33	−15.5%
5/17/40	124.20	−20.57	−14.2
11/8/29	236.53	−36.98	−13.5
4/8/32	62.90	− 9.28	−12.9
10/7/32	62.67	− 8.89	−12.4
9/16/32	67.10	− 9.09	−11.9
10/2/31	96.88	−12.98	−11.8
11/19/37	118.13	−14.96	−11.2
6/20/30	221.92	−27.77	−11.1
5/27/32	47.47	− 5.84	−11.0

LARGEST MONTHLY DOW GAINS AND LOSSES SINCE OCTOBER 1928 BY POINTS AND PERCENT

Top Twenty Gains Since 1928 By Points

Month	DJIA Close	Points Change	% Change
Jul 97	8222.61	549.82	7.2%
Nov 96	6521.70	492.32	8.2
Apr 97	7008.99	425.51	6.5
Jan 97	6813.09	364.82	5.7
Jun 97	7672.79	341.75	4.7
May 97	7331.04	322.05	4.6
Nov 95	5074.49	319.01	6.7
Jan 96	5395.30	278.18	5.4
Dec 91	3168.83	274.15	9.5
Sep 96	5882.17	265.96	4.7
Jan 87	2158.04	262.09	13.8
Jan 94	3978.36	224.27	6.0
Jul 89	2660.66	220.60	9.0
May 90	2876.66	219.90	8.3
Sep 95	4789.08	178.52	3.9
Jan 89	2342.32	173.75	8.0
Feb 95	4011.05	167.19	4.3
Apr 95	4321.27	163.58	3.9
Jul 87	2572.07	153.54	6.3
Jul 95	4708.47	152.37	3.3

Top Twenty Losses Since 1928 By Points

Month	DJIA Close	Points Change	% Change
Oct 87	1993.53	−602.75	−23.2%
Mar 97	6583.48	−294.26	− 4.3
Aug 90	2614.36	−290.84	−10.0
Mar 94	3635.96	−196.06	− 5.1
Nov 91	2894.68	−174.42	− 5.7
Nov 94	3739.23	−168.89	− 4.3
Jan 90	2590.54	−162.66	− 5.9
Sep 90	2452.48	−161.88	− 6.2
Nov 87	1833.55	−159.98	− 8.0
Feb 94	3832.02	−146.34	− 3.7
Aug 92	3257.35	−136.43	− 4.0
Nov 73	822.25	−134.33	−14.0
Jun 94	3624.96	−133.41	− 3.5
Sep 86	1767.58	−130.76	− 6.9
Jul 96	5528.91	−125.72	− 2.2
Jun 91	2906.75	−120.75	− 4.0
Jul 86	1775.31	−117.41	− 6.2
Aug 95	4610.56	− 97.91	− 2.1
Aug 88	2031.65	− 97.08	− 4.6
Sep 93	3555.12	− 96.13	− 2.6

Top Twenty Gains Since 1950 By %

Month	DJIA Close	Points Change	% Change
Jan 76	975.28	122.87	14.4%
Jan 75	703.69	87.45	14.2
Jan 87	2158.04	262.09	13.8
Aug 82	901.31	92.71	11.5
Oct 82	991.72	95.47	10.7
Apr 78	837.32	79.96	10.6
Nov 62	649.30	59.53	10.1
Nov 54	386.77	34.63	9.8
Aug 84	1224.38	109.10	9.8
Oct 74	665.52	57.65	9.5
Dec 91	3168.83	274.15	9.5
Jul 89	2660.66	220.60	9.0
Feb 86	1709.06	138.07	8.8
Apr 68	912.22	71.55	8.5
Apr 83	1226.20	96.17	8.5
May 90	2876.66	219.90	8.3
Jan 67	849.89	64.20	8.2
Nov 96	6521.70	492.32	8.2
Jan 89	2342.32	173.75	8.0
Jul 80	935.32	67.40	7.8

Top Twenty Losses Since 1950 By %

Month	DJIA Close	Points Change	% Change
Oct 87	1993.53	− 602.75	− 23.2
Nov 73	822.25	− 134.33	− 14.0
Sep 74	607.87	− 70.71	− 10.4
Aug 74	678.58	− 78.85	− 10.4
Aug 90	2614.36	− 290.84	− 10.0
Mar 80	785.75	− 77.39	− 9.0
Jun 62	561.28	− 52.08	− 8.5
Oct 78	792.45	− 73.37	− 8.5
Jan 60	622.62	− 56.74	− 8.4
Nov 87	1833.55	− 159.98	− 8.0
May 62	613.36	− 51.97	− 7.8
Aug 81	881.47	− 70.87	− 7.4
May 56	478.05	− 38.07	− 7.4
Jan 78	769.92	− 61.25	− 7.4
Sep 60	580.14	− 45.85	− 7.3
Oct 79	815.70	− 62.88	− 7.2
Nov 74	618.66	− 46.86	− 7.0
Jan 70	744.06	− 56.30	− 7.0
Aug 66	788.41	− 58.97	− 7.0
Sep 86	1767.58	− 130.76	− 6.9

Top Ten Gains 1928–1950 By %

Month	DJIA Close	Points Change	% Change
Apr 33	77.66	22.26	40.2%
Aug 32	73.16	18.90	34.8
Jul 32	54.26	11.42	26.7
Jun 38	133.88	26.14	24.3
Jun 31	150.18	21.72	16.9
Nov 28	293.38	41.22	16.3
Sep 39	152.54	18.13	13.5
May 33	88.11	10.45	13.5
Feb 31	189.66	22.11	13.2
Aug 33	102.41	11.64	12.8

Top Ten Losses 1928–1950 By %

Month	DJIA Close	Points Change	% Change
Sep 31	96.61	− 42.80	− 30.7%
Mar 38	98.95	− 30.69	− 23.7
Apr 32	56.11	− 17.17	− 23.4
May 40	116.22	− 32.21	− 21.7
Oct 29	273.51	− 69.94	− 20.4
May 32	44.74	− 11.37	− 20.3
Jun 30	226.34	− 48.73	− 17.7
Dec 31	77.90	− 15.97	− 17.0
Feb 33	51.39	− 9.51	− 15.6
May 31	128.46	− 22.73	− 15.0

LARGEST YEARLY DOW GAINS AND LOSSES SINCE 1928 RANKED BY POINTS AND PERCENT

Best Twenty Years Since 1928 By Points

Year	DJIA Close	Points Change	% Change
1996	6448.27	1331.15	26.0
1995	5117.12	1282.68	33.5
1989	2753.20	584.63	27.0
1991	3168.83	535.17	20.3
1993	3754.09	452.98	13.7
1986	1895.95	349.28	22.6
1985	1546.67	335.10	27.7
1975	852.41	236.17	38.3
1988	2168.57	229.74	11.8
1983	1258.64	212.10	20.3
1982	1046.54	171.54	19.6
1976	1004.65	152.24	17.9
1958	583.65	147.96	34.0
1997	6583.48	135.21	2.1
1992	3301.11	132.28	4.2
1972	1020.02	129.82	14.6
1980	963.99	125.25	14.9
1954	404.39	123.49	44.0
1967	905.11	119.42	15.2
1961	731.14	115.25	18.7

Worst Twenty Years Since 1928 By Points

Year	DJIA Close	Points Change	% Change
1974	616.24	−234.62	− 27.6
1966	785.69	−183.57	− 18.9
1977	831.17	−173.48	− 17.3
1973	850.86	−169.16	− 16.6
1969	800.36	−143.39	− 15.2
1990	2633.66	−119.54	− 4.3
1981	875.00	− 88.99	− 9.2
1962	652.10	− 79.04	− 10.8
1957	435.69	− 63.78	− 12.8
1960	615.89	− 63.47	− 9.3
1984	1211.57	− 47.07	− 3.7
1978	805.01	− 26.16	− 3.1
1953	280.90	− 11.00	− 3.8
1956	499.47	11.07	2.3
1952	291.90	22.67	8.4
1979	838.74	33.73	4.2
1951	269.23	33.82	14.4
1950	235.41	35.28	17.6
1970	838.92	38.56	4.8
1968	943.75	38.64	4.3

Best Twenty Years Since 1950 By %

Year	DJIA Close	Points Change	% Change
1954	404.39	123.49	44.0
1975	852.41	236.17	38.3
1958	583.65	147.96	34.0
1995	5117.12	1282.68	33.5
1985	1546.67	335.10	27.7
1989	2753.20	584.63	27.0
1996	6448.27	1331.15	26.0
1986	1895.95	349.28	22.6
1955	488.40	84.01	20.8
1991	3168.83	535.17	20.3
1983	1258.64	212.10	20.3
1982	1046.54	171.54	19.6
1961	731.14	115.25	18.7
1976	1004.65	152.24	17.9
1950	235.41	35.28	17.6
1963	762.95	110.85	17.0
1959	679.36	95.71	16.4
1967	905.11	119.42	15.2
1980	963.99	125.25	14.9
1972	1020.02	129.82	14.6

Worst Twenty Years Since 1950 By %

Year	DJIA Close	Points Change	% Change
1974	616.24	−234.62	− 27.6
1966	785.69	−183.57	− 18.9
1977	831.17	−173.48	− 17.3
1973	850.86	−169.16	− 16.6
1969	800.36	−143.39	− 15.2
1957	435.69	− 63.78	− 12.8
1962	652.10	− 79.04	− 10.8
1960	615.89	− 63.47	− 9.3
1981	875.00	− 88.99	− 9.2
1990	2633.66	−119.54	− 4.3
1953	280.90	− 11.00	− 3.8
1984	1211.57	− 47.07	− 3.7
1978	805.01	− 26.16	− 3.1
1997	6583.48	135.21	2.1
1994	3834.44	80.35	2.1
1987	1938.83	42.88	2.3
1956	499.47	11.07	2.3
1992	3301.11	132.28	4.2
1979	838.74	33.73	4.2
1968	943.75	38.64	4.3

Best Ten Years 1928–1950 By %

Year	DJIA Close	Points Change	% Change
1933	99.90	39.97	66.7
1928	300.00	97.60	48.2
1935	144.13	40.09	38.5
1938	154.76	33.91	28.1
1945	192.91	40.59	26.6
1936	179.90	35.77	24.8
1943	135.89	16.49	13.8
1949	200.13	22.83	12.9
1944	152.32	16.43	12.1
1942	119.40	8.44	7.6

Worst Ten Years 1928–1950 By %

Year	DJIA Close	Points Change	% Change
1931	77.90	− 86.68	− 52.7
1930	164.58	− 83.90	− 33.8
1937	120.85	− 59.05	− 32.8
1932	59.93	− 17.97	− 23.1
1929	248.48	− 51.52	− 17.2
1941	110.96	− 20.17	− 15.4
1940	131.13	− 19.11	− 12.7
1946	177.20	− 15.71	− 8.1
1939	150.24	− 4.52	− 2.9
1948	177.30	− 3.86	− 2.1

WEB-VESTING—GET FREE QUOTES, COMPANY DATA, RESEARCH, AND MORE THROUGH THE INTERNET

Your computer can be used to perform sophisticated financial analysis or simply to retrieve stock quotes and basic company information. We suggest signing up with one of the services that provides unlimited Internet access. There are already well over 100 million pages of information available on the Internet. We've selected some of the most useful sites for investors. But remember that the World Wide Web is in its infancy and new sites are being added every day. One beautiful thing about many web sites is that they will link you to other sites with related information at the touch of a mouse. Here are some of the best sites for a variety of market information.

Wall Street City   *www.wallstreetcity.com*

David Brown, co-author of *Cyber Investing* and also the CEO of Telescan, earlier this year merged his supersite Wall Street City with TIPnet, a premium service. Quotes, semi-log charts and company snapshots are available on all US, Canadian and foreign stocks, plus options, futures and mutual funds. You can also maintain a 150-stock portfolio for free. Most importantly, for a fee you can screen stocks as professionals do by using the *ProSearch* database of all listed stocks, to choose which companies had rising earnings four quarters in a row, low multiples and price/sales ratios, good relative strength and many other criteria from nearly 300 different factors. If you desire, you can backtest any combination of criteria to see what has worked in the past. Or else, let *wallstreetcity.com* tell you what's working right now. Their best search in the last twelve months was optionable stocks which would have gained a 109.4% return for the period.

Quote.com   *http://www.quote.com*

Here you can get unlimited free quotes and daily, weekly and monthly charts on all US and Canadian listed securities plus headlines of the company's press releases. Maintain a portfolio of seven stocks, see intraday charts of major averages and obtain data on most active stocks, new highs and lows, and volume alerts, all free. Information on all mutual funds from Morningstar and Lipper is also available. For just $9.95 a month you can maintain two portfolios of 50 stocks each with net worth calculated. View them anytime and have them e-mailed to you after the market closes. Features are constantly being added.

Market Technicians Association   *http://www.mta-usa.org*

Everything you ever wanted to know about technical analysis, technical indicators and software is provided by this non-profit organization. Links to over 150 sites with access to portfolio and stock internet resources and on-line trading and market discussion groups. See graphs on all commodities, connect to top analysts such as John Murphy, Ralph Acompora, John Bollinger, and others.

Goldsheet   *http://www.goldsheet.simplenet.com*

Goldbugs will be delighted to find data on 700 mining-related companies and funds including symbol, exchange, proven and probable reserves. Has links to 1,900 mining-related sites which include 625 mining company home pages and 40 gold newsletters.

Hoover's Online   *http://www.hoovers.com*

Company profiles from a database of over 2,500 companies. $9.95 per month but some data is free. Lists other useful Web sites with links, plus a 10,000 company directory.

Zacks Analyst Watch   *http://www.zacks.com*

Free index to current brokerage research reports. For a fee subscribers get the famous earnings estimate service and more.

INVESTools   *http://www.investools.com*

Market letters on line.

Westergaard Online   *http://www.westergaard.com*

Research and commentary on small companies.

Stocksmart   *http://www.stocksmart.com*

Quotes, charts on 30,000 stocks US and worldwide.

NETworth   *http://www.networth.quicken.com*

Quotes, charts and news on US stocks and mutual funds.

Yahoo
http://www.yahoo.com

The popular search site also has quotes, short and long term charts and news for each company at a single stroke.

Briefing.com
http://www.briefing.com

Quotes, and your own portfolio of 25 stocks. Lots more on 8,300 companies for $6.95 a month.

Securities and Exchange Commission
http://www.sec.gov

The EDGAR data base makes available every corporate document filed with the SEC.

EDGAR Online
http://www.edgar-online.com

This outfit, like a few others, simply gives you, for a modest fee, what the SEC offers for free. But their searching software is easier to use, they manage to get new filings on line quicker than the government, and they have a notification service that will send you an e-mail message any time a company on your "WatchList" list makes a filing.

Federal Reserve Bank St. Louis
http://www.stls.frb.org

Gives you access to the FRED database which can also be downloaded. Get the Consumers Price Index monthly figures since 1946 or all the Discount Rate changes since 1934 and 30 other interest rate categories. Help yourself to similar data on employment, gross domestic product, population, exchange rates, plus most monetary and business indicators. Direct links are provided to all the Federal Reserve branch banks and most of the US Government sites.

Global Financial Data
http://www.globalfindata.com

The most extensive, long-term data on stock market indexes (especially foreign markets), interest rates, inflation, etc. available anywhere. Some of it is offered free.

Dorsey, Wright & Associates
http://www.dorseywright.com

A site for professionals and point & figure aficionados. Tom Dorsey is the author of this edition's Best Investment Book of the Year (see page 92). Several thousand brokers case this site to find breakouts, shakeouts, double tops and bottoms, catapults, reversals and other patterns being formed by stocks. You can see the NYSE bullish percent chart and sector bullish percent charts. Last time we looked golds were heading towards zero. Monthly fees are charged but there's a two-week free trial.

Horsesmouth
http://www.horsesmouth.com

Brokers only. Commentaries and analysis by the foremost independent financial experts.

Pinnacle Data Corp.
http://www.pinnacledata.com

Order any financial, stock market, commodity, economic or monetary database here.

The Trader's Magazine
http://www.traders.com

Technical Analysis of Stocks and Commodities magazine.

Wall Street Research Net
http://www.wsrn.com

Over 250,000 links.

Investor Guide
http://www.investorguide.com

Free comprehensive site, many links.

Silicon Investor
http://www.techstocks.com

All about tech stocks.

New York Times
http://www.nytimes.com

Barron's
http://www.barrons.com

The Economist
http://www.economist.com

CNN*fn* The Financial Network
http://www.cnnfn.com

Many of the major news organizations are now on line. This site has current market and other developments, "hot stories," opinion and more.

CNBC
http://www.cnbc.com

Obtain daily guest list for CNBC.

Time Warner's Pathfinder Network
http://www.pathfinder.com

Time's umbrella site for *Fortune, Money,* and *Hoover's Business Profile.*

New York Stock Exchange
http://www.nyse.com

Nasdaq
http://www.nasdaq.com

Vancouver Stock Exchange
http://www.vse.com

Big Charts   http://www.bigcharts.com

Work & Money (Christian SM)   http://www.csmonitor.com/work

THE IDEAL BUSINESS

1) **Sells the world**, rather than a single neighborhood or even a single city or state. In other words, it has an unlimited global market (and today this is more important than ever, since world markets have now opened up to an extent unparalleled in my lifetime). By the way, how many times have you seen a retail store that has been doing well for years, then another bigger and better store moves nearby, and it's kaput for the first store.

2) Offers a product which enjoys an **"inelastic" demand**. Inelastic refers to a product that people need or desire—almost regardless of price.

3) Markets a product which **cannot be easily copied**. This means that the product is an original or at least it's something that can be copyrighted or patented.

4) Has **minimal labor** requirements (the fewer personnel, the better). Today's example of this is the much talked about "virtual corporation." The virtual corporation may consist of an office with three executives, where literally all manufacturing and services are farmed out to other companies.

5) Operates on **low overhead**. It does not need an expensive location; it does not need large amounts of electricity, advertising, legal advice, high-priced employees, large inventory, etc.

6) **Does not require big cash outlays** or major investments in equipment. In other words, it does not tie up your capital (incidentally, one of the major reasons for new-business failure is under-capitalization).

7) **Enjoys cash billings**. In other words, it does not tie up your capital with lengthy or complex credit terms.

8) Is **relatively free of all kinds of government regulations** and strictures (and if you're now in your own business, you most definitely know what I mean with this one).

9) Is **portable or easily moveable**. This means that you can take your business (and yourself) anywhere you want—Nevada, Florida, Texas, Washington, South Dakota (none have state income taxes) or hey, maybe even Monte Carlo or Switzerland or the south of France.

10) **Satisfies your intellectual needs**. There's nothing like being fascinated with what you're doing. When that happens, you're not working, you're having fun.

11) Leaves you with **free time**. In other words, it doesn't require your labor and attention 12, 16 or 18 hours a day (my lawyer wife, who leaves the house at 6:30 AM and comes home at 6:30 PM and often later, has been well aware of this one).

12) Is one in which your **income is not limited by your personal output** (lawyers and doctors have this problem). No, in the ideal business you can sell 10,000 customers as easily as you sell one (publishing is an example).

That's it. If you use this list it may help you cut through a lot of nonsense and hypocrisy and wishes and dreams regarding what you are looking for in life and in your work.

The above was written by Richard Russell, publisher of Dow Theory Letters, PO Box 1759, La Jolla CA 92038. Incidentally, many points listed above should be taken into consideration when you are looking for great stock investments.

STRATEGY PLANNING & RECORD SECTION

CONTENTS

PORTFOLIO AT START OF YEAR

DATE ACQUIRED	NO. OF SHARES	SECURITY	PRICE	TOTAL COST	PAPER PROFITS	PAPER LOSSES

PORTFOLIO AT START OF YEAR

DATE ACQUIRED	NO. OF SHARES	SECURITY	PRICE	TOTAL COST	PAPER PROFITS	PAPER LOSSES

ADDITIONAL PURCHASES

DATE ACQUIRED	NO. OF SHARES	SECURITY	PRICE	TOTAL COST	REASON FOR PURCHASE PRICE OBJECTIVE, ETC.

ADDITIONAL PURCHASES

DATE ACQUIRED	NO. OF SHARES	SECURITY	PRICE	TOTAL COST	REASON FOR PURCHASE PRICE OBJECTIVE, ETC.

ADDITIONAL PURCHASES

DATE ACQUIRED	NO. OF SHARES	SECURITY	PRICE	TOTAL COST	REASON FOR PURCHASE PRICE OBJECTIVE, ETC.

ADDITIONAL PURCHASES

DATE ACQUIRED	NO. OF SHARES	SECURITY	PRICE	TOTAL COST	REASON FOR PURCHASE PRICE OBJECTIVE, ETC.

ADDITIONAL PURCHASES

DATE ACQUIRED	NO. OF SHARES	SECURITY	PRICE	TOTAL COST	REASON FOR PURCHASE PRICE OBJECTIVE, ETC.

SHORT-TERM TRANSACTIONS

Pages 169-176 can accompany next year's income tax return (Schedule D). Enter transactions as completed to avoid last minute pressures

NO. OF SHARES	SECURITY	DATE ACQUIRED	DATE SOLD	SALES PRICE	COST	LOSS	GAIN

TOTALS:
Carry over to next page

SHORT-TERM TRANSACTIONS (continued)

NO. OF SHARES	SECURITY	DATE ACQUIRED	DATE SOLD	SALES PRICE	COST	LOSS	GAIN

TOTALS:
Carry over to next page

170

SHORT-TERM TRANSACTIONS (continued)

NO. OF SHARES	SECURITY	DATE ACQUIRED	DATE SOLD	SALES PRICE	COST	LOSS	GAIN

TOTALS:

Carry over to next page

SHORT-TERM TRANSACTIONS (continued)

NO. OF SHARES	SECURITY	DATE ACQUIRED	DATE SOLD	SALES PRICE	COST	LOSS	GAIN

TOTALS:
Carry over to next page

LONG-TERM TRANSACTIONS

Pages 169-176 can accompany next year's income tax return (Schedule D). Enter transactions as completed to avoid last minute pressures

NO. OF SHARES	SECURITY	DATE ACQUIRED	DATE SOLD	SALES PRICE	COST	LOSS	GAIN

TOTALS:

Carry over to next page

LONG-TERM TRANSACTIONS (continued)

NO. OF SHARES	SECURITY	DATE ACQUIRED	DATE SOLD	SALES PRICE	COST	LOSS	GAIN

TOTALS:

LONG-TERM TRANSACTIONS (continued)

NO. OF SHARES	SECURITY	DATE ACQUIRED	DATE SOLD	SALES PRICE	COST	LOSS	GAIN

TOTALS:
Carry over to next page

175

LONG-TERM TRANSACTIONS (continued)

NO. OF SHARES	SECURITY	DATE ACQUIRED	DATE SOLD	SALES PRICE	COST	LOSS	GAIN

TOTALS:

BROKERAGE ACCOUNT DATA

	MARGIN INTEREST	TRANSFER TAXES	CAPITAL ADDED	CAPITAL WITHDRAWN
JAN				
FEB				
MAR				
APR				
MAY				
JUN				
JUL				
AUG				
SEP				
OCT				
NOV				
DEC				

INTEREST/DIVIDENDS RECEIVED DURING YEAR

AMOUNT	STOCK/BOND	FIRST QUARTER		SECOND QUARTER		THIRD QUARTER		FOURTH QUARTER	
		$		$		$		$	

INTEREST/DIVIDENDS RECEIVED DURING YEAR

AMOUNT	STOCK/BOND	FIRST QUARTER	SECOND QUARTER	THIRD QUARTER	FOURTH QUARTER
		$	$	$	$

PORTFOLIO AT END OF YEAR

DATE ACQUIRED	NO. OF SHARES	SECURITY	PRICE	TOTAL COST	PAPER PROFITS	PAPER LOSSES

PORTFOLIO AT END OF YEAR

DATE ACQUIRED	NO. OF SHARES	SECURITY	PRICE	TOTAL COST	PAPER PROFITS	PAPER LOSSES

PORTFOLIO PRICE RECORD

Place original purchase price above stock name

STOCKS / Week Ending	1	2	3	4	5	6	7	8	Dow Jones Industrial Average	Net Change For Week
JANUARY 2										
9										
16										
23										
30										
FEBRUARY 6										
13										
20										
27										
MARCH 6										
13										
20										
27										
APRIL 3										
10										
17										
24										
MAY 1										
8										
15										
22										
29										
JUNE 5										
12										
19										
26										

Enter weekly closing prices for stocks in your portfolio

STOCKS / Week Ending	9	10	11	12	13	14	15	16	17	18
JANUARY 2										
JANUARY 9										
JANUARY 16										
JANUARY 23										
JANUARY 30										
FEBRUARY 6										
FEBRUARY 13										
FEBRUARY 20										
FEBRUARY 27										
MARCH 6										
MARCH 13										
MARCH 20										
MARCH 27										
APRIL 3										
APRIL 10										
APRIL 17										
APRIL 24										
MAY 1										
MAY 8										
MAY 15										
MAY 22										
MAY 29										
JUNE 5										
JUNE 12										
JUNE 19										
JUNE 26										

PORTFOLIO PRICE RECORD

Place original purchase price above stock name

STOCKS / Week Ending	1	2	3	4	5	6	7	8	Dow Jones Industrial Average	Net Change For Week
JULY 3										
10										
17										
24										
31										
AUGUST 7										
14										
21										
28										
SEPTEMBER 4										
11										
18										
25										
OCTOBER 2										
9										
16										
23										
30										
NOVEMBER 6										
13										
20										
27										
DECEMBER 4										
11										
18										
25										

Enter weekly closing prices for stocks in your portfolio

STOCKS / Week Ending	9	10	11	12	13	14	15	16	17	18
JULY 3										
10										
17										
24										
31										
AUGUST 7										
14										
21										
28										
SEPTEMBER 4										
11										
18										
25										
OCTOBER 2										
9										
16										
23										
30										
NOVEMBER 6										
13										
20										
27										
DECEMBER 4										
11										
18										
25										

WEEKLY INDICATOR DATA (First Half)

Week Ending	Dow Jones Industrial Average	Net Change For Week	Net Change On Friday	Net Change Next Monday	S & P Or NYSE Comp.	NYSE Ad- vances	NYSE De- clines	New Highs	New Lows		90- Day Treas. Rate	30- Year AAA Rate
JANUARY 2												
9												
16												
23												
30												
FEBRUARY 6												
13												
20												
27												
MARCH 6												
13												
20												
27												
APRIL 3												
10												
17												
24												
MAY 1												
8												
15												
22												
29												
JUNE 5												
12												
19												
26												

See instructions on page 188

WEEKLY INDICATOR DATA (Second Half)

Week Ending	Dow Jones Industrial Average	Net Change For Week	Net Change On Friday	Net Change Next Monday	S & P Or NYSE Comp.	NYSE Ad-vances	NYSE De-clines	New Highs	New Lows		90-Day Treas. Rate	30-Year AAA Rate
JULY												
3												
10												
17												
24												
31												
AUGUST												
7												
14												
21												
28												
SEPTEMBER												
4												
11												
18												
25												
OCTOBER												
2												
9												
16												
23												
30												
NOVEMBER												
6												
13												
20												
27												
DECEMBER												
4												
11												
18												
25												

See instructions on page 188

MONTHLY INDICATOR DATA

MONTH	DJIA Next to Last Day Prev. Mo.	DJIA Fourth Trading Day	Point Change These 5 Days	Point Change Rest Of Mo.	% Change Whole Period	% Change Your Stocks	Prime Rate	Trade Deficit $ Bil.	CPI % Change	% Unemployment Rate
JAN										
FEB										
MAR										
APR										
MAY										
JUN										
JUL										
AUG										
SEP										
OCT										
NOV										
DEC										

INSTRUCTIONS:

Weekly Indicator Data (page 186-187). Keeping data on several indicators may give you a better feel of the market. In addition to the closing DJIA and its net change for the week, post the net change for Friday's Dow and also the following Monday's. Watching their performance vis-à-vis each other is fascinating (see pages 56, 132 and 133). Tracking either of the S&P or NYSE composites, and advances and declines, will help prevent the Dow from misleading you. New highs and lows are also useful indicators. All these weekly figures appear in weekend papers or *Barron's*. Data for 90-day Treasury Rate and 30-year AAA Bond Rate are quite important to track short- and long-term interest rates. These figures are available from:

Weekly U.S. Financial Data
Federal Reserve Bank of St. Louis
P.O. Box 442
St. Louis, MO 63166
http://www.stls.frb.org

Monthly Indicator Data. The purpose of the first four columns is to enable you to track (and possibly take advantage of) the market's bullish bias early in the month (see page 64, 66 and 134). Prime Rate, Trade Deficit, Consumers Price Index, and Unemployment Rate are worthwhile indicators to follow. Or, readers may wish to use those columns for other data.

IF YOU DON'T PROFIT FROM YOUR INVESTMENT MISTAKES—SOMEONE ELSE WILL

No matter how much we may deny it, almost every successful person in Wall Street pays a great deal of attention to trading suggestions—especially when they come from "the right sources."

One of the hardest things to learn is to distinguish between good tips and bad ones. Usually the best tips have a logical reason in back of them, which accompanies the tip. Poor tips usually have no reason to support them.

The important thing to remember is that the market discounts. It does not review, it does not reflect. The Street's real interest in "tips," inside information, buying and selling suggestions, and everything else of this kind, emanates from a desire to find out just what the market has on hand to discount. The process of finding out involves separating the wheat from the chaff—and there is plenty of chaff.

How to Make Use of Stock "Tips"

1 The source should be **reliable**. (By listing all "tips" and suggestions on a Performance Record of Recommendations, such as below, and then periodically evaluating the outcomes, you will soon know the "batting average" of your sources.)

2 The story should make sense. Would the merger violate anti-trust laws? Are there too many computers on the market already? How many years will it take to become profitable?

3 The stock should not have had a recent sharp run-up. Otherwise, the story may already be discounted and confirmation or denial in the press would most likely be accompanied by a sell-off in the stock.

PERFORMANCE RECORD OF RECOMMENDATIONS

STOCK RECOMMENDED	BY WHOM	DATE	PRICE	REASON FOR RECOMMENDATION	SUBSEQUENT ACTION OF STOCK

(continued on next page)

PERFORMANCE RECORD OF RECOMMENDATIONS

STOCK RECOMMENDED	BY WHOM	DATE	PRICE	REASON FOR RECOMMENDATION	SUBSEQUENT ACTION OF STOCK

FINANCIAL DIRECTORY

Broker, Lawyer, Accountant, Banker etc.

NAME AND ADDRESS	AREA CODE	NUMBER

(over)

FINANCIAL DIRECTORY

Broker, Lawyer, Accountant, Banker etc.

NAME AND ADDRESS	AREA CODE	NUMBER

(over)